D0476139

THE MATTERHORN

by

GUIDO REY

Translated from the Italian by

J. E. C. EATON

Revised and two additional Chapters by

R. L. G. IRVING

BASIL BLACKWELL · OXFORD

MCMXLVI

First printed in this Edition
October 1946

PRINTED IN GREAT BRITAIN IN THE CITY OF OXFORD
AT THE ALDEN PRESS

CONTENTS

LIST OF ILLUSTRATIONS

INTRODUCTION

A WHOLE book about a mountain!

However great the latter be, it will seem to many a small subject for a large volume.

But let them read, and they will see that with every page the subject gains breadth and height, that the mountain grows more and more alive and acquires the importance and the attractive virtue of the hero of a poem, and that at last the work seems all too short; for in it is gathered a treasure of knowledge, of observations, and of ideas, only to be found in those books that are the spontaneous product of a great passion and of long experience, the intellectual offspring of a man's whole life.

One of the first chapters of the book, based on valuable documents which no other besides the author has handled, full of life and moving as a drama, filling our minds with admiration and awe, tells how the now famous mountain — one of the strangest and most wonderful in the world — which was once almost unknown outside the region it dominates, drew little by little the attention and awoke the admiration of travellers of all nations, who successively approached, studied, and described it, and bequeathed to others the fascination it exercised over their minds; how the old and widely spread conviction that its summit was on all sides inaccessible was succeeded by the hope of conquest, now by one, now by another route, which in turn were abandoned and resumed; it tells of the long succession of the earliest unsuccessful attempts, of hopes dashed to the ground and rising again, of patient preparations, of mortal anxiety, of the rivalry and the struggles of the different expeditions, foiled by every kind of natural and fortuitous mishap; it tells the story of the two attempts, at last successful, made almost simultaneously from the Italian side and from the Swiss, in which the pride of a daring Englishman and the patriotic feeling of a great Italian met here and there in conflict, and the former's triumph was tragic, and the revenge of the vanquished was no less glorious than the first conquest.

But all this, sufficient matter indeed for a book, forms but a part of Rey's work. It is preceded by a most telling picture of the people who live under the great mountain's sway, as they were before their Matterhorn became the fortune and the glory of the valley, poor and austere, almost shut off from the world, simple and rude in their habits, believing in wondrous legends of giants and fairies; to whom the mighty pyramid towering over their hills was as a mysterious and terrible monster, to be for ever a mystery; and from among these people there stand out weird figures, now lost to us these fifty years and more, whose very mould had disappeared: innkeepers, shepherds, hunters, solitary and simple old priests, who in our imaginations are almost confounded with the personages of the fables told and believed in by their people while they lived. In the relation of the long struggle for the conquest of the peak, the author shows us, with new details and the happy touch of an artist, all the pioneers, actors, and their helpers, present and afar off, illustrious and obscure, in the memorable enterprise; among them there pass before us guides, scientists, artists, priests, Tyndall and Whymper, the abbé Gorret and the geologist Giordano, the hunchback of Breuil and Quintino Sella — a group of figures that are indelibly impressed on our memories in a hundred different ways, in strenuous thought, in violent effort, in pain, in fatigue, in triumph; and behind each one of them we see the formidable Titan, from whose brow they have torn the veil of ancient mystery, and on whose summit they have planted their banner.

After relating the ascents of the pioneers, the author tells of his own, and of his attempts by new routes, and these are the finest pages in the book. In their graphic descriptions we seem, indeed, to follow the daring climber step by step, and in them the strange psychical phenomena produced by the fatigue and the dangers of great ascents are analysed and portrayed with such success, that we struggle with him in dangerous places, we feel the horror of the abyss, we tremble for his life, and when we see him win through to safety we breathe again: we are soothed and rejoice as at a victory of our own.

Throughout the book, with the rapidity of weather changes in the

Alps, we have a succession of triumphs and mishaps, smiling and gloomy aspects of nature, episodes of ascents, pleasant, sad, and terrible; and alternating with these in natural sequence, description and narrative, history and poetry, argument and anecdote; and throughout all is manifest in varying form the versatile and acute mind of the author, brooding over all and drawing from all lessons for himself and for others. And in every page, even where he quits for a time the mighty and silent protagonist of the book, there vibrates like a subdued musical accompaniment a deep and exquisite feeling for the mountains, which at last enters into the soul even of him who has as yet had no inkling thereof, and admits to his mind a host of new ideas, a new curiosity, an earnest longing (happy is he if his age still allows him to satisfy it; sad, if such time for him is past) for the unknown world to which the author attracts and raises him. In this feeling for the mountains Guido Rey lays his whole soul bare.

After reading his book we see that if not this then some other great passion, action-compelling and prolific, must needs have set him aflame; that, had chance and circumstances allowed, he would have explored Africa or the Polar regions, or founded a colony, or sought new paths of commerce afar off, or have yielded himself up to some science or some art, with a success only equalled by his ardour.

Opportunity turned him towards mountaineering, the birth of which in his land coincided with his early youth; but in it the nobility of his mind led him to seek not so much the delights of the eye and of fame, as that solitude which inspires great thoughts and the joys that are born of effort and danger and the triumph of the will; he did not climb from a vain desire for strong emotions, but to strengthen his own intellect and to probe by those emotions the depths of his nature. In the mountaineer are bound up the poet, the painter, the thinker, the citizen; in him are a heart open to all fine feelings, a mind thirsty for all knowledge, an observer who on the mountains sees far into a thousand things around him and within him that most men do not see, and which serve as food for his own mind and reveal a stimulating and illuminating line of thought to others. In him, too, there is the writer.

Pedantry may find fault with phrases and words in his book, and the subtle critic may discover there inequalities and lack of sequence, and even in parts lack of art. But it has the effectiveness which is only to be found in the books of those who have a deep feeling for their subject, and who have revolved it in their minds for many years, have developed it lovingly, living again the life and almost doing again the work they describe.

Where lack of art there is, this very lack is pleasing: it is replaced by sincerity, and the writer's ingenuousness is original and graceful. You observe his occasional pursuit of an elusive phrase required to express a complex thought or a hidden sentiment, with the same curiosity and sympathy with which you mentally accompany the climber up a difficult pitch; and for those few passages where his pen is uncertain or halts among details that appear superfluous, you are well repaid by many beautiful, clear, and facile passages that flow and glisten like springs of mountain water. A fragrance of Alpine herbs and flowers is wafted up from those pages; on your brow, bent over the book, blows the keen, pure breeze of the Matterhorn, and you feel the coolness of pines and snows, and almost as you read you feel the air grow fresh about you.

In this book more than any other on such a subject, we feel the strange and pleasurable effect produced on the reader by the constant sight of the author going before and helping him on his upward way like a stalwart guide, and the gradual but continuous uplifting of his thoughts and all his sentiments, the steadfast straining of all his aspirations and all his efforts towards a goal that is hardly to be won and that towers alone above the world. At intervals throughout the book we seem, our imagination captured and dominated by the mountain, to hear, as in the illusion of a dream, the rumbling of avalanches, the cleaving of glaciers, the shriek of the storm, and to catch as through a sudden rent in the clouds lightning glimpses of mighty walls of rock and of boundless spaces on the horizon. From time to time our thoughts turn to common books that portray social life, as if we looked down from a summit bright with the dawn on to the misty plain, and after this downward glance we breathe the limpid air with a more intense delight, rejoicing in the silence and the solitude, drunken with freedom and grandeur.

From these vivid descriptions of bodily and mental struggles, of privations and fatigue cheerfully endured, of strenuous and ingenious efforts to overcome the formidable and often insidious obstacles that nature sets in the way, there seems to emanate something of the writer's own confidence and daring, his indomitable perseverance in his purpose, that stirs our blood and braces our nerves, sending us back more resolute to begin or resume our work, more ready to meet and master any difficulties or dangers in our path. And what is most wonderful of all, it is ever a modest and gentle voice that tells us of these doughty deeds.

A fine book, and certainly a useful one. It will admit him who knows not the mountains into a world strangely different from that he dwells in, a world in which he will find characters, passions, forms of virtue and of mental greatness hitherto unknown, and will teach him how Italian mountaineering was born, whose first glory was the conquest of the Matterhorn itself, and will give him the quintessence and the noblest fruits of the love of mountains.

Those who have passed among the mountains without studying them, and who have kept but vague memories of their beauty, together with much unsatisfied curiosity, will find here a great store of topographical and historical notes in pleasant form; and a profusion of quotations skilfully selected and suitably distributed will make known to them the existence of a European Alpine literature, scientific and artistic, rich and varied, whose works they will feel moved to seek out.

New-fledged mountaineers will learn here from an incomparable master how daring must be wedded to prudence, with what foresight bold undertakings must be prepared for, how from a pursuit which for many is a mere physical exercise may be derived the highest intellectual pleasures, strength and courage for life's battles and a treasury of memories for the comfort of their old age.

And all will rejoice to acquire an intimate acquaintance with a fellow-countryman, who has earned the exceptional distinction of having ascended the highest peaks in the Alps, reached a rare degree of culture and become a writer in a brief leisure vouchsafed him by his business; a man to whom the motto 'Excelsior' has not been merely his climbing motto, but the guiding principle of his whole life; an Italian who possesses, besides the best qualities of his own race, all those with whose lack we are reproached by peoples of graver and firmer temperaments; a tranquil mind, a good and fearless heart, a poetic soul governed by an iron will.

EDMONDO DE AMICIS

EDITOR'S NOTE AND ACKNOWLEDGMENTS

I HAVE left Mr. Eaton's translation unchanged, apart from a few minor alterations. For the illustrations I tender my warmest thanks to M. Charles Gos, who has procured for me many photographs and reproductions from his brother M. Emile Gos (those facing pp. 22, 23, 38, 39, 55, 70, 71, 86, 103, 119, 134, 135, 182, 198, 247, 266, 275), from the comte de Suzonnet (facing pp. 103, 119, 150, 199), from M. André Roch (facing pp. 166, 167, 183, 215, 230, 231, 274), and from M. Marullaz (facing pp. 87, 214).

I am greatly indebted also to the Editor of the *Alpine Journal* for the illustrations facing pages 7 and 246, for the photograph of Guido Rey and for much material which has been invaluable in the preparation of the two additional chapters.

R. L. G. IRVING

Winchester, June 1946

CHAPTER I

THE PIONEERS

"Felices animos, quibus haec cognoscere primis
Inque domos superas scandere cura fuit!
Credibile est illos pariter vitiisque locisque
Altius humanus exeruisse caput."

OVID, *Fast*

In the beginning the mountain was enclosed in a mighty range, as is the work of art in the rude block of marble. The revelation of its wondrous form cost the Sculptor many thousand years of labour. None stood by to applaud; the Creator alone, unsatisfied, laboured at His task with the ceaseless, strenuous toil of the artist who hurries not, content if his work but grow beautiful and great. With frost and snow, with rain and sun He perfected His monument; with these He cut the grooves on its mighty walls, carved the gigantic battlements of its summit, and sharpened its sky-piercing apex; while time, the great colourist, was clothing the completed parts with a mysterious veil of hues that varied with the changing lights of the sky, and enamelling with a brown metallic rust the mighty serpentine strata, painting with a fair golden colour the limestone masses, and making bright the delicate slabs of mica.

Huge streams of ice enclosed the giant's base and filled the valleys, chiselling on their lofty walls the marks of their passage; thence they flowed down to the plains, carrying before them a mighty offspring of blocks, stones, and mud. These were the fragments of Alpine monuments — fragments so huge as to build other smaller mountains on the distant plains.

Then the ancient, inhospitable, and savage landscapes on the mountain's side were succeeded by others more smiling and more gentle. The large, turbid stream in the main valley, the clear torrents in the lesser, flowed again in the beds which the glaciers had once filled, and the mountain-sides, made fruitful by the waters, gave joyful birth to new woods and meadows.

The earth was now ready to receive man, its future lord. What manner of man was he, who venturing up the lonely valley in pursuit of his quarry, first viewed the vast and lofty pyramid?

Maybe 'twas not the Matterhorn as seen to-day, a dilapidated and wrinkled ruin, but a far vaster and more colossal peak. That wild man doubtless gazed on it in admiration and in wonder, and heard with terror the thunder of the avalanches. On his return to his home below, he told his family assembled in their cave of the wondrous things revealed to him above; of the sweet-smelling pine woods, of the flowering pastures, of the glistening glaciers, of huge eagles, of strange goats with mighty curving horns, of snakes and dragons; and how he saw a peak so sharp and lofty that no man had ever viewed its like, and how on the mountain there dwelt a demon that yelled and hurled down rocks.

The first families went up to dwell at the giant's feet, driven upwards by fear of other men more fierce and strong than they, who overran the lower valleys; or they were drawn thither by the good pastures for their flocks. They were rude shepherds, long-haired, clad in sheepskins, mighty hunters of wild beasts, and to them was vouchsafed long contemplation from the upper pastures of the mysterious pyramid, now smiling in sunshine, now frowning in cloud; and maybe they worshipped it as the throne of the mysterious god Penninus, ancient genius of these Alps.

The centuries rolled by; the peoples at the mountain's foot took names: Salassi they were called on this side, Seduni on the other.

Up through the main valley came the legionaries of Rome, building bridges, daringly conceived and executed, and setting up their solid milestones by the way. The ancient Salassi succumbed after prodigies of valour, and the Imperial eagle's claws rested on the Alpine capital. Hordes of barbarians came down from across the Alps and passed by, raging and destructive; Augustus' massive walls, his theatres and his temples fell. Other temples arose with a new faith, other strongholds with new ideals of life, of art, of love. But in their turn the fragile towers of Challand's manors fell to pieces; and after ringing for a short space with the clash of arms and the harmony of song, the halls of the knights and troubadours were left in ruins and solitude.

Thus in rapid alternations of periods obscure and glorious, of perfect peace and fierce strife, the centuries went by; the grey and ancient Dora rushed down towards the plain, roaring and telling of the glories of the valley, from the mythical legend of Cordelus, a comrade of Greek Herakles, founder of the first Salassian city, to the true history of Santo of Mentone, who built the first Alpine refuges on the lofty passes, beside the pagan altars. And at the upper end of that short valley, whence rushed headlong the Marmore torrent, the great mountain towered alone, clad in the shadow of a holy awe.

But already men had given the peak a name, though confusedly: Mons Silvius they called it, and perhaps the name was derived from an illustrious Roman leader, or more simply, from the woods that embraced the mountain's foot.[1] The name was at any rate a generic one, applied to the whole range of which the mountain formed a part, rather than to the mountain itself; a family name, not yet a personal one; for the ancients did not know, as we know, each separate summit; they recognized the fearful peaks only where these vouchsafed a passage across the Alps, and 'twas the passes, and not the lofty summits, which earned a name and propitiatory altars to their gods. Thus the pass which opens out to the east of the mountain and which connected the valley of Augusta (Aosta) with the land of the Seduni was famous of old, while the lofty peak was unknown.

There is no certain proof that the pass, now called the St. Theodul, was ever crossed by the Romans; it was, however, surely known during the early, dark, and troubled centuries of our era to the fugitives from Augusta, who, when the protection of Rome failed them, sought in despair up on the bleak pass a refuge from the barbarians who were sowing death down in the great valley; they carried their treasures with them over the rough glaciers of the Silvio and lost them on the way, or buried them up there amid the rocks of the pass; and now from time to time these treasures return, after so many centuries, to the light of day.[2]

The sisters of St. Catharine are said to have crossed the Silvio when, in the twelfth century, during times of cruel war, they abandoned their rich possessions and the convent of Vallesia, and crossed over to the valley of Augusta, taking refuge in the modest hermitage of Antey.[3]

The pass became known to the Valdostan pilgrims who travelled, praying as they went, to the shrines of the Valais and of Schwyz, urged by their faith to cross these snows; perhaps they raised their eyes in terror to the gigantic and threatening mountain, and thought that to brave the dangers of its glaciers was an expiation of their sins. Other rude and unknown people ascended the Monte Silvio: German families migrating into Italy, soldiers occupying the pass in years of war[4] or pestilence; and on their return they told fearsome tales of demons and of saints, of chasms yawning at every step of the way, of wondrous echoes, of sudden-forming clouds, and of destructive avalanches rushing down the mountain flanks. The obscure record of these passages was consecrated by the popular legend of Ahasuerus, the unresting traveller who had crossed the pass at least three times, at intervals of hundreds of years, and had cursed it.[5]

But none admired the Cervin; neither the mystic terror of the pious pilgrims, nor the calm and stolid contemplation of the shepherds of Val Tornina and Praborno[6] had given birth to the idea of its sublime beauty. The Monte Silvio was not made for man.

To us in our time it seems strange that men's souls should have remained so long untouched by Nature's weighty and serene teaching in the mountains, and that they should have been so fettered by mean or stupid prejudice as not to rise to the simple and natural enjoyment of the beautiful and great; that it should have needed some of those rare moments when wider and clearer visions of truth and beauty seem to reveal themselves to the minds of men, before certain noble spirits came up into the mountains with feelings other than those of base repulsion and superstitious fear. It was men inspired by the bracing breeze of the Renaissance who first felt the mysterious fascination of the mountains and a desire to know their dangers.

Aegidius Tschudi, oldest of Alpine topographers and historians, was the first to make mention of the pass in his work, *De Prisca ac Vera Alpina Raethia*, published at Basel in 1538. He approached the Cervin as a student when in his Alpine travels he reached the summit of the pass. There are traces of this visit of his to the Silvio in a fragment of his autobiography which precedes the second book of the *Gallio Deceived*, another of his works, in which the pass is described[7] at length; but he does not seem to have paid any particular attention to the lofty Matterhorn. And even Josias Simler, who is considered the ancient father of mountaineering, is silent concerning the wondrous mountain. In his work, *De Alpibus Commentarius*, published in 1574, he wrote (p. 74): 'Apud Sedunos mons est quem quidam Siluium nuncupant, Salassi Rosae nomen ei imposuere: in hoc monte ingens est glaciei perpetuae cumulus per quem transitur ad Salassos', and briefly added: 'et tamen illi adhuc altiora et magis rigida juga imminent.' More than this he did not say. The Cervin remained for yet two centuries in deepest oblivion, till a man, nurtured amid the new ideals that heralded the Revolution, came and observed with understanding eye the secrets of the lofty monument, and revealed its beauty to mankind.

This was Saussure, the same who already had discovered and studied another colossal hill in the Alps, Mont Blanc.[8] In 1787 Horace Benedict de Saussure a Genevese philosopher and geologist, climbs to the top of Mont Blanc; two years afterwards he reaches the foot of the Cervin, and is filled with admiration.

But the Cervin has no cause to fear him; he, the one ardent dream of whose life had been for so many years the conquest of the highest Alpine summit, and who had at last realized his dream, is not moved in the presence of the marvellous pyramid by the desire to ascend it; he has no hope of measuring its altitude by taking the barometer to its summit. 'Its precipitous sides', he writes, 'which give no hold to the very snows, are such as to afford no means of access.'[9] Yet a great scientific interest, a boundless admiration blaze up in him, in the presence of 'the proud peak which rises to so vast an altitude, like a triangular obelisk, that seems to be carved by a chisel'. His keen and searching eye fixes itself on that gigantic rib, which protrudes in its nakedness from the skin which covers the earth, and which reveals to him endless secrets of the anatomy of that great body. His mind, ever eager for novelty, boldly and intuitively grasps the causes which gave to the peak its present precipitous and fleshless form: the Cervin had not come thus, like a perfected crystal, from the hands of Nature; the centuries had laboured to destroy a great part of that which ancient convulsions of the earth had built.

And the sage meditates on the immense forces which split up and swept away all that the pyramid has lost, and finds again afar its mighty *débris*, brought down in ruins from above into the sub-Alpine valleys and hollows.[10] He plans to return next year for a closer examination of the magnificent rock.

In order to realize how little the valleys and passes surrounding the mountain were at that time known we must read Grüner's work on the Swiss[11] glaciers, in which the valley of Matt (Zermatt) is described. 'On fait six lieues sur la glace pour se rendre de Paraborque, qui est dans le Val Vicher, à la vallée de Tornenche; ce chemin est rempli d'élévations, de cavités et de crevasses difficiles et dangereuses pour les voyageurs. . . . Les passages dont j'ai parlé ne sont praticables que dans les plus grandes chaleurs de l'été; partout ailleurs cette vallée de glace est inaccessible; personne n'ose s'y risquer, et je ne peux en donner ni dessein ni description détaillée.'

To Marc Bourrit, a Genevese who passionately loved the mountains, who had preceded Saussure himself in certain investigations round Mont Blanc, the Cervin seems to have been at that time unknown.

During his travels among the mountains of the Valais, in search of a mysterious valley of immense glaciers,[12] he had drawn nigh to it, making his way from Bagnes towards the Mont Vélan, and, from the heights of Chermontane, he had seen the enormous group of peaks 'weather-worn, and in great measure free from snow, beyond which the Lombard plain must lie.'

But in the joyous narrative of the discovery there is no mention of the Cervin's name. Bourrit intended to return and explore that chain, but was forestalled by Saussure.

The latter, the first time, had come from Ayas to the Col des Cimes Blanches, whence the Cervin had been revealed to him in all its grandeur; descending to Breuil, he ascended to the Theodul, taking with him a certain Jean Baptiste Hérin, the first Valtournanche guide whose name appears in a traveller's book.[13] On his second

Guido Rey

Villa Rey
with Jomein and the Matterhorn

journey, which took place in 1792, he comes to the Val Tournanche, studying and describing it; he ascends to the Theodul Pass, where he spends three days, analysing the structure of the Cervin, whose height he is now the first to measure, and collecting stones, plants, and insects. Nothing escapes his careful observation, from the sparse lichen that clings to the rocks to the tiny but vigorous glacier fly that flutters over the cold snows, and whose existence at such heights is full of mystery. At night he takes refuge under the tent erected near the ruins of the old fort at the top of the pass.[14] During these days he ascends the Little Cervin, which he names the Cime Brune du Breithorn.

The appearance of this first traveller and his long stay on the pass made a lasting impression on the imagination of the mountain folk; for many years the great man lived in the memories of the shepherds of Breuil — as M. Hirzel-Escher, who passed there in 1822, testifies — and they were wont to speak of him with a kind of veneration; the modest wooden hut where he lodged at Breuil bears to this day the name of Maison de Saussure.

This was his seventh journey in the Alps, and his last; he has left us in his writings a treasury of profound and inspired observations; but, amid his earnest scientific research, every page shows his boundless enthusiasm for the beauties of the Alps; he seems to repay the mountains with passionate love for the knowledge they bestow upon him. In him the scientist frequently changes into the poet and the painter; his narrative is smooth and plain, free from outbursts of conventional enthusiasm; but his simple and quiet language bring home to us the mountain calm in all its completeness. And that is why the *Voyages* is full of vivid interest even for the uninitiated, and why this work has preserved its freshness and its youth for all these years, and is to this day a model for him who studies mountains and writes of them.

Töpffer has pointed out, as a noteworthy fact, that he who has best understood and interpreted the Alps, one of the few who have infused into their style the characteristics and the grandeur of the mountains, was a student of positive science, a man accustomed to the use of the barometer and hygrometer, and that of all the poets and artists who came after to sing of these same places and to paint them, not one has been able to equal him. To us, to whom it is given to follow the different phases of the slow growth of human interest in the Alps, it seems natural that (before all others) the geologists should have sought the Alps, for they were the first handbooks of their science.

De Saussure was not content with platonic contemplation of Alpine landscapes, which filled with a poetic calm and comforted the troubled soul of his great fellow-citizen Rousseau.

The geologist must needs touch the summits, test them with his hammer, take away with him fragments of them, wrestle hand to hand with the mountain, in order to pierce its mystery; and that is why the science of geology was the real mother of mountaineering.

The publication of Saussure's book, in 1796, revealed to all scientists and travellers the beauties of places till then almost unknown.

The first inquirers began to come to the Cervin. They came from afar: there is a record of a party of Englishmen who in the summer of 1800 crossed the Great St. Bernard, a few months after the passage of Bonaparte; they came to Aosta and thence to Valtournanche, slept at the châlets of Breuil, and traversed the Theodul Pass, which they called Monte Rosa.[15] The Cervin was to them an object of the most intense and continuous admiration.

Mr. Cade, one of the party, who described the journey, relates that on their way up the valley they everywhere attracted the attention of the good mountain folk, who would leave their work in the fields and come running up, curious to see these rare wayfarers and to ask them questions.[16] To the inhabitants accustomed to the isolation of these unknown valleys the arrival of those travellers, with their outlandish form of dress and their strange speech, must have presented a curious spectacle. They felt that these travellers were rich, they were even at times inclined to think them richer than they were; with their rough good sense they could not understand why people who had every comfort in their homes should come and adventure themselves in a poverty-stricken country among inhospitable mountains; why people, who had at their disposal good roads and horses and carriages, should walk up toilsome paths, and they wove about them the most absurd hypotheses.

At that time the mountains, for those who dwelt among them, were divided into two zones: the useful, that which produced the grass of the pastures and the timber of the forests, where mines were found, where the mill-wheel could revolve, which gave easy communication with the neighbouring valleys, and where at the furthest the chamois could be hunted; and the useless, that which stretched up to heaven from the line of eternal snow.

And at the sight of those travellers braving without any apparent object the dangers of the glaciers, the mountain folk were led to imagine a thousand divers and fantastic reasons for their coming, but never the real one of pleasure and study. When they surprised the geologist chipping the rocks with his hammer and filling his pockets with useless pebbles they suspected him of being a seeker after treasure; the botanist storing grasses in his mysterious green box was an alchemist; and those others who were sketching or looking intently about them, taking notes of everything, were the secret agents of some foreign Government, or at best they were cranks or madmen. Therefore they looked upon them with suspicion.[17]

When we reflect on the ease with which we travel in the Alps at the present day, when the railways bring us rapidly to the foot of the mountains and far up the valleys, carriage roads wind up to a height of 5,000 feet, a decent inn is to be found in almost every village, and we climb the peaks with an excellent guide-book like Martelli's or Vaccarone's or Bobba's in our hands, we think with admiration of those travellers, unpractised and misjudged, who after much journeying forced their way into regions (almost unknown) of bad paths and worse quarters; who, full of new-born wonder, came among the Alpine folk who were still living the same obscure lives as of old, all unknowing that poets and men of science were celebrating their mountains in song and studying their beauties and their secrets, unconscious of the new love that was arising in the civilized world for their rude houses and their inhospitable rocks.

Some of these travellers doubtless had with them that primitive guide-book to Switzerland by Johann Gottfried Ebel, which was published at Zürich towards the end of the eighteenth century, and translated and adapted to the use of the English in 1818, and which was as the Alpine travellers' A B C. Among the very detailed information which it gave as to the way in which the dangers of the Alps should be met, we find the following curious rule: 'Before venturing into a difficult passage, gaze your fill at the precipices until the impression which they may make on your imagination passes off, and until you have made yourself able to look upon them unmoved.' In it tourists were specially enjoined, if they wished to draw pleasure and profit from their excursions, to salute in a friendly manner all those whom they met by the way, and to converse affably with the mountain people, in order to put away all pride and vanity, leaving at home all the prejudices of caste and high birth, and bringing with them into the high mountains the man alone. In this book Val Tournanche is only mentioned incidentally in the indices; the Cervin appeared in it under the three names of Silvius, Matterhorn, and Mont Cervin, and was briefly described as one of the most splendid and wonderful obelisks in the Alps. On Zermatt there was this curious note: 'A place which may, perhaps, interest the tourist is the valley of Praborne; it is bounded by huge glaciers which come right down into the valley; the village of Praborne is fairly high, and stands at a great height above the glaciers; its climate is almost as warm as that of Italy, and plants belonging to hot countries are to be found there at considerable altitudes, above the ice.' The routes in that first guide-book were for the most part incomplete and poorly described. Murray's Handbook, which was destined to be the model of all guides for Alpine travellers, only made its first appearance in 1838, and Johanne's *Itinéraire* in 1841.

The railways, where there were any, terminated a hundred miles from the Alpine centres, and no one had even dreamt of tunnelling through the mountains. Aosta could only be reached by many stages in a coach; it took three days to go from Turin to St. Vincent; at the present day the journey from Paris to Zermatt requires eighteen hours. Brigands prowled about Ivrea, bears and wolves infested the neighbourhood of Châtillon.[18] The journey was neither comfortable nor safe, and now and then it was necessary to draw one's pistol from one's pocket, as happened to the painter Brockedon, who, in 1821, came into conflict with the brutal customs officials of Paquier.[19]

Now the bears and the brigands have disappeared, and the customs officials have become good fellows.*

In those days an exceptional strength of character, together with a certain spirit of adventure and of eccentricity, were needed in order to face the vicissitudes of Alpine journeys. The state of mind in which our ancestors ventured into the unknown regions of the snows was very different from that of the climbers of the present day. Perhaps they called to their aid a superfluous degree of heroism, and saw dangers where we see only a few difficulties; but in exchange for their discomforts and impediments, they enjoyed the unforeseen; the valleys were revealed to them in all the poetry of solitude, in unprepared primitive simplicity; the mountains whispered shyly to them the secrets they had not yet told to others.

A great feeling of curiosity, of uncontrollable admiration, the joyfulness and enthusiasm of youth opening the mind to new ideals, are manifest in the pages written by these pioneers.

A new world began to show itself.

Those strangers, men of noblest intellect, climbing the Alps, and reaching the summits of the passes, gazed eagerly out over our land: from the cold, snowy heights their glances sought the country where the orange blooms, and already they seemed to see a bluer sky on our horizon and gentler slopes in our valleys; far below lay the mirage of fair Italy, eternal dream of northern minds.

They were the first to tell us that our valleys contained wondrous monuments, and teach us to admire them. The mountain people had thought them seekers after treasure, and they were not wrong, because these men discovered and bequeathed to us a treasury of enthusiasm and study which is still unexhausted.

Mr. William Brockedon, who came here in 1825, considered the crossing of the Theodul Pass from Breuil to Zermatt a difficult undertaking, and caught fever on his return.[20] He tells us that on

* [Some of them became decidedly less 'good fellows' under the Fascist régime. – R.L.G.I.]

the way over the glacier small wooden stakes were fixed to point out the dangerous places and the right road; when two stood together it was a sign that on that spot was a bridge of ice over a crevasse, and that the greatest care was needed. On the ascent he suffers from the rarefaction of the atmosphere, and has to halt at every step. When he arrives panting, exhausted, on the top of the pass, he gazes 'on the beautiful pyramid of the Cervin, more wonderful than aught else in sight, rising from its bed of ice to a height of 5,000 feet, a spectacle of indescribable grandeur'. In this 'immense natural amphitheatre, enclosed from time immemorial by snow-clad mountains and glaciers ever white, in the presence of these grand walls the mind is overwhelmed, not indeed that it is unable to contemplate the scene, but it staggers under the immensity of those objects which it contemplates'. Thus does Brockedon give expression to his enthusiasm, and the same feelings must have inspired those others who at that time drew nigh to the Cervin.

Those who made their way up through the Val Tournanche to the foot of the mountain were few in number. Mr. Coolidge, a most diligent collector of old and new stories of the Alps, mentions during those years, besides Brockedon, only Mr. Hirzel-Escher, of Zürich, who crossed the Theodul in 1822, starting from Breuil, accompanied by the local guide, Jean-Baptiste Menabraye[21] and a French gentleman from Algiers, who in 1837 made the same ascent. The greater number came from the Valais up the Visp valley to Zermatt.

In 1813 a Frenchman, M. Henri Maynard, had climbed to the Theodul and attained the virgin summit of the Breithorn; he was accompanied by numerous guides, among them old J. M. Couttet, of Chamonix, the same who had gone with Saussure to the top of the Little Cervin in 1792.

In 1821 the ascent of the Breithorn was repeated by the illustrious English astronomer, Sir John Herschel, with a Chamonix guide, and again in 1830 the summit was attained by Lord Minto, with a gang of twelve Chamoniards. All these thought they were ascending Monte Rosa.

Lord Minto left a diary of his journey, full of curious notes of great value for the history of early mountaineering.[22] He took with him a small piece of blue paper in order to compare it with the colour of the sky at different altitudes; it was the same piece that Dr. Paccard had taken with him on the first ascent of Mont Blanc.

On the pass he found the four walls of the hut that Saussure's guides had built, and he spent the night there. Overtaken by bad weather he returned to Zermatt, whose worthy inhabitants received him with acclamation and joy at seeing him return alive from a night spent among the glaciers of the Cervin. Lord Minto called the Theodul Pass the Mont Cervin, and the Cervin the Matterhorn; the Breithorn he called Monte Rosa.

It was only when he reached the top of the Breithorn that he became aware of his error, by the discovery of another distant summit, towards Macugnaga, which he supposed to be higher than his own. From up there he saw Mont Blanc, but, turning his gaze on the Cervin, he gave voice to his great wonder: 'It is impossible,' he said, 'for words to convey any idea of the immensity of this pyramid, regular and symmetrical in form, as if it had been designed by an architect, and rising to a prodigious height above the glacier on which it rests.'

Above all the eye of those early worshippers was struck by the rare, symmetrical form of the mountain, which did not seem the blind, indifferent work of Nature, but the masterpiece of a whole thinking, restless people, which had given to it a human impress, expressive of its own power.

Dr. Forbes writes: 'It is so very different from what we have been accustomed to find in natural scenery, that among the ideas that crowd the mind in first contemplating it, those of Art and the Artificial come with the rest.'[23]

Their stupefaction, their loss of mental balance, manifested themselves in the most fervid exclamations, in the boldest imagery.

Some compared it to a ruined tower, some to an obelisk piercing the sky, some to a sphinx that keeps mysterious watch in silent space on its pedestal of ice; some, again, to the bust of a giant with weary shoulders and mighty flanks, wrapped round the elbows in the wide folds of a white veil that sweeps down from his head in majestic curves till it covers his feet (Töpffer); some there were who saw in it the form of a couchant lion, and some of a rearing horse (Ruskin); some called it the Leviathan of mountains, and others the monument that an archangel had erected to himself before he left the earth.

Others, again, it inspired with visions of ancient mythology. To John Ball the summits of Monte Rosa seemed like the solemn conclave of the Scandinavian gods, whose white beards flowed down even to their feet, and the Cervin was the mythical hero who burst into the midst of the majestic assembly; to Dollfus Ausset the Cervin was among the other peaks as Achilles among the Grecian heroes. drawing to himself alone the glances and the admiration of all mankind. It was the marvel of marvels, as Hinchliff felt himself compelled to say.

The writings of these pioneers are full of its great name; the bare and inert rock is gradually quickened into life by men's enthusiasm, and clothes itself with the bright veil of their dreams.

'Stronger minds,' remarks Edward Whymper, 'felt the influence of the wonderful form, and men who ordinarily spoke or wrote like rational beings, when they came under its power seemed to quit their senses, and ranted and rhapsodized, losing for a time all common forms of speech.'

Among the poets of the Cervin during these years (1834 to 1840) were Elie de Beaumont, a famous French geologist; Desor,[24] a naturalist of Neuchâtel, who went up there with a party of friends, two of whom, Agassiz and Bernard Studer, had names illustrious in science; Engelhardt, a native of Strassburg, who was so filled with admiration for Zermatt and its neighbourhood, that he returned there at least ten times (from 1835 to 1855), and described these places in two valuable volumes,[25] drew panoramas and maps, and collected most minute notes on the mineralogy and botany. He was one of the earliest and warmest friends of Zermatt.

Zermatt was at that time a quiet little village, and travellers found simple hospitality there at the parish priest's, or at the village doctor's, Herr Lauber by name. Besides students there came only a few collectors of Alpine crystals, insects, and plants, of which they reaped a rich harvest, and which they afterwards sold. Of tourists pure and simple there was as yet no sign, and Desor was able to write at that time: 'In the visitors' book (Herr Lauber's), which is in its first year, I saw that the names of the five or six travellers who had preceded me all belonged to persons known to me, being Swiss botanists and zoologists; decidedly this valley is not yet infested by tourists!'

In 1841 there comes James David Forbes, professor of natural philosophy at the University of Edinburgh. An eminent philosopher and geologist, and a most observant traveller, he continues, in his journeys and his writings, the work of Saussure. He is full of admiration for the Cervin, and he calls it the most wonderful peak in the Alps, unscaled and unscalable. These words, pronounced by a man noted among all his contemporaries for his thorough knowledge of mountains, show what men's feelings then were towards the Cervin, and how at a time when the idea of Alpine exploration was gaining ground in their minds, the Cervin stood by itself as a mountain apart, of whose conquest it was vain even to dream.

And such it remained till long after this; as such it was described by John Ball twenty years later in his celebrated guide-book. Incidentally I may point out that Forbes calls it the Mont Cervin and rarely uses its German name of Matterhorn.

Professor Forbes ascended the Theodul in 1842, climbed the Breithorn, and came down to Breuil and Paquier; as he descended from the savage scenery of the Mont Cervin, the Italian landscapes of the Val Tournanche seemed to him like paradise.[26]

Meanwhile Gustave Studer, the geographer, together with Professor Ulrich, was describing and mapping the topographical features of the Zermatt peaks. And behold, amid the chorus of those who found in the Cervin subjects for study, there arises the voice of one who demands of it nought but a simple, pure delight for his eye and his soul; he is an artist and a philosopher, and the author of the exquisite *Voyages en Zig-zag*, Rudolph Töpffer of Geneva.

I have again opened the pages of that golden book, once the delight of my youth, to see what was the Cervin's message to that noble and high-souled man, and I have found them still as full of freshness and wholesomeness and honesty as before; and I remember the time when, reading them eagerly and gazing at their curious engravings, I dreamt ever of lengthy marches in joyous company, up through green valleys and over lofty passes, of delicious meals beside Alpine lakes, and of suppers in the simple mountain inns, eaten with the sauce of the exhaustless gaiety and tremendous appetite of youth. In that book I have, as it were, found again an old friend, who perhaps was the first to inspire me with an eager desire for the mountains.

Töpffer, who first accompanied and guided youth to the Alps for purposes of education and amusement, began his zig-zag journeys in 1832, but it is only in 1840 that he mentions the Cervin. 'Déjà on parle de la Vallée de Zermatt qui s'ouvre à Viège, et des glaciers du Mont Cervin, comme offrant des beautés et des horreurs d'un caractère plus grand ou plus intéressant que ce que l'on va voir à Chamonix et dans l'Oberland.' Happy was he who lived at a time and in a place that gave him, almost at a stone's throw from his own home, unknown and wonderful objects to discover!

Two years later Töpffer and his pupils came to Zermatt. He has described this journey of his in a chapter entitled 'Voyage autour du Mont Blanc', one of the finest he has written, the most complete, the fullest of experience; it seems as if, foreseeing the nearness of his end he had wished to collect in these last pages of his the most exquisite reminiscences, the most fervent interests of his whole life.[27] Here he sings a real hymn of praise to the Cervin. In pages at once comprehensive, precise, and magnificent he describes its form, comparing it with a huge crystal of a hundred facets, flashing varied hues, that softly reflects the light, unshaded, from the uttermost depths of the heavens. Then mastering himself, he asks whence comes this emotion that he feels: 'D'où vient donc, d'où vient l'intérêt, le charme puissant avec lequel ceci se contemple?' And he answers this question with a profound analysis of man's sensations in the presence of the mountain: 'Ce n'est pourtant ni le pittoresque, ni la demeure possible de l'homme, ni même une merveille gigantesque pour l'œil qui a vu les astres ou pour l'esprit qui conçoit l'univers! La nouveauté sans doute, pour des citadins surtout; l'aspect si rapproché de la mort, de la solitude, de l'éternel silence;

notre existence si frêle, si passagère mais vivante et douée de pensée, de volonté et d'affection, mise en quelque sorte en contact avec la brute existence et la muette grandeur de ces êtres sans vie; voilà, ce semble, les vagues pensées qui attachent et qui secouent l'âme à la vue de cette scène. . . . Poésie sourde mais puissante, et qui, par cela même qu'elle dirige la pensée vers les grands mystères de la création, captive l'âme et l'élève.' And he concludes with a profession of his faith: 'Plus d'un homme qui oubliait Dieu dans la plaine, s'est ressouvenu de lui aux montagnes.'

Töpffer's book was illustrated by Calame, his master and friend, with drawings of the Cervin, executed in the romantic style of the period. It is an artificial Cervin, of conventional beauty, and of too slender a shape, that we see in those early drawings, as also in Engelhardt's; a fantastic Cervin, fearfully smooth, such as it might appear in a troubled dream to a mountaineering novice planning to ascend it; a picture corresponding rather with the exaggerated effect it produces on the astonished mind of the artist, than with the real form of the mountain.

But about this time there came a man who studied the Cervin in its structure and form, and who sketched it and described it in all its parts with the curiosity of the artist and the insight of the scientist. This was John Ruskin, a new and original type of philosopher and geologist, painter and poet, whom England was enabled to create during that period of radical intellectual reforms, which led the way for the highest development of her civilization. Ruskin was the Cervin's poet *par excellence*. When, as a boy of fourteen, he was taken by his parents to visit the Alps, he became filled with so great an enthusiasm and so burning a love for them, that the traces of their inspiration appear in many parts of his numerous works; some verses which he wrote at that time tell how the mountains revealed a new life to him, which would last till he entered the gates of death.

As a child he had become enamoured of the drawings of Turner, painter of mountains, of sunsets, of architecture, and of the sea, who was at that time much talked of in England, and of whose merit Ruskin was afterwards a strenuous and successful defender.

Side by side with this passion of his for art, that for scientific research had developed in him, especially in respect of geology, and at the age of fifteen the reading of Saussure's *Voyages*, a gift from his father, gave him the greatest delight. In that noble and profound book he seemed to find the complement of the visions he had had of Turner's fantastic water-colours, and the explanation of his stormy outlines and wondrous colours. They were his keys to that which he happily called mountain architecture.

In this spirit he came to the Alps, and he never wearied of returning to them. He went to Zermatt in 1844, and it is to be noticed as a curious fact, that the first time he saw the Cervin it did not please him.[28] The wonderful mountain on its lofty pedestal in the very heart of the Alps was, perhaps, too far removed from the ideal he had formed of the mountains; but he returned, studied and dreamt for long at its feet, and at length he pronounced it 'the most noble cliff in Europe'.[29]

Round about the noble cliff we see him busily analysing the perspective of its outlines, calculating the angles of inclination of its various ridges, intent on determining which point is the real summit;[30] we see him deducing its internal structure from the twisted curves of the strata, which appear on its lofty walls, and seeking to read the mountain's true nature in its outlines.

Edward Whymper, examining a drawing of the Cervin executed by Ruskin in 1848, remarks in it certain details, which a draughtsman pure and simple would have neglected, and which only he who climbs its rocks and struggles hand to hand with the mountain discovers to be the essential features of its anatomy.

Ruskin would have been an ideal illustrator of books on mountaineering; by the side of his concise, analytical, and yet emotional drawings, the pleasant and poetical syntheses of Töpffer and Calame appear superficial; but he was no mountaineer, nor a great friend to mountaineering; other ideals filled his soul; he drew sketches of the mountains merely as an illustration of his teaching of the beauty of natural forms, which was the object of his whole life. In his work on Modern Painters he makes continual use of the mountains as an example of beauty and an incentive to morality. In laying down the principles which are to guide him in his description of the historic Stones of Venice, he quotes as a model the mighty mass of rock, which he considers more sublime than any human building, and it is strange to us, when we open that wonderful book of his (*Stones of Venice*), so full of the ancient splendour of the city of lagoons, to read almost at the beginning this passage:

'But there are sometimes more valuable lessons to be learned in the school of nature than in that of Vitruvius, and a fragment of building among the Alps is singularly illustrative of the chief feature which I have at present to develop as necessary to the perfection of the wall veil.

'It is a fragment of some size; a group of broken walls, one of them overhanging; crowned with a cornice, nodding some hundred and fifty feet over its massive flank, three thousand above its glacier base, and fourteen thousand above the sea — a wall truly of some majesty, at once the most precipitous and the strongest mass in the whole chain of the Alps, the Mont Cervin.'

And elsewhere he again dwells tenderly on this idea of the Cervin as an architectural work (in a passage in which he likens it to an Egyptian temple).

Certainly the style of Ruskin's admiration and teaching is very different from Saussure's classical simplicity and Töpffer's calm romanticism; the occasional intricacy of his writing, and the mystic hymns with which he ends some of his chapters, may be less pleasing to more prosaic students of the Alps; yet they cannot but rejoice that this great genius has let fall the life-giving dew of his admiration on one of their ideals, and has been the first to create a new worship, and to weave about the Cervin lofty dreams of art and beauty.[31]

We have said that Ruskin was no friend to mountaineering; it is to him that we owe the celebrated definition of difficult ascents, comparing them with greased poles, up which men climb in rivalry to gain the small prize hanging from the top; the climbers of Mont Blanc were alluded to by him in this ironical simile. He had never known the mysterious, ineffable joy of conquering a virgin peak; to him also the Cervin was inviolable; he was content with admiring it. Nevertheless the publication of Ruskin's work certainly produced a great impression at the time on educated people in England, and spread wide a desire to see the mountains to which the young apostle of beauty had dedicated his throbbing, enthusiastic pages. We may infer as much from the frequent discussions to which his work gave rise, and from the quotations therefrom in Alpine writings and guide-books printed in the following years.

Other men of high attainments followed, paying to the Cervin their tribute of admiration and research; John Ball, that tireless and learned traveller and writer of works on travel, afterwards the first president of the English Alpine Club;[32] Jacob Siegfried, who about that time was the first to cross the Allalin Pass; Von Tschüdi, author of *The Swiss Guide* (Schweizer führer), published in 1855; the brothers A. and H. Schlagintweit, who stopped for three days on the Theodul in order to make observations, and attempted the highest peak of Monte Rosa; Adams Reilly, who made the first accurate map of the southern slopes of Monte Rosa; and others besides.

Every one of these high souled and determined men left behind him a part, however small, of his enthusiasm and his experience. We at the present time think it natural, on reaching the foot of the Cervin, to wonder how soon we shall be able to climb it; but then it needed the sum of those men's admiration to prepare slowly this new sense of desire. Mr. Coolidge remarks that the presence at Zermatt in 1851 of Alfred Wills, one of the foremost champions of English mountaineering, marked the close of the timid attempts, and the beginning of the era of conquest.[33]

The army of students and poets was now about to be succeeded in the tourney at the Cervin's feet by the company of the real climbers, the knights errant girding themselves up for the conquest of the fair virgins of the Alps; they were not urged on by the love of science or of art alone, but also by an inexplicable passion whose fascination, whose very existence, lay in the difficulty of the struggle. They entered the lists brandishing their new weapon, the ice-axe, and escorted by their faithful esquires, the new guides. The battle began with the highest peak of Monte Rosa, and it lasted fully nine years (1847-1855)[34].

The passes and peaks round Zermatt were explored little by little. Monte Rosa was conquered; but the Cervin remained still the mysterious mountain of the past; the idea that it might be accessible to man[35] had not yet arisen, but its mystery filled men's minds more and more.

'L'ascension au Mont Cervin (Matterhorn) est possible: un ballon d'une enveloppe excessivement solide, cuirassé pour ainsi dire et d'une forme spéciale, maintenu par une forte corde qui se déroulerait lentement et qui, à volonté, pendant l'ascension, permettrait au touriste aérien de diriger l'embarcation et d'arriver à la cime par des circonstances météorologiques de calme plat', wrote Dollfus-Ausset, an Alsatian scientist, in 1855.

They were still in Utopia; and the same year a poet, hearing in imagination the unconquered Cervin calling to Monte Rosa vanquished by man, poured forth this song:

> Frère, console toi! Le Mont Cervin te venge!
> Pour me vaincre jamais, il faudrait qu'un archange
> Prêtât son aile à l'homme, ou qu'un rapide éclair
> Le saisît palpitant et l'emportât dans l'air;
> Il faudrait que son corps, léger comme un fluide,
> Pût s'élever sans peine aux régions du vide.
> Jusque là, même en rêve, il n'essaiera jamais
> De peser un instant sur mes âpres sommets.
>
> . . . .
>
> Je ne laisse arriver à mon sublime faîte
> Que les soupirs ardents du juste et du poète;
> Que les flots du déluge, et les esprits du feu
> Et mon front ne fléchit que sous l'ombre de Dieu.

Ten years later man trod the Cervin's summit.

And meanwhile what had been done by us Italians? Though dwelling close to the Cervin, though masters of one half of it, we were leaving to foreigners the joy of admiring it, the credit of studying it. The wondrous Alps appeared to be unknown to us; their fascination had not yet been revealed to us. Thus it is with the flash of a lofty lighthouse, which lights and guides far distant ships, but is invisible to those who stand at the foot of its tower.

Italians, indeed, had at that time much else to think about and do; they had before them a great and difficult task — the creation of

Italy — and their efforts were directed towards this goal, their thoughts were all absorbed by this ideal. The notion that by strengthening their limbs with gymnastic exercises youths became vigorous to take part in their country's battles, had already arisen. Leopardi had poured out the following hymn to a victor in the pallone:

> Te rigoglioso dell'età novella
> Oggi la patria cara
> Gli antichi esempi a rinnovar prepara.

(Filled with pride in the new age, thy dear country prepares thee to follow the example of the ancients.)

And the pupils of the gymnasium at Turin, founded by Ricardi of Netro, a future hero of Goito, sang with enthusiasm the hymn that Felice Romani, the patriotic librettist of the 'Norma', wrote for them about 1840:

> I sudati ed aspri ludi
> Affrontiam sereni e lieti,
> Alle prove degli atleti,
> Afforziam le membra e il cor.
> A palestra ancor più rude
> Pronti un dì farem passaggio,
> Chè la forza dà coraggio
> E il coraggio dà valor..

Joyful and unmoved We face the strenuous and rough games. With athletes' struggles we strengthen our limbs and our hearts. Some day we will readily pass to a yet rougher arena, for strength gives courage, and courage valour.

Poor verses, but a fair song bravely and calmly sung by youths who were full of faith and hope! Would it were sung by us on the lofty peaks with the same untainted enthusiasm with which our fathers chanted it during their first school walks on the hills around Turin, under the guidance of one of the first teachers of gymnastics, Obermann.

VALTOURNANCHE

J. B. MAQUIGNAZ
one of a famous family of
Valtournanche guides

Memorial Tablets at Valtournanche

Jean-Antoine Carrel
Daniel Maquignaz
Chanoine Georges Carrel
Antoine Maquignaz
John Joseph Maqui
Sig. Giovanni Bobb

But the lists of the Alps were not yet open, and the destiny in store for those young men was the redemption of their country. Their alpenstock was a rifle; the summits for which they strove with the alien, to which the youth of Italy raised their longing eyes, were the Cathedral of Milan, bristling with countless spires, that shone white as the snow of Mont Blanc; and the Campanile of Venice, rising straight and smooth from the green lagoon, like a Dolomite tower above the silent lakes of the upper Cadore. On these heights the Italians, who were making ready for that last difficult ascent of the distant Seven Hills, for which they had so long yearned, wished to plant their banners. And already the victims of their brave attempts and of their first glorious efforts were counted by hundreds.

Their glances and their thoughts were at that time only turned towards the Alps, as to a bulwark against the foreigner, on which Garibaldi's chasseurs were to repeat the heroic feats of the soldiers of the Duke of Savoy on the Col de l'Assiette.

The poetry of that time mirrored the minds of the people, and in the verses of Giovanni Prati the mountains wept at the misfortunes of their native land. No man as yet thought of the mountains for the mountains' sake. Those few, poets or men of learning, who sallied forth from the circle of the subalpine cities to seek among the Alps inspiration or knowledge, did not venture to leave the paths that led up through the bottoms of the valleys. The high mountains were not yet in the conscious possession of the Italians; they were like a wondrous piece of scenery painted at the back of the stage, with the actors missing.

If we read the letters of Francesetti of Mezzenile, written in 1820,[36] we are surprised to find ourselves confronted by a would-be mountaineer. He seems a youth who as yet knows not love, but is already full of desire; he does not aspire to conquest, and is content to gaze at his lady and to praise her beauty.

The modesty of the prologue to his letters betrays his fear of being unworthy of the beauty he describes, a shame-faced concealment of the enthusiasm which might appear childish and vain to others, almost a fear of derision; feelings that are not unknown to us at the present day, with all our experience. And, going on from aspirations to deeds, we find some noble conceptions, men who were true mountaineers: the Italians Pietro Giordani, in 1801, Vincent and Zumstein in 1819, Gnifetti and his companions in 1842, had been the first conquerors of the peaks of Monte Rosa, at whose feet they had been born, and in the same year (1842), the Abbé Chamoix, also a son of the mountains, had climbed his fair Tersiva. These exploits made no noise, nor did the climbers boast of them. In the same way Alpine history is silent concerning chamois hunters, who in pursuit of their game had more than once ascended, unconscious pioneers, peaks where no man had set his foot before them.

But Italian history does mention a mountain hunter, the greatest of all, 'Bella speranza del regno. Primogenito figlio di Carlo Alberto Re. Varcate più montagne erte, asprissime. Famose per natura o per subalpino valore. Qui salì ai XXII. di Luglio MDCCCXXXIII.'

These lines, which the Commune of Susa caused to be engraved in marble and placed on the summit of the Roche Melon, 3,500 metres high, in memory of the first Alpine ascent of the young Duke Victor Emmanuel, correspond with those others of two centuries before, which commemorated the ascent of that peak by Charles Emmanuel II, 'followed by his courtiers, in the flower of his age, full of fervent devotion, in order to adore the Virgin, his protectress, from the highest spot in his States'.

The princes of this true Alpine race made a habit of braving the hardships of the Alps; they were accustomed to fight in their mountains, to cross and recross the high ranges in winter and in summer, on which, as on a crystal pivot, rested the scales of their ancient policy, until to our great good fortune, the balance inclined to the side of Italy.

Victor Emmanuel II professed publicly, perhaps before any other in Piedmont, a passion for the mountains. Before 1842 he had already climbed, under his father's guidance, to the foot of Monte Rosa, in the Gressoney Valley; later on he came by the pass, at that time seldom used, of the Fenêtre de Champorcher, to Cogne, on whose heights he learned to love hunting the chamois and the bouquetin. This sport, which he began to follow in 1850, was afterwards assiduously followed by him in the great Italian group of the Grand Paradis, which he covered with a network of well-made paths, right up to the glaciers. He was a lover of the chase, and sought in the Alps the joy of laying low his nimble quarry with a straight shot from his rifle, rather than that of ascending them; but he yearned after them also for the sake of the rough life and the difficult passages which he found there, and which satisfied the need he felt to strive and conquer. And the talk to which the young king's hunting expeditions gave rise in Piedmont, the anecdotes which were told of his simple life upon the heights, of the kindly affability of his converse with the Alpine folk, and above all the confidence which was felt in him, the goodwill with which his every action was followed in Italy, as if his country's weal depended upon it, undoubtedly assisted in inspiring other noble hearts with a desire for the Alps, and in attracting the attention of the multitude to the hitherto unknown mountains. Something beautiful and great there must have been up there for Victor Emmanuel to return thither every year; and men's glances were turned with curiosity and respect, upwards to the white summits among which the king sought new strength to serve his people.

Italy, busied for so many years with the winning of her liberty, had lagged in many respects behind other nations; but as she was now attaining step by step unity and a consciousness of her own strength, she felt the need of an intellectual revival and of aspirations towards a higher civilization. In that generous spring-time of ideals it seemed to men of high attainments that the love and exploration of mountains, the struggle with rocks and ice, might be made a mighty instrument of progress. It seemed to them good that youths should mount to the summits of the Alps to cry out joyfully to the peoples over the border that all Italy, or nearly all, belonged to the Italians. And the Alpine Club sprang from the mighty brain of Quintino Sella, like Minerva from the head of Jupiter, armed at all points.

CHAPTER II

THE THREE INNS

'The snows of Mont Blanc and the cliffs of the Matterhorn would have their charm in the midst of a wilderness; but their beauty is amazingly increased when a weather-stained châlet rises in the foreground; when the sound of cow-bells comes down through the thin air; or the little troop of goats returns at sunset to the quiet village.'
LESLIE STEPHEN, *The Playground of Europe.*

I CAN see in my mind's eye one of those romantic travellers of the first half of the century, come from afar to venture among the Alps, in the days when they were known only through the studies of a few men of science or the vision of certain poets. I can see him climbing for the first time up the lonely valley path, his mind filled with the dream of an idyllic peace, of a free and primitive life, awakened in him by the writings of Haller[1] and Rousseau; he recalls in memory the poetic images of the bold chamois hunter in *Manfred* and of the mountain heroes in *William Tell*; the sweet melodies of 'Linda' and of the 'Sonnambula', which he lately applauded in the theatres of the town, still ring in his ears. It seems to him that the lives of the men who inhabit those small châlets, who breathe so pure an air, who slake their thirst at such crystal-clear springs, amid natural scenes so full of light and sound, must needs be full of harmony and peace; that the hearts of the mountain people must be as tranquil and as noble as the objects which surround them. And already he dreams that the happiness of the pastoral life is about to be revealed to him, that at some turning of the path a joyous band of Alpine folk will rush forth, and that some Linda or Amina in a velvet bodice will appear among the flowers at the window of a châlet and sing a greeting to him.

But, when he enters the village street, he sees that things are not as the poet has portrayed them; a sense of something forbidding, almost akin to terror, is conveyed by the sight of the low, dark houses, huddled one against the other for purposes of mutual protection against the cold and of resistance to the shock of the winds; the garments of the hill-folk are poor and ragged; their forbidding faces are never lit up by a smile; their life is a hard one, as is that of all things which live and grow in those high places, and man's fate up there is like that of the pines, which fill the fissures of the rocks with their deep-burrowing roots, suck up their nourishment from the barren soil, and grow in serried groups strong enough to stand the weight of the snows, and live till the hurricane uproots them or the avalanche sweeps them away; or else die slowly of old age when the sap of life is in them no more. No man notices that there is a pine the less in the forest, or a cross the more in the little cemetery. Perhaps the troubles and the worries that pertain to town life are not apparent in the mountains, but there is instead a sort of stupor, of dull, continuous suffering.

The summer is short: the rest of the year is winter, and the mountain dweller patiently awaits in his closed stable the sun's return; the time for harvest is short, and the work of gathering it in is heavy; the placid joys of labour do not seem to brighten men's lives in these high places, but hopeless resignation to fate shapes their course.

In the midst of the wretched hovels rises the church, which differs from them but little, save for its belfry, whose bells fill the air with their sad or joyful peals, and which presides over the births, weddings, and funerals of this small group of men in their isolation from the world.

And the religion of these men appears one of terror to the thoughtful stranger, when he enters the little church and finds it full of strange baroque images and fearsome paintings of sacrifices and torments, and sees the women in their white veils grouped together praying with the gloomy fervour of an ancient faith, and hears the voice of a minister of God threatening his people with the vengeance of heaven, while the avalanche thunders without, and exhorting the faithful to despise earthly riches and human vanities, while they have no joys and but few wretched possessions.

In the upper part of the valley where the path grows rougher and skirts dangerous ravines, he frequently meets with small black crosses that commemorate some accident, and, if he forces his way to the very summit of the pass, he sees that it is bestrewn with bones that lie bleached among the snows; and he feels that here death is nearer to men than elsewhere. The idyllic dream vanishes: Amina becomes in reality a woman who descends the weary path bent double under a heavy load of hay; and in place of the strong and healthy mountaineers, who are at work far off in the fields or pastures, there appears before him an object of pity and disgust, a grotesque and misshapen creature that holds out its hands for alms: the cretin.

To this day we who read the writings of the early travellers are grieved to find in them a feeling of pity, and at times of contempt, for the rude inhabitants of the Alps; and when John Ruskin came, he, with his exquisite sensibility of feeling, was touched, more intensely than any other, by the contrast between the bright glory of nature in the mountains and the squalid poverty of those who dwelt among them; the chapter entitled 'The Mountain Gloom',[2] which is withal one of the finest he wrote about the Alps, seems to be the poet's cry of anguish when disillusioned; he sees the cruel realities of life take the place of his long-cherished visions.

But I think that neither the first roseate vision of the poets nor Ruskin's dark picture was a true reflection of the lives of our mountain people, whose lot was not more miserable than that of all other tillers of the soil; for them, as for the others, the meadow blossomed year by year, and the grain ripened; fatigue brought health-giving sleep, that gave oblivion of their woes; a religion suited to their simple minds afforded them hope and resignation. Little sufficed them, because their wants were few; theirs was a poverty free from shame; theirs was a primitive equality founded on labour that was necessary and the same for all. They lived by the exchange of commodities, like a people of ancient times; money the corruptor was almost unknown; the strictest economy ruled their whole lives; a rigorous climate and a niggardly soil provided necessaries, but no superfluities; and yet they loved that narrow strip of sky that was enclosed by the rugged outlines of the peaks, and the little patch of soil where they were born, and where they wished to die.

The Swiss who were enrolled in foreign armies were wont to be so grievously overcome by home-sickness at the sound of the ancient chant of the Alpine shepherds, that it became necessary to forbid it to be sung in their ranks, because its notes caused them to weep, desert, or die.[3] And among the ennobling lessons which the mountain people have taught the men of cities is a great love for their native place; for them their little village is the centre of the world. It is certain that we do not dream of our comfortable houses, nor of the sumptuous buildings, nor of the hum of the streets in our towns with the same eager longing with which the native of the Alps yearns in exile for his hovel, for the little white church tower, for the peace of its valley and its songs.

It is not difficult, even at the present day, to imagine the village of Valtournanche as it was fifty or a hundred years ago.* The natural scenes which surround it are unchangeable, and the work of man among the rugged mountains progresses right slowly. There are now a few forests the less in the valley,[4] and in exchange there are the telegraph posts and the carriage roads; the church has been repaired and the old tower restored; here and there a châlet freshly done up and roofed with new tiles introduces a patch of brightness among the brown and grey mass of the old houses; but all around are the same meadows, the same fields of rye or potatoes, supported on the slopes by low stone walls, and the same rocks rise bare and threatening above the village. The road leading up the valley was, till after the middle of the century, the same wretched mule-track which De Saussure had used in 1792. Paquier was the chief hamlet, the Grande Paroisse, the highest church in the valley, the mother of a brood of little scattered villages whose inhabitants scratch the barren mountain soil for the little nourishment that it was in its power to give.

The Valtorneins — such is the local name of the inhabitants — were shepherds and tillers of the soil; the chase afforded them recreation from their arduous labours, and smuggling yielded them a rare, risky, and uncertain profit. Little news came up from the

* [Written before the influx of motorists and the development of Breuil as a winter sports resort—R.L.G.I.]

plain; they had heard of Bonaparte's swift passage through the great valley down below; they had learnt of the various changes of government by the alterations in the arms over the tax-collector's office, or by the watchwords of liberty written up on the tavern doors; they had heard an echo of the great wars in the simple tales brought up thither by some relative or friend who had been discharged from the Sardinian army or survived Napoleon's campaigns.

There lives still in the valley the memory of those veterans, who after following willy-nilly the French eagles, after deserting them even, boasted themselves loudly to be the soldiers of the Grande Armée; among the rest was a certain Bernard Meynet, known as Kikolin, and an Aymonod, nicknamed des Clous, who had belonged to a regiment that had been sent to Spain, and who told the story of his journey so well that he seemed a professor of geography and history. So say the old men who used to know him.

They knew that they had a king to whose house they had been loyal for centuries, a king who desired soldiers, a government which exacted taxes; the salt that gave savour to their soup was dear, and the tobacco that they smoked in their pipes and that reeked in their pouches was indifferent; across the Theodul Pass there was better and cheaper for sale, but the guards — the *préposés* — did their best to prevent any from coming across the mountains. Authority was represented by the custom-house officer, who was also the policeman. He was in charge of their property, while the parish priest took care of their souls. But the supreme family authority, the queen bee of the hive, was in those days the mother, who kept the money, prepared the food, sewed the men's clothes, washed the linen, dressed the children, beat them, and made them say their prayers. The men had many other things to do; almost all the Valtournanche families had some small farm in the great valley, near the stony banks of the Dora, between Châtillon and Chambave; the land there was divided between the inhabitants of Paquier, Chamoix, Madelein, Antey, and the other little communes of the Valtournanche, in a quasi-freehold granted them of old by the feudal lord of that district; and at Châtillon the church of the Valtorneins was that of Our Lady of

Grace, whither they descended in solemn procession, preceded by their venerable white banner, when it behoved them to pray to Heaven for rain.

It was these possessions of theirs in the plain, *du plan*, which they valued, and still value, greatly, because from them they obtain those fruits of the earth which their poor native soil 5000 feet above the sea does not produce: walnuts, chestnuts, maize for their polenta, a little wheat to knead with the rye for their bread which they bake once or twice a year; their brown bread which must last them six or twelve months, and which, when it has grown hard, they have to cleave with hatchets or soak in milk to soften. The bread-baking was a solemn function in each family, and its tradition is still religiously preserved. Those possessions entailed the descent of a part of the family, in spring for the ploughing, in autumn for the harvest.

Happy was he who owned also a patch of those pergola vines, supported on the hillsides by stone walls, and upheld by small white posts, which give so ancient, so Italian a character to the vineyards of the Aosta valley. *La vigne du plan!* It was the pride of a whole family; it yielded a few barrels of rough but genuine wine which sufficed for the whole year, and, when any was over, it was not sold, but given to the less fortunate.

But there were bad years sometimes; old men remember a terrible winter; for two years, owing to a disease of the vines, no wine had been made; the wheat and potato crop had been poor throughout the whole Aosta valley; the Swiss had come over in the autumn to buy, and the small proprietors had been obliged to sell them all their produce in order to pay their taxes; the spectre of winter and famine and the proclamation of new taxes terrified and excited the poverty-stricken people; the parish priests preached the duty of charity from the pulpit and collected alms for the poorest families. It was the terrible winter of 1853; the popular excitement overflowed unexpectedly in the sad and useless insurrection of December 26th, when a handful of the hill-folk, descending with weapons and sticks from Champorcher, and joined on the way by contingents from the other lateral valleys, awoke once more at the gates of the good city of Aosta the terror that half a century before had been inspired there by the peasant hordes of the famous Régiment des Soques.

About the time of the feast of St. Bernard of Mentone, in the middle of June, the greater number were wont to depart for the high pastures with their own flocks, or to take service in the common 'Alps' as shepherds or cheese makers; and up they would go from pasture to pasture, as the season permitted, and as the grass was gradually eaten off, up to the highest places, where the grass is scanty and the pastures are dangerous for the flocks, up almost to the moraine, to the foot of the Château des Dames, the Tournalin, the Cervin. Often they would take with them the youngest member of the family, as a *lappa borra.*[5] The child found fresh milk and good air, cost its family but little, and grew up strong and healthy, with rosy cheeks, in the smiling sunlight. And thus were bred the men who were to conquer the Cervin.

A son of Valtournanche, the clever and learned Abbé Amé Gorret, whose name is well-known and dear to climbers, and by whose courtesy I obtained the greater part of these notes on the customs of the valley, has described the life of those children who were taken up to the highest châlets, poetically recalling the memories of his own childhood in the châlet of Cheneil: 'Combien ce Cheneil me rappelle de doux souvenirs! C'est un châlet de consorterie entre vingt-sept particuliers. Autrefois les mères de famille y allaient passer l'été avec leurs enfants; c'est là que j'ai été élevé. Nos mères n'avaient guère à s'éloigner de la maison; elles soignaient le lait et les poules, et rapiéçaient nos habits; nous enfants, nous servions tous de bergers. Ces jours me sont encore si présents! Aussitôt jour, nos mères nous appelaient, elles nous faisaient la prière et le dîner en même temps; à l'arrivée du soleil nous allions manger notre blanche bouillie sur le roc devant la maison, nous bourrions nos poches de pain, et nous partions gais et affairés après nos vaches. Arrivés aux pâturages, quelle joie, quels amusements bruyants! Le jeu du bacculô ou fiolet, spécialité de la vallée d'Aoste, le jeu du Colin Maillard, ou Ciappo fo (attrape fou), les défis pour la course, pour sauter les torrents, pour gravir les rochers, tous jeux de véritable gymnastique. Le soir nous ramenions nos vaches à la maison, et le lendemain nos plaisirs recommençaient.'

At Michaelmas they would come down, deliver the children to their mothers, together with the summer's pay and the sheets still fragrant with hay; then they would be off again for the vintage. For the feast of All Souls they would all be back at the village.

These periodic migrations, which still continue to a certain extent, are a real characteristic of the population of the Valtournanche. As the Abbé Gorret writes of it: C'était la vie de nos bons et robustes ancêtres avant l'invasion des touristes et la fondation des cantines et des auberges, vie passée en famille à l'usage patriarcal, loin de tout bruit. Durant les émigrations temporaires ce n'étaient que brèves réapparitions à la maison pour décharger, entre les mains de la mère de famille, la petite bourse de l'argent gagné, et chez le curé le poids des consciences.

Life in the summer was one of fatigue high up on the sunlit pastures, in sight of the glaciers and the sky, in the winter one of repose in the darkness of the stable. During the latter season, when the little châlets are buried in the snow, when long, silver festoons hang down from the eaves, when the torrent is silent in the grip of the frost and the steps of the rare wayfarers are no longer heard on the soft layer of snow that covers the path, when the sun is only seen for a few hours above the horizon, the mountain people take their rest. Only at times, on fine days when the sun shines bright but cold on the vast white canopy and makes the trees with their icy beards glisten, do they leave their houses and go forth up the valley to look for the heaps of wood that they have made ready in the summer, and the hay they have stored in the highest châlets that they may bring it down on the useful highway of the snow; and the loaded sledges slide silently down the deep chute between two white walls.

This is the season when feast days are celebrated in the family circle: Christmas, the New Year, and, the most solemn of all, that of St. Anthony; on that day the old wine and the new flow merrily, gloomy hearts brighten with unwonted gaiety; and in the evening, in the largest room called the poêle, the only warm room in the châlet, two or three families of neighbours are gathered together, and while the old folks chat, the young man eyes the maiden who already owns his heart. He has known her from a child, he has seen her in the summer brave and strong up on the 'Alp'; he knows that she loves children, that she does not fear hard work, that she is thrifty, and that her feminine vanity is content with a piece of bright-coloured silk to put round her head, and a pair of little golden rings to adorn her ears. She is the woman for him; they exchange the first light words which shape the course of their whole future. Sometimes a musician puts a ribebba to his lips, and dancing begins; a dance full of gravity, with serious faces, stiff bodies, the partner held respectfully at a distance, feet sliding in a monotonous cadence, until the old mother says it is time to go and packs everyone off to bed.

But not every day is a feast day. In the long winter evenings, following days of torpor, when, owing to the fury of the storm, no man has been able to put his head outside the door, in the warm stable, whose windows are stopped with straw, while the oil burns slowly in the little lamp, the old grandfather tells the family the tales he has learnt from his forefathers. They are tales old and beautiful as mythology; none knows whence they come; they are a strange mixture of pagan and Christian ideas, a survival of traditions that live on in mountain regions with a tenacity unknown elsewhere.

They are the usual tales of fairies (*fayons*) dancing in a ring at dawn on the grass where the dew-drops hang like pearls, and leaving there the traces of their gay festival; or the souls in purgatory wandering by night flame-like up and down the quiet, winding torrent; or, again, of miserly dwarfs who at sunset hour come forth from the cave where their treasure lies concealed, and who from afar seem to see gold and gems scattered among the rocks and sparkling in the last rays of the sun.

The thought of riches buried in the bosom of the mountain has always fired the imagination and kindled the desire of the poor mountain folk, and to this day we may see, near certain mysterious rocks in almost inaccessible places, the traces of laborious but misguided seekers after treasure.

It was known to all that up there, near the Becca (as the Cervin was called), where the storms were born and whence the clouds arose black as the smoke of hell, the devil himself abode; he it was who unceasingly hurled rocks down into the valley. And the old man who was telling the tale would lower his voice as he pronounced that name; a shudder would run through the audience; the children, already in bed, would listen in the shadow with their eyes wide-opened by curiosity and fear. He would tell of the Wild Man, and this legend was the dearest of all to the Valtourneins, because it was full of the savour of their own lives. It had all the appearance of a true tale:

One day the *Omo Servadzu* came up thither: whence he came and when no man can tell, for at that time there was no living soul in all the valley. He was the first man, and he must have been a wise one, because he foresaw the storms and was learned in many matters: the shepherds, attracted little by little by his presence, came up with their flocks, and he began to educate the small community, and to instruct them in the useful things of life; he taught them how to cure the diseases of their cows, how to make toothsome cheeses, good creams, and the other products of milk. The shepherds at once loved and feared him.

That strange man lived in the châlets of l'Eura, which means the wind; they are the furthermost, the highest, at the foot of the Becca; when the weather was fine he might be seen caring for the flocks, and moving about with a little sack of salt, which he sprinkled on the grass; and the shepherds were confident that all was well under his supervision; but when the wind began to blow fiercely he would hide himself, and no man knew where he lay concealed. Whence arose the local proverb, 'When it rains, it rains; when it snows, it snows; when the wind blows, the weather is bad, and it is well to do as the Wild Man does — hide oneself'. 'Fo fare commen l'omo servadzu et se cazé.'

When the men of the mountain thought they had learnt everything, they offended him grievously, and he disappeared as he had come, taking with him certain secrets, which to this day are sought for in vain — how to make use of the buttermilk and how to mend the broken limbs of the goats.

Another legend there is that is strangely analogous to this one. It is said that once upon a time a giant (named Gargantua) lived in the Aosta valley; he was a kindly genius of the valley, which in his time was full of flowering meadows, and in it the shepherds played ninepins with balls of butter or with discs of cheese; there was such an abundance of milk that it formed rivulets, at which the lambs quenched their thirst. The climate was mild; there were years in which the flocks were able to stop up at the highest pastures, at Breuil, till near Christmas; the old grandfathers remembered them; in those days all were happy and contented; evil was unknown.

The fancy of primitive peoples has always delighted to attribute to heroes the mighty works that the forces of nature have performed, and at times tradition has darkly seen glimpses of a period in the earth's geological history which science has subsequently explained and fully established.

Now the legend tells how in those far-off days the mountains did not present, as they do to-day, an alternation of towering peaks and deep clefts; one simple, uniform ridge, as lofty as the Becca itself, extended over the place where the Cervin now stands and shut in the small valley below. One day the giant was seized with the desire to see the country that lay beyond the mountain; it was but a step for him to cross the lofty barrier; he strode over the range, and while one foot was still on this side, and the other rested in the country of the Swiss, it befell that the surrounding rocks all fell to pieces. The narrative does not say whether this was brought about by the enormous weight of the giant's body, or by other causes. The pyramid of rocks which was caught between his legs alone remained upright. Thus was the Becca formed.[6]

A murmur of incredulity went the round of the audience when they heard the end of the tale; but the old narrator, stung to the quick, rebuked the unbelief of his young hearers; these things were related by our forefathers; they were believed in by them, who knew more than we do, and who were better men than we.

In those days the kindly Deity loved the Val Tournanche, because its inhabitants were simple and devout, and He sent them protectors from time to time, and saints who performed miracles.

That was the time when the hermit of Tornaleis,[7] by dint of much kneeling in prayer, left the impress of his knees on the rock, as may be seen to this day; it was the time of the famous St. Theodul. He was a great saint indeed, sturdy and strong, who crossed the mountains in summer and in winter, and surpassed the devil in cunning: a true mountaineer! And the old man told the tale, a hundred times re-told, of St. Theodul, Bishop of Sion, in the Valais.

One day St. Theodul, who was already a bishop but not yet a saint, crossed over from the Valais into the Val Tournanche, using the pass that afterwards received his name; he came to visit his brothers in Christ, Evantius and Juvenal, who led the life of hermits, the one on the heights of Châtillon, the other on those of Fenis.

It befell that on his way through Breuil he stopped in those poor châlets, where the shepherds received him with respect, and shared with him their modest provisions. In return the bishop gave them his episcopal blessing, and went on his way.

On his return he stopped once more at the châlet, and found that misfortune had come upon the house; a child had been bitten by a terrible serpent, and the mother was weeping hot tears in her helplessness to save her little one. Then the bishop, moved to pity, invoked the Grace of God, murmured a prayer over the wound, and forthwith the child recovered.

Theodul then left the house amid the repeated thanks of the good people, and, raising his hands, blessed that plot of soil, and commanded that serpents and other venomous beasts should flee to the other side of the torrent. Immediately a great hissing was heard in the air, and serpents, scorpions, and toads were seen departing.

Theodul's piety, his good works, and the miracles he was wont to perform made him famous in the valleys of Viège and of Tournanche. The devil, by nature envious of all virtue, sought by every opportunity to diminish the holy man's prestige and to cause him annoyance. One day at Praborne, while his lordship was on his way up to the pass, Satan approached him respectfully and offered to go part of the way with him. Theodul agreed; as they went on their way, talking of various matters, the devil boasted that he was more powerful than a bishop. Theodul was quite unmoved; he said

THE TWO PROTAGONISTS

Edward Whymper

Jean-Antoine Carrel

The Abbé Gorret

Professor Tyndall

he knew that he was a miserable sinner, frail as other men, and requested his companion to give him a proof of his power; and as they were passing certain châlets, he pointed out a great cauldron which the shepherds used for cheese-making, and promised him, on the word of a bishop, that if he succeeded in carrying it on his shoulders across the pass as far as Paquier, he would be his slave for ever after. No sooner said than done; the devil shouldered the cauldron and toiled laboriously up the glacier, but when he drew near the pass, where the ascent is steeper, he slipped and rolled with his cauldron right down to the bottom of the valley.

There might be some doubt of the accuracy of this story, on account of the devil's unwonted simplicity and the dubious honesty of the conduct of the bishop, who is suspected of having tripped him up; but we have an authentic proof of it in an ancient painting in the church at Crépin, that depicts the devil in the act of tumbling down the glacier with the cauldron, and the bishop rubbing his hands with delight.[8]

The old story-teller used to relate another tale, which was current in the valley of Viège, and which also dealt with the devil's tricks, and with certain bells that Theodul brought through the air from Rome to Sion, flying across the pass; and this one, too, ended in the discomfiture of the evil spirit, as popular comedies close with the triumph of virtue and the punishment of vice.

And so these tales were appreciated by the simple audience, who rejoiced at the ridicule with which the devil, their enemy, was covered, and were filled with a sense of safety and of pride by the thought that the machinations of Satan could in nowise prevail against their patron saint.

And through the veil of legend they dimly saw the fears, the articles of faith, the deeds of their remotest ancestors, as if the events of long ago appeared through a rift in the mist of ignorance. The spirit of legend was in their minds, handed down to them by their forefathers like a hereditary instinct. They loved it because in their native shrewdness they felt that it was alive and human, because it described places familiar to them, and because it told of dangers and struggles which formed a part of their own lives.

The Cervin itself often appeared in the legends; all these stories seemed to be its offspring and to hover still about its mysterious rocks. But modern life and countless modern ideas invaded the valley by the roads that were now so easy for the traveller, and a blast of positivism withered for ever the primitive flora; legend's last hour had struck, even at this height.

When the first shepherds of Breuil had thought that they knew more than the Wild Man, and had offended him, he had disappeared. And so it befell with the demon of the Cervin: when no longer believed in, he departed. The winged dragons turned to stone in the depths of their caverns; the timid fairies, who had found their last refuge in these places, vanished slowly, reluctantly, from these haunts, where they had lived so peacefully; but, as they went, they lighted up the valley once more with a last glimmer of truest poetry.

To us late comers it is rarely vouchsafed to catch a glimpse of this beauty. Knowledge of the ancient stories grows gradually less; so also the old style of dress, the tail coat, and the breeches, tight at the knee, have disappeared; they were relics of the previous century which had long survived in this corner of the earth whither the fashions come fifty years late.

One single thing still remains: the dialect, the fine, vigorous, Valtornein patois, the pride of the valley. There are still a few who believe in the demons of the Cervin, but they conceal their belief in their hearts, being almost ashamed to believe. Once only, being with a young guide on the Col du Lion, whilst we watched dense mists rising from the chasm of Tiefenmatten, as from an enormous seething cauldron below, and threateningly enveloping the flanks of the Cervin, I heard the guide exclaim, 'J'avais bien dit que là-bas il y avait les bacans!' He meant evil spirits. That terrible scene conjured up visions of a malignant power in his untutored mind; and I myself, under the spell of that simple man, who was simple indeed but stronger than I, felt my blood run cold, as if I myself believed. And this showed me how easy it was for the wonderful phenomena of nature to have been attributed by these primitive-minded men to maleficent forces against which it was necessary for the saints to descend with their miracles.

From that height, whence a single glance takes in all the peaks in the valley, and whence they all seem huddled close together, it is easy to understand the story of the three hermits who, standing each on a different summit, had agreed to say a prayer each day at the same moment, and threw over to each other their single hatchet for splitting their wood.

Up there, where the Theodul Pass seems so near to the green pastures of the Jomein, we can understand the birth of the legend of a mysterious city which once stood on the pass, among flowering meadows, and is now buried under the ice.

The Abbé Gorret calls his fellow Valtorneins 'le peuple le plus casanièrement nomade qu'il m'a été donné de connaître'. And indeed, while they spent three-quarters of the year in wandering about, they dearly loved their native soil, owing to the innate desire of the mountain folk to possess the land, which is here more precious than elsewhere; instinctively they loved the house where they were born, because it received and sheltered them in the season of foul weather; in fine weather the whole valley was their home, a short valley which can be traversed from end to end in ten hours' walking. But in the course of those ten hours you pass from the warm, sunlit vineyards of Chambave to the windy pastures of l'Eura; from Châtillon, where the oleanders bloom and the Italian thyme may be picked, to Breuil, where the edelweiss grows, and to the Theodul, where the *Ranunculus glacialis* and the sparse lichen of Iceland cling to the rocks

And in their constant wanderings up and down the valley, in their alternation of diverse kinds of labour and of cultivation, the mountaineers of Val Tournanche gained a more open mind and wider knowledge than the stay-at-home inhabitants of the neighbouring valleys. In their lives was the motion which makes clear and pure the rushing waters of the torrent; the curse of cretinism rarely visited them; whilst it prevailed to a sad extent in the other tributary valleys of the Dora.

Of great utility also was the continual passing to and fro of people from other places, who for purposes of trade or religious motives crossed the Theodul Pass, which was then known as the Mont

Cervin Pass, or simply as the Mont Cervin.[9] These were cattle-dealers from the valley of Viège, who were wont every autumn to drive herds of cows and oxen across the pass, to the fairs in the Aosta valley; these parties were guided by certain men, named Joseph Taugwalder and Peter Burchner, who were thoroughly familiar with the col; or they were men of Ayas and of Valtournanche, loaded with great wineskins, who crossed the pass to Praborne, in order to sell the Valdostan wine, which was much prized there; and it is said that, on their arrival at Praborne, the skins were not always as swollen nor as heavy as when they left Paquier

They were smugglers who crossed the snows of the Mont Cervin into Piedmont, with their *bricolla* full of tobacco, coffee, chocolate, the finest English muslins, Swiss watches, and the famous gunpowder of Bern; or pilgrims who faced the hardships of the road or the dangers of the glaciers on their way to Sion, the holy city of the Valais and to Einsiedeln, in Canton Schwyz, to fulfil a vow at the sanctuary of Our Lady of the Hermits, to whom the Valdostans, and especially the Valtorneins, owed an ancient allegiance.

Old men relate that in the great ice plateau, which lies below the pass on the Swiss side, at a place called Tour de Gomba, there was a miraculous echo. When the way was doubtful, owing to thick mist, the pilgrims would join their voices together in order to ask the saint whether they were on the right road. If they had gone wrong, however little, the saint would be silent. When he answered they were safe.

It has been believed that the pass was easier formerly than it is in our time.[10] We cannot know of all the victims whom the glacier claimed in past centuries, but it is certain that the passage of people who were unacquainted with the place, and were poorly provisioned and clad, cannot have been unattended by disasters and misfortunes. In the village they told of a party of muleteers lost on the pass. A mule, which arrived alone with its load at Zermatt, made the disaster known, but no one of the party was ever seen again. The traveller, Hirzel-Escher, was shown the place where a Piedmontese noble, a fugitive in 1820 owing to political offences, had met with his death amid the ice. They related how in 1825 a merchant with his horse disappeared for ever in the glacier, and they regretted most of all that he had with him ten thousand francs.

Hinchliff, passing over the glacier in 1855, discovered the sad remains of a party which had undoubtedly perished many years before. Scattered about over an area of eight or ten yards they found shoes of the kind worn by peasants, and pieces of rough woollen stuff; a sack protruded partially from the snow; bleaching human bones lay strewn about in all directions, mingled with the skeletons of mules and horses. They had been surprised by a snowstorm while trying to cross the pass, and had perished of cold and exhaustion.[11] The description Hinchliff gives of the attitudes in which he found the corpses of some of these victims makes us think with horror of their sufferings. 'Guides and all,' writes the English climber, 'looked at this melancholy sight in perfect silence; no one knew anything of the lost party, nor had our guides ever heard of their bones being there. What a scene of suffering must have been here!' These were the first unknown victims of the Cervin. Their bones disappeared by degrees, buried in the snow, engulfed or swept away by the glacier; other parties were preparing to cross the pass, ignorant or careless of the other's fate.

At Praborne they would muster in large numbers, fifteen or twenty, with horses and mules, to attack the pass; even at the present day the old men of Valtournanche remember those assemblies of rude Valaisans, who were mostly guided by a certain Brantschen,[12] an old man who knew the pass well and was the only one who could speak a few words of French, and such French!

They took their provisions with them, and, in the kitchen that was lent them by the parish priest of Paquier, they boiled their salt meat together with a few unpeeled potatoes, and this made the civilized Valtorneins smile. On the way back, if the sky was cloudy, they caused themselves to be accompanied up to the pass by men of Val Tournanche; these were the earliest guides. But their mothers and their sisters wept at seeing them depart, and invoked the mercy of Heaven for them. At that time the guide's calling did not exist in the valley, nor did that of innkeeper. The only refuge for wayfarers was the priest's house, the *curé*.

About 1850 a worthy man, the Rev. Father Bore, was chief priest at Paquier; he was one of the many simple mountain priests who fulfil their mission of instructors and consolers in the high-level villages. Poor amongst the poor, mentally superior to their neighbours, often men of culture and lovers of study and of books, sometimes men of genius, they spend their life of self-sacrifice, stifling the secret rebellion of their souls, in alleviating the sufferings of others. But they too are sons of the mountains, and therefore their modest Alpine parish is dear to them; they love their flock because they know how kindly is its nature for all its roughness; they live obscure in the healthy air of their native valley, and, when their mission is at an end, they will rest at the foot of the church tower, and a small head-stone will record their names in that churchyard which they have looked upon from their window every day of their lives.

A great affection, almost a feeling of jealousy, has always bound the Valdostan clergy to their own Aosta, where they are educated, and to their mountains where they are born and where they fulfil their mission. It is largely due to them and to their conservative instinct, that the ancient tongue, the French, is preserved in the valley.[13]

I do not dislike the tenacity with which the Valdostans cling to the speech of their forefathers; it pleases me because they are none the less true and ardent Italians; they adhere to it in the pride of an ancient people, jealous, like islanders, of the purity of their race. For them it is not the language of France, but their own, the tongue which was spoken of old in the castles of their Counts, and which has been heard for centuries past under the arches of their humble churches and of their simple schools, an emblem of uninterrupted traditions and of immemorial fealty to a royal race. It is the shield with which the modern Salassi protect themselves from the on-slaught of modern corruption.

Italian mountaineering owes a great debt to the Valdostan priests of that period. Some of them had ascended the peaks at a time when mountaineering was as yet unknown to us; afterwards when it came into being and made known to all that the climbing of mountains had its intellectual and moral uses, those sturdy, untiring priests, who were already inured to hardships and familiar with the mountains and their difficulties, were more ready than all other men to further the good work.

Perhaps it afforded them an unexpected comfort, a new occupation for their monotonous lives, a thrilling pleasure which was not forbidden them by their austere rules, a pure and lofty ideal in harmony with their faith; perhaps they were filled with a sense of noble pride because the men of the plains had at last learnt to love their mountains. And in some of them was kindled a noble enthusiasm for that ideal, which became a part of their lives; their names are written in letters of gold among the first of Italian mountaineers: Chanoine Carrel of Aosta, the Abbé Chamonin of Cogne, the Abbé Chanoux of the Little St. Bernard.

But the chief priest, Bore, was a stranger to these new enthusiastic ideals; during the twenty-six years he spent at Paquier his efforts were wholly devoted to his modest but holy mission. Those who knew him say that his was a head of iron and a heart of gold, that he was inflexible but gentle, rough but full of kindness at the core. He was the cause of the rebuilding of the priest's house and of the church, and he himself with his strong arms joined in the work among his parishioners;[14] and he restored the fine tower which makes the view of the village so picturesque; he established schools in almost all the sections of the Commune, and when he died (1858) there was not one child in the neighbourhood that did not know how to read and write.

An unpublished autobiography of a candidate for admission to the seminary at Aosta describes to us the elements of the teaching in Valtournanche. It was in 1846; the youth, destined by his parents, simple mountain folk, for the Church, was admitted by the stern parish priest to his house, in order to begin his studies under the guidance of the *vicaire's* cane. The latter, after following the trade of a chimney-sweep in Piedmont, had found his vocation in the seminary, and was full of willingness to impart to his rustic pupil what little he himself knew. I let the young student speak for himself:

'S'étant assuré que je savais déjà passablement lire, le vicaire me fit de suite attaquer simultanément les deux grammaires, la française et la latine. La grande difficulté était que ni l'un ni l'autre nous n'avions les livres requis pour cela. Le curé réussit à nous déterrer dans sa bibliothèque ses vieux livres des premières classes; nous voilà donc définitivement enfoncés dans l'étude. Le papier coûte, se salit vite et dure peu; il faut aviser et chercher à s'en passer. Nous finissons par découvrir une belle pierre calcaire, au grain très fin et onctueux, et voilà plus d'une semaine à lui donner le poli voulu. Entre chaque leçon, frotte la pierre. Pour encre une décoction de toutes les baies noires que je rencontre dans les buissons. Une énorme plume d'aigle me dura trois ans.

'C'est un riant souvenir maintenant quand je me rappelle que quatre à cinq fois par jour je devais aller à la fontaine pour laver mon cahier et ensuite le faire sécher, détruire mon devoir aussitôt accompli.'

This boy, who wrote his Latin essay on a stone with an eagle's feather for a pen, was destined later to write on the rocks of the Cervin, together with other worthy comrades, one of the finest pages in the history of Italian mountaineering; he was Amé Gorret.

Other boys were growing up at the same time in the little classes of Valtournanche. I like to think of the future conquerors of the Cervin seated on small benches in the humble room that was used for a school, unruly and impatient for the lesson hour to come to an end, that they might run out and give chase to the squirrels in the trees, or set snares for the birds; paying more attention to shepherding the flocks on the pastures, or to watching for the marmot near its hole, than to the catechism or the grammar lesson on the narrow benches. I can imagine their leader, a Carrel, already restless, already a bersagliere, the author of all the naughty tricks played in and out of the school, of all the excursions up the hills, of the snow-fights, the terror of masters and school-fellows. A Bich, calm, thoughtful, and docile, a Maquignaz, taller and thinner than his comrades, more silent and more serious; slow to learn, but having once learnt it, knowing his lesson well. Standing before them, with his terrible cane in his hand, a rough master who warned them that if they were not good the Cervin would devour them.

At that time the Cervin was nought but an ogre that threatened the farmer with storms and the hunter with snow; no one of those children dreamt that man could ascend it; they knew that not even the chamois ventured on to the Becca. The education of the future heroes progressed on primitive lines; stripes, ear-pullings, an occasional application of the master's toe — these methods were those then in vogue in all the schools in Piedmont, and, after all, they were not so bad, for they were the ones which fashioned soldiers for the redemption of Italy, and guides for the conquest of the Cervin. 'If you are not good the Cervin will devour you!' the master would repeat, as he raised his threatening cane. And the mountain did in truth devour some of them: it claimed the whole soul, held them in bondage all their lives, made them famous and then — slew them.

Paquier. — Murray, in his Guide Book of 1852, writes that there was no hotel at Valtournanche, but that the *curé* took in travellers, ladies as well as gentlemen; five or six francs were the *obol* that it was customary to leave him for bed, supper, and breakfast. The first hotel in the valley was then a priest's house. It appears, however, that the parish priest Bore was more inclined to receive the muleteers of Praborne than strangers, who were more exacting, owing to the comfortable life they were accustomed to and the fatigue of the long journey. And Murray, in his '54 edition, comments on the good priest's hospitality in these terms. 'Very bad accommodation.'

Alfred Wills, who subsequently became one of the foremost English climbers, supplies such discouraging particulars of the rudimentary simplicity of these lodgings that I do not venture to quote them. Fortunately the parish priest Bore remained in ignorance of these unflattering expressions concerning his house and himself.

We should take into consideration that these strangers, mostly Englishmen, were some of the most civilized and of the richest of the men of the nineteenth century, and that they came up among these humble people, who were still leading a life of almost medieval simplicity; they were accustomed to the most scrupulous northern cleanliness and they came to a district where soap was not looked upon as an article of prime necessity. Since that time the Italians have made much progress, and, on the other hand, the English of the present day, being more accustomed to travel and to the discomforts of Alpine life, are more easily satisfied; but those ancestors of theirs, men of unbending type, tenacious of their habits, who brought with them all the needs and prejudices of their civilization, must have been ill at ease in the wretched beds at the priest's, or in the shepherds' hayloft; the rough grissini at the Paquier *curé's*, and the golden polenta at the hamlet of Breuil, cannot have flattered their palates. This explains the outbursts of indignation which appear in the Guides and other books of that period.

But in 1855 King[15] finds in Valtournanche* a little house, which had been recently fitted up as a hotel, entitled the 'Mont Cervin', where the landlord does his best to please his guests with the modest resources at his disposal, and the wine is good. So says King. It may seem childish to pass in review the opinions of travellers on the goodness of the wine and the greater or less degree of cleanliness of the lodgings in Valtournanche, but when a reliable man like Mr. King arrives, and tells us that in that year a good little hotel has been opened, we feel, as it were, a sense of pride, and our Italian hearts swell, unaccustomed as they are to gentle words of praise. The hotel was kept by Nicolas Pession, and belonged to him and his brothers. King relates thus his impressions: 'Our beds were shown us in the two corners of the room used as a *salle à manger* — one a berth in the wall, as in a Highland cabin; but they answered all the purpose, and, moreover, were tolerably clean.' And, last of all, the bill was most moderate; it is well to record this fact, and point it out to hotel keepers of the present and the future: one franc for each bed; four dinners, four suppers, breakfast, two dozen eggs, beer, etc., eight francs in all!

It is true, alas! that not all the travellers who came afterwards took away with them so favourable an impression, and that Hinchliff in the same year found the hotel dirty,[16] and that in the following year a Mr. Longman described it as the most miserable of hotels,[17] and considered that the host had the appearance of a real Italian bandit. Poor honest Pession! The same illusion which made the sky

* The old name Paquier for the village was replaced by Valtournanche. In this book the valley will be Val Tournanche.

appear of a deeper blue to the stranger who approached the Alpine frontiers of Italy, showed him a brigand in the garments of a peaceful innkeeper. Some, who stopped and spent the night there, took the precaution to bar the door of their room with their alpenstocks, and others, again, passing by, declared that only dire necessity would induce them to cross the threshold. No matter: Valtournanche had its inn as had Zermatt.[18]

This was the first step forward; the inn was destined to progress gradually, the landlord to learn better the art of making himself attractive to the travellers who began to frequent the valley, till the exacting Murray Guide Book was able to declare it 'homely, but clean and cheap'; the highest praise, this, for an Alpine hotel, as we understand them. And from thenceforward the inn, under its altered name of the Monte Rosa Hotel, had also its humble place in the great story of the Cervin.

In the modest room which did duty as *salle à manger* in the Monte Rosa Hotel, a few years ago I was waiting for fine weather. At the present day it is all newly done up, but then it was the old historic room, papered with blue-flowered wall-paper, the same the first-comers had known; there, too, on the small chimney-piece stood the two little painted plaster cats who, with their round, unmoving eyes, had watched the first admirers of the Cervin go by; two weeping willows, made of ornamental green paper, framed a mirror covered with pink gauze, which prevented both indiscreet flies from contaminating the glass and the vain traveller from gazing at himself therein.

It was raining in the valley, the mountain summits were covered with snow. With my forehead pressed against the panes of the little window, I was watching the dismal mists come floating up the valley; it was a day of failure, one of those which make one hate the mountains. I was thinking sadly of the time I was losing, of the climbing projects that were becoming illusory; there were no newspapers, and a few old volumes, loose and torn, among them the first numbers of the *Bollettino del Club Alpino*, which I knew almost by heart, formed the only resources of the library.

On a plank, near the cleared dinner-table, was an old collection of loose leaves; it was like an account book, or a washerwoman's list.

Driven by my boredom I opened it: a fragrance of cheese, wine, and tobacco arose from those loose, crumpled pages. It was the old visitors' book, and on the first page was the inscription, written in large letters by a local scribe: 'Noms et prénoms de Messieurs les Voyageurs qui passent à Valtournanche pour traverser le Col St. Théodule pour Ayas, les Cimes Blanches, Valpelline, &c. Dès le 17 Août, 1860.' I thought at first it was one of the ordinary commonplace hotel books, which are all alike:

> Exactly! page on page of gratitude
> For breakfast, dinner, supper, and the view![19]

The usual praises of the cooking, of the host's courtesy, of the moderation of the bill; the usual expressions of admiration into which the most matter-of-fact man breaks out before the beauties of the mountains; when for the first, and perhaps the only time in his life, he has felt, after dinner, that he is a poet.

But something worthy of respect was discoverable in those old pages, for all their homeliness; on the crumpled sheets, written with ink yellowed by age, the words had acquired the status of antiquity; by degrees I was led to recall those dead words to life, and I found myself, not unmoved, in the presence of some of those unexpected revelations which occasionally flow from a simple name or a date. I remarked first of all that the Cervin was not mentioned in the inscription; at that date it was not yet spoken of in Valtournanche.[20] In the first pages the visitors' names were written in columns, in excellent order, without remarks or comments; they are mostly Englishmen's names. Then by degrees the travellers' pen became less reserved, and it was curious to observe how the statements written down by one were often corrected or derided by him who followed in the register; there were ironical comments, and emphatic denials one day of that which another man had emphatically affirmed the day before; outbursts of international antipathies, or of antipathies between travellers of the same nationality who did not know one another and were destined to follow one another about the world from hotel to hotel, without perhaps ever meeting or understanding one another.

One climber came down from the Theodul and ingenuously described his impressions; another followed and commented thus: 'Peut-on être monté si haut et en être redescendu si bête?' But on one point all are agreed, and that was in their unqualified praise of the eggs *à la reine*, a dish dating from the foundation of the hotel, and vaunted in every European language on every page of the book. 'Chef d'œuvre!' exclaimed one, and another declared it a 'plat inimitable qu'on ne peut faire qu'à Valtournanche'.

But among the commonplaces of these outbursts there stood out the respected and welcome names of those foreign mountaineers whom I had learnt to know and to admire through their writings and their expeditions: the signatures of Bonney, of Adams Reilly, of Barnard the painter of the Cervin, of Tyndall, Craufurd Grove and Hawkins, of Leslie Stephen, of Mathews and Morshead, of Freshfield and Mummery. They all came to admire our Cervin and some to ascend it.

Behold the name of Edward Whymper; he came by for the first time on August 28th, 1860, from Biona in the Valpelline, on his way to Breuil. He was there again on August 27th in the following year, and wrote in a firm, bold hand in the book 'Edward Whymper, *en route* for the Matterhorn'. This was the expression of his faith. The resolute man's hopes were already high, but four years yet were to pass before he conquered. But immediately after his entry another hand, less firm and noble than his, had written in the register these lines in English: 'This gentleman is always attempting the impossible, and then he curses everybody because he fails in his . . . attempts.' And another, full of envy, adds ironically, 'Of course he went, and saw, and conquered'. These remarks seemed like the satires and the insults which the *canaille* formerly hurled at the hero in his triumph, on his way to the Capitol.

At this point the interest in the book became most poignant, as if an old man had been telling me tales of an ancestor of mine whom he had known, for I now came upon the names of the very few Italians who had come up here during those years, when the very idea of mountaineering was still unknown in Italy, and, among many names that were strange to me, the following woke an echo in my heart, for they were names of friends, and dear to me as such. In 1860 there was Count Caesar Merani, a Tuscan; in 1861 Giovanni Barracco, a Calabrian, who subsequently accompanied Quintino Sella on the first Italian ascent of Monte Viso; then a party of three men of light and leading from Milan: G. Visconti Venosta, C. Prinetti, and R. Bonfadini; and further on the Abbé Benedetto Rignon of Turin, and G. Battista Rimini, a topographer in the Royal Corps of the General Staff of the Army, and one of the first and most enthusiastic members of the Italian Alpine Club.

It was not yet the habit of the Turinese to come and spend the hot season in this valley; so that while at Courmayeur and Gressoney, where more progress had been made, the hotels were, during those years, crowded with town dwellers who had fled from the heat of the capital, the Valtournanche host but rarely saw Italian travellers passing through; it was only in 1865, the Cervin year, that their numbers increased. Evidently the fame of Whymper's disaster and of Carrel's victory had echoed even in our cities and attracted men curious to see the bloodstained, glorious Cervin.

In the pages of the book, which were at first written in foreign languages, notes in Italian now begin, and there appear, alas! only now the first sketches with which we, natives of the land of art, rejoice to illustrate our enthusiasm. In that year there appeared in the book the actors in the high comedy of the Cervin. Felice Giordano, who came up to contest the victory with Whymper, wrote his name; Amé Gorret wrote his and those of his companions who planted the Italian tricolor on the summit on July 17th. And as I gazed upon those names, written immediately after the contest, I was filled with an intense interest, a deep emotion, and the names seemed to me to be redolent of all the pristine enthusiasm of that day.

Ah! Gorret's heart must have overflowed with joy when he signed that page! How sad must Giordano's have been when he turned his face to the plain without having taken part in the conquest! I thought how, at the table where I sat, those brave men met to celebrate the victory. I saw the Abbé drinking a toast with the bersagliere, I heard the shouts and paeans of joy with which the Valtorneins greeted the good news; the commonplace list which I held in my hands seemed to me a golden book of glorious deeds, and the little room a sanctuary in which the noble passions of those valiant men still hovered. A breath of new life had blown down the valley from the Becca, and caused the peaceful mountain folk of Valtournanche to thrill with proud hopes.

But in that year the Matterhorn had overcome the Cervino; the Englishmen reached the summit three days before the Italians; the rival Praborne, thanks to the intelligent enterprise of the Swiss, was about to become the great Zermatt, one of the most important Alpine centres, to which travellers flock from all parts of the world. Valtournanche remained lonely and quiet in its grassy corner.

That is how we who love the mountains for the simplicity of the life we lead among them, for the peace we find in their stern solitudes, would have it remain, a small obscure village, nestling under the pines. The old Monte Rosa Hotel too, we would have it always as we see it now, as it was known to the first ardent lovers of the Alps, a typical Italian inn, with the outside staircase, in the old style, with the gay green shutters, and the wooden balcony from which I had my first view of my own Punta Bianca.[21] On no account must anyone remove the old log bench outside, on which the guides and village elders come to sit and smoke their pipes and share their stock of mountain lore.

Jomein. — 'Three miles higher still there stood the hamlet of Brividum, whose environs are rich in excellent pastures; at the present day there are also the huts of Breuil, which are only habitable in the summer, and even then days are not so rare in which men and beasts are seized with a fit of shivering as a sudden wave of cold air passes over them. The old name of the place, therefore, expresses very well the *brivido* (shivers) of the Tuscans, and the same word indicates the same idea and sensation.' Thus wrote Durandi in 1804.

I will not concern myself with the correctness of this or other suggested etymologies. Nor will I inquire whether the correct name be Breuil, as Saussure always wrote it, and as modern maps have it, or Breil, as the Chanoine Carrel called it, and as the inhabitants of the valley pronounce it. It is certain that when, fatigued by the steep ascent, we reach the little plateau of Breuil, after emerging from the close valley, we are met by a feeling of unwonted coolness, even in the hottest days of summer; the flat, open space is exposed to the winds of the Cervin, the waters which flow over it bear with them the cold draught of the mountain air, and the sight of the glaciers close at hand helps to intensify the sensation of coolness; the traveller who is as yet unhardened hastens to wrap himself in his shawl, while the climber quickens his step, rejoicing in his heart because he has recognized the keen air of 7000 feet; and already he sees afar, somewhat higher up, the smoking chimneys of the well-known hospitable hotel, holding out promise of a good supper.

But when Saussure came, there was no hotel, and no man could have predicted that so fine a one would have been built up there, near the wretched hovels where the great Genevese had received hospitality. 'Nous retrouvâmes au Breuil,' he writes in 1792, 'notre bon hôte Erin, et notre petite et mauvaise chambre sans lit, et sans fenêtre, et toutes les privations et les petites souffrances dont l'accumulation ne laisse pas de causer beaucoup d'ennui.'

Equal hardships beset Brockedon, who came up in 1825, and, while waiting to cross the Theodul, spent three days in bad weather at the huts of the Jomein, which he calls the Mont Jumont, and passed the nights on a wretched bed of insufficient hay, which he shared with innumerable parasites, amid the exhalations of the stable underneath, covered by a disjointed roof through which filtered the starlight and the raindrops. For food he had only three eggs, some milk, and black bread that had been baked six months before. The worthy Mr. Brockedon assisted the good woman, the hostess, to cook the polenta, but did not taste the mess; repugnance overcame hunger.

At the present day the fumes of an exquisite *cuisine*, which delight the nostrils and whet the appetite, are wafted up the staircase of the Mont Cervin Hotel; the weary climber finds a hot bath ready and sleeps in a soft bed in a neat and cheerful little room, and the telegraph affords communication between this place, formerly so wild, and the civilized world. But here also the beginning was humble and progress very slow.

THE MATTERHORN
from the Becca di Guin

Pic Tyndall
from near the Col du Lion

Mr. King, who passed this way in 1855,[22] relates that in the châlets of Breuil one floor had been fitted up with simple comforts; there were two small rooms, with beds, a table and a few benches, which afforded the traveller 'as good a night's quarters as a mountaineer ought to expect'.

This was the so-called 'Logement de Saussure', done up and embellished, and in an old journal of that year I find it described as 'Hôtel recommandable d'Ambroise d'Hérin'. Certain victuals, in addition to the usual food of the mountain folk, were obtainable at that time also at the Michellina, a small house belonging to the Jomein pastures. However, Chanoine Carrel wrote at that time: 'Le Breuil est un séjour charmant; c'est fort regrettable qu'on ne puisse s'y loger. Mais que les voyageurs se rassurent; j'ai l'assurance que cette année, 1855, on y bâtira une modeste auberge confortable. Le plan en est dressé et les engagements sont pris.'

It was Signor Favre, of Aosta, who had this first inn[23] built among the pastures of the Jomein, and we immediately find it mentioned with much approval in travellers' notes, under the name of the Mont Jumont Inn, a name which was changed two or three years later into the present one of Mont Cervin Hotel. Mr. Cole[24] writes thus about the little Alpine inn: 'Good food, good rooms, and great civility. What more could man desire at 6600 feet above the sea, in the year of grace 1858?'

And Mr. Tuckett, who came past there in the following year, rejoiced to find that a comfortable and hospitable house had replaced the wretched huts which had been the only refuge open to him four years before. Signor Favre's hotel-register has been lost. I regret it immensely, because it would give us a great store of valuable information about the first development of mountaineering in this region; we may deduce as much from the fact that several important accounts of ascents, which were published in the earliest volumes of the *Bollettino*, were drawn from that register. There remains to us the new visitors' list, which bears the same relation to the former one as the fashionable intelligence in a newspaper does to the ancient songs of the troubadours. I have turned over its pages a hundred times during the long days I have spent waiting at the hotel, and I have found in it few things that have made me think and many that have made me laugh; but those who wrote them are still living, and their modesty forbids that I should quote in these pages passages from their prose or poetry.

We shall meet with the Jomein again and again at every stage of the Cervin's history: it was Whymper's and Tyndall's starting-point for their attempts; it was the scene of the preparations for the Italian expedition. In my narrative that dear name will recur on every page, as it recurs frequently and lovingly to my memory. I still remember the little narrow room, with its white plaster, as I saw it the first time I came, in which a worthy woman with a scarf on her head served me with the simple food that she herself had prepared.

One day I found that a fine dining-room, all panelled with pitch-pine wood, had taken the place of the old room, and that the first black-coated waiter had appeared at the hamlet of the Jomein. The hotel grew still larger, and the dining-room became capable of holding two hundred guests. But notwithstanding these improvements, the place has remained simple, the life there keeps hearty, and free from the luxury of cities, which the stern presence of the Cervin would not brook. In that place one sole thought, one sole image impress themselves on the minds of climbers and non-climbers: the great mountain, attractive but terrible, an inexhaustible theme for conversation, is the cynosure of every eye, it is for ever making fresh appeals to the emotions. It seems as if every guest at the hotel looks upon the Cervin as being in some measure his own, and feels a pride in it like him who enjoys the familiar friendship of a great man. And at break of day he hastens to see if the Cervin be visible: when the Cervin smiles the whole hotel smiles; when it dons its gloomy covering of cloud a veil of sadness seems to descend on all things.

Such unison of feeling naturally produces among the guests a harmony which is rare in large hotels. The height and isolation of the place helps to promote this union; the Jomein is 2070 metres above the sea, a height at which Quintino Sella wished that the conventional forms of civilized salutation should be abolished. It is far from all inhabited centres; the flower-decked plateau on which the hotel stands is bounded on either side by torrents which flow down, the one from the Theodul, the other from the Cervin, and the little valleys in which they run offer solitary nooks to lovers of quiet. There you may find those modest but charming little flowers, the white Alpine viola, the mountain sempervivum with its golden corolla, and the curious saponaria which covers the hottest slopes with its bright yellow blossoms. In a few steps we reach the cover of the thick pine-woods, whence, through the dark foliage, we see the white, glistening glaciers; while if we ascend a few hundred metres we find ourselves on the wild, bare mountain-side, before a boundless view of peaks and sky, and there, in the remote solitude, we forget the hotel and our daily life.

Every now and then we see the arrival of parties of climbers and guides from the neighbouring summits; their faces bear the mask that the sun sets upon them in the high mountains; they have in their eyes a strange reflection of the distant horizon they have seen on the heights, and their drawn features seem still to show traces of the emotions they have felt. And the whole hotel appears to thrill at their arrival.

For these reasons the Jomein is dear to me. I have returned there continually for more than ten years, and each time I discover new picturesque poetic nooks. Between me and these spots a deep intimacy has grown up. When I am far from them, and I think of the mountains, my thoughts always end by straying to that place. I half close my eyes and I see it once more; and so, when I have a pencil in my hands and absent-mindedly let it run over a blank page, the outline of the Cervin appears.

Few places can claim so deep an affection from me as this, which has given me so many hours of freedom and health, and which is bound up with some of my dearest dreams of Alpine life. There, in its quiet little rooms, I have mastered my hot impatience at delay, I have cradled my hopes of an undertaking long desired, I have tasted the undefiled joy of victory, I have concealed the bitterness of a defeat which to-day is as dear to me as a triumph. I have looked upon it as I came from the city, from the bottom of the plateau of Breuil, a tiny spot at the foot of the Cervin, and it has seemed to me a strong fortress whence I could begin my campaign; I have seen it from the lofty summits of the mountains which surround it, a white point barely visible, vertically under my feet, promising me rest after the contest; I have yearned for it during the long descent; I have seen from lofty bivouacs its light, lit for me, shining down in the dark valley, as the lighthouse shines for the storm-tossed mariner, and moving, as if to tell me that down there someone was thinking of me as I wandered among the mountains. . . .

I think I am suffering from home-sickness for the Jomein!

The St. Theodul. – One day as I was ascending to the Theodul Pass, my guide, who had turned aside from the ordinary way, found in the valley at the foot of the glacier two small pieces of wood, rudely carved, one of which represented a clenched hand in the act of clasping some object, and the other, which fitted exactly into the empty space in the hand, was shaped like a small carved staff. The guide, as he handed them over to me, gave it as his opinion that they must have belonged to the statue of a warrior grasping a sword.

From time to time old relics, such as coins, and rusted arms and horseshoes, are found on the way up to and at the top of the pass. They are vestiges of travellers of yore, records of unchronicled struggles, of hasty flights, of misadventures. Therefore I examined those relics, in the hope of learning, from the mode of their fashioning, to what period they belonged. They must have been of very great antiquity, because the wood was black and utterly rotten; but as they had no artistic stamp I was unable to decide whether they had been made five lustres or five centuries before; the ruder things of every age are all alike. I put the two pieces of wood into my pocket, and kept them, owing to that feeling of respect that we have for those things which contain a mystery; but I thought no more about them.

One day, as I was reading the narrative of Philibert Amadeus Arnod, bailiff of Aosta and judge of the Aosta district, which was written in 1691, and discovered in the archives by Luigi Vaccarone, I came across a passage in the midst of an interesting description of the pass that turned my thoughts again to the wooden hand: 'A la sommité l'on y trouve une vieille et grossière statue de bois, appelée St. Theodule, que l'on dit par l'ancienne tradiction avoir esté mise en ce lieu par les Vallésiens soub un motif de vénération et de protection envers le dit saint.'

This was a revelation to me; I looked for the old hand, fitted the other piece into it, and immediately saw the hand of the Bishop of Sion, grasping his pastoral staff; there was no doubt about it, I was in possession of the saint's left hand. Some of the excrescences of the wood, though rotten, suggested the shapes of the arabesques which usually adorned the upper part of the crook of pastoral statues in the fifteenth and sixteenth centuries. I rejoiced at the thought of being in the presence of a fragment of the statue which the devout Valaisans had carried up so many centuries before, and my fancy easily conjured up the image as it must have been, with its cloak and mitre, when, from its rude niche of heaped-up stones, it solemnly gave its blessing to the ancient visitors to the Mont Cervin.

I had then a vision of the traffic on that remote pass as it developed under the protection of the saint's image. Up from the Val Tournanche came long lines of pilgrims, weary and breathless from the steep ascent, on their way to Sion, the little Valaisan Jerusalem; bands of armed men came stealthily up from both sides of the pass, and met and fought on the summit: these were the men of the Viège valley and those of the Aosta valley, who fitfully carried on their traditional contest.[25] Parties of Zermatt muleteers and Châtillon merchants came past; they brought with them long beams, with which they bridged the crevasses;[26] all the way up the slope the air resounded with the oaths that were hurled at the mules when they sank into the snow under the weight of their load, and, terrified, refused to proceed. A crowd of Germans came across, who were sent by a bishop of Sion to colonize his fiefs in the Lys valley and to found Gressoney; on reaching the pass they looked with curiosity on Italy, and on the neighbouring heights behind which their new home lay concealed. Then came the soldiers of Victor Amadeus II, who, with the assistance of the Valaisans, hastily built a wall of defence to prevent the brave Waldenses, who had been cast out of

Piedmont, from returning to their native valleys; and that lofty outpost was called the 'Monservin Fort'.

At times there came men walking with stealthy steps, ever seeking cover and watching till the mist or the darkness should grant them a favourable opportunity to cross the pass and safely store their precious load, without being seen by other men who stood motionless and waited for them hour by hour behind a rock.

On the snows of the pass, before the holy niche, hands already frost-bitten were stretched out despairingly towards the image; women weeping with the cold, amid the thick mists, prayed that by its intercession a ray of sunshine might come to lighten the perilous way; hymns of thanksgiving arose from the pilgrims when on their return they beheld from the heights the green meadows of their native valley, and saw that the end of their weary march was near at hand.

Amid the oaths of the muleteers, the prayers of the pilgrims, and the challenges of the sentries of the Monservin, the wooden saint, motionless within his humble niche, continued to give his blessings, an emblem of peace on the desolate pass.

Then there were the long, lonely winters. How many of these did the little statue pass up there? Did some sacrilegious hand, impelled by the cruel cold, snatch it from its altar and burn it like a common log of wood? Or did a blast of wind, which tore the niche asunder, hurl the saint into the air and scatter his limbs on the glacier that swallowed them up and carried them afar in its bosom?

To us nought remains but the mysterious hand, broken and blackened, grasping a splinter of the pastoral staff like the hilt of a sword.

After the disappearance of the saint, a ray of new light is shed upon the pass and brightens it. It is the pure light of science; the ruins of the rampart built by the fanatical muleteers of Savoy are now used to prop the tent of Saussure; the self-same stones serve to build a peaceful shelter for the learned Genevese[27] in his studies.

Among the guides who accompanied Saussure on his second journey round the Cervin was one J. Jacques Meynet, of Valtournanche. It seems as if he took fire at the flame of enthusiasm that burnt in Saussure, and was from that day forth bound by a special affection for that inhospitable region of the pass, and that that flame was transmitted as an heirloom to all his humble family. In fact, about sixty years later, one J. Pierre Meynet, a nephew of the above, was on the pass repairing the remains of Saussure's hut, when he found some straw and certain coins still there.

Engelhardt, the constant visitor to Zermatt, is the first to mention the fact; during his journey in 1851 he had been told at Zermatt that a house was being built on the very top of the pass. 'This piece of news', he writes, 'is too interesting not to be mentioned: a native of Valtournanche, named Minette, encouraged by the increasing number of visitors to these parts, has lately put up a tent on the pass, and there visitors now find unexpected refreshment and a refuge for the night.'

It was also reported that an Englishman, of high standing in the diplomatic service, whom Engelhardt believes to be no other than Robert Peel, English ambassador to Switzerland during the Sonderbund War, had spent a night up there, and was so surprised and pleased at the hospitality he met with, that he gave his host a twenty franc piece, and promised to lend him six thousand more if he built a house up there. Whether or not the worthy Minette received Sir Robert Peel's money is not known, and the Valtorneins never believed that he did. The humble architect of the Theodul remained as poor as he was before, with no other resources than his own arms and those of his wife, a worthy woman of Zermatt, who shared his labours and his hopes.

The travellers who ascended to the pass marvelled to find on its highest point, in a place that was but ill protected by a few rocks protruding from the glacier, that wretched little tent, all patched and repaired, and, under the tent, the man and his wife who served them with good bread, cheese, a glass of cognac, or a certain wine that was as sharp and as light as the air on the pass. And, while the woman busied herself in their service, the man would point out to them a rude stone building barely begun; it was his daily task, the aim of his life to complete it; it was to be a hotel with four well-closed little rooms, and beds, and it was to be called the 'Hotel Bouquetin'.

All through the summer this courageous couple braved, under their frail canvas shelter, the wind, the cold, and the blizzard, at 3300 metres above the sea. Whenever their modest stock of provisions was exhausted the old man made his way down to Valtournanche, or to Châtillon, to replenish it, leaving his wife to guard the tent alone on the wind-swept pass. Mr. Wills, who found Meynet up there in 1852, describes him to us: he was an old man of lofty stature, sound of limb, straight as a pine-tree. His bronzed countenance, furrowed by the hand of time, his vivacious grey eyes, his piercing glance, the folds of skin round the mouth that stood out as if carved in wood, his long grey beard that flowed down to his chest, and a certain gravity of bearing, gave him an appearance of dignity and strength, so that he seemed like the wild monarch of that desert. A long, ragged grey smock reached down below his knees, and a strange goat-skin cap covered his head; he seemed another Robinson Crusoe on his desert isle. He spoke excellent French, and his conversation and his ideas were far superior to those usually pertaining to men of his condition.[28] And when some traveller showed an interest in him, he opened his heart and poured forth his enthusiasm for the glories of his pass, and described in glowing terms the wondrous sights he enjoyed up there, and proclaimed aloud that by building a refuge for those who could not otherwise have viewed those sublime scenes of nature, he had shown himself a benefactor to the human race. And then he would humbly ask for a contribution towards the construction of his house on the snow; it was not, he said, the greed for gain that impelled him, but the wish to make known the beauties of a sunrise on his pass. 'Gentlemen', he would say, 'I work for humanity!' and he told how he purposed to walk about the world, to London, to Paris, on a pilgrimage collecting funds for his undertaking. He must have been an oddity in the completest sense of the word, and a man of great intelligence. The old men of Valtournanche remember him still.

He had made some study of Latin, was acquainted with the laws of prosody, and was wont to adorn his speech with classical quotations. His life is full of strange mysteries; no man knows why he abandoned his studies in their midst; he did a little of everything;

he was for a few years schoolmaster at Paquier, he was engaged in commerce with some of his friends; but it appears that neither trade, nor teaching, nor his speculations in building in the high Alps were profitable to him, because he was generally penniless. Poor dreamer! His ideas were in strong contrast with those of his fellow-citizens, who were less excitable and more practical; and yet he belonged to the same breed, he possessed their gifts of self-denial and self-respect, he was a symbol of their rude idealism, their natural and unconscious love of the beauty of the mountains, he embodied their timid hopes of a happier destiny for their valley.

From time to time such strange men appear among the rude peasants; had they been born among educated people they would perhaps have been poets and artists; up in the mountains they are looked upon as visionaries, as harmless madmen, at whom children point their finger, and whose strange doings are related in the rustic village assemblies for two or three generations.

He was rarely seen in the village; he would descend to get provisions, and then return to his hermitage, where, wrapped in the peace of the lofty glacier, he would dream of the future. He came before his time; had he lived twenty years later, he had perhaps become another Seiler of Zermatt. But, modest though he be, he counts for something in the valley's progress; he too has a right to a humble place among the worshippers and the prophets of the Cervin. Without having shared the heroic inspiration that shortly after was breathed upon Carrel, he foresaw the day when the multitude should come over the pass, proclaiming the wonders of the mountains and bowing low before the majesty of the Cervin. Like all the pioneers, he did not see the fulfilment of his dream. One fine morning the good Meynet departed from his valley, leaving his stone house on the col incomplete and roofless, and never returned to gaze from that spot on the glories of the sunrise. The strangest surmises were made concerning his disappearance; some said he had been robbed and slain by brigands, others that he was roaming about the world preaching the beauty of the Theodul; other things were said that it skills not to repeat.

'The harmless and adventurous enthusiast has disappeared,'

exclaims Wills, on his return to the pass some time after, 'and the cabin, in the midst of the glacier, remains as he left it, and will remain so until the violence of the storm has prostrated its walls, or some successor shall be found to inherit the old man's enthusiasm and love of nature.'

The successor came, and he was again a Meynet.

The old J. Pierre, before leaving his native land, had made over the possession of the Theodul to his cousin Ant. François Meynet, a notary of Aosta, and son to the J. Jacques who had accompanied Saussure; and, in the deed of sale, dated December 28th, 1852, are written these solemn words: 'A cabin which the vendor, animated by sentiments of humanity, has had the excellent and daring idea of building for the purpose of harbouring travellers.'

The new owner caused the hut to be covered with a roof, added a small wooden hut hard by, and entrusted the whole to the care of his brother, J. Baptiste. Thus those who passed by in 1855 found another greybeard there, another enthusiastic and eccentric Meynet, who extended hospitality to travellers and expounded to them the beauties of the Alpine scenery. The spirit of the old Minette lived again in his successor.[29]

The tradition of the ancient founder was carried on. The new greybeard delighted to relate to his guests the story of his campaigns in Napoleon's army, in which he had served under Marshal Junot. He opened his heart to Mr. Hinchliff, disclosing all his paternal pride in his two sons who were fighting on Crimean battlefields, and, drawing some excellent wine from a small cask that was concealed in the wall, he insisted on the Englishman's drinking with him to the success of the allied armies; and the Englishman and the Piedmontese fraternized up there at 3300 metres above the sea, thinking of their fellow-countrymen fighting side by side in a distant land.

That must have been a great day for the good Meynet — on whom Hinchliff there and then jestingly conferred the title of Count of the St. Theodul — one of those rare moments which made up to him for his long hours of frozen solitude.

A feeling of deep sympathy is awakened in us when we read these unimportant records of Alpine life in simpler times, when the innkeeper was a peasant somewhat more intelligent, and the guide a mountaineer somewhat bolder than the rest. Neither existed as yet professionally, and the traveller who came more frequently into contact with the rude inhabitants of the mountains, and who was not as yet separated from them by that kind of interpreter, the modern hall porter of the large hotel, took an interest in them and their way of life much greater than at the present day.

It is this community of life with the natives of the Alps which lends such beauty to the writings of Saussure and the climbers of the good old times. At the present time accounts of Alpine expeditions contain other ideas, other conceptions of noblest import, which were then undreamt of; but those other things are no longer there, and it is a sad loss because they were so full of beauty!

It is well worth while at the present day to record the struggles, the hopes, the humble resources and the modest joys of those early innkeepers on the high mountains, because the record helps to broaden the minds of modern Philistines, who, when they arrive in panting crowds on the pass, consider it a matter of course that there should be a house to harbour them, and cry out if the bread be stale, or if the grog be not ready for their refreshment. Let these gentry think of Saussure, who spent three days and three nights on the pass before the hotel existed; let them think of old Minette and his brave wife, who spent three long months in every year up there under a miserable tent, for the good of humanity.

Baptiste was succeeded in 1857 by his son, J. Augustin, in the 'government' of the Theodul. The testimonials written at that time in the visitors' book of the hotel on the pass by certain Valtournanche friends are full of enthusiasm for J. Augustin[30] and his brave sisters. It would seem that the Valtorneins were beginning to see that the visionary Meynet was right.

Travellers came up to the pass each year in greater numbers; the rush to the mountains had begun; waves of travellers broke over Zermatt, and the spray was hurled up as far as the pass. The worthy Meynet must have been well pleased — not, indeed, that the hotel yielded much profit, because the carriage of fuel and provisions to so great a height was a costly matter and the season was short; but thenceforth the Theodul was much frequented and the evenings were cheerful.

When business was most flourishing and the hotel increasing its custom by leaps and bounds, we see the rise of another dynasty, that of the Pessions, who laid claim to the lordship of the Theodul. With reference to the contest between the Meynets and the Pessions for the possession of that barren islet of rock, there appeared for the first time in our Alpine literature the question of the ownership of glaciers; the law stretched its arm up to that height, where nature had seemed to be superior to human jurisdiction and the civil code to have renounced its sway.

The Pession family, who owned an 'alp' beside the glaciers of the pass, claimed possession, showing an extract from the land-register which indicated Switzerland as the boundary of their 'alp'. The matter was brought before the court and was settled by a compromise, according to which the Pessions paid for the improvements, and the Meynets gave up the 'county' of the Theodul to the Pessions, who, in partnership with the Perruquets and others, hold it still.[31]

Parallel with the history of the early innkeepers runs the equally modest one of the first guides. The guides, as we understand them, did not yet exist in the valley; they were men who showed the way, stout carriers of baggage, mostly jovial fellows who chatted, smoked, and . . . drank. The few travellers who came to Paquier before 1848 were sometimes forced to wait whole days at the priest's before a guide — and such a guide! — was found and brought to them. He had perchance that very instant put off his smuggler's pack; it was all one to him to drive the Zermatt herds and the mules of Valdostan merchants over the snows of the pass, or to drag the unpractised climber on his way. There was no question of roping on the glacier; the iron-shod stick was an article of luxury.

At Paquier and in its neighbourhood those who were thoroughly conversant with the way over the Theodul Pass could be counted on the fingers of one hand. It was called 'traversing the Mont Cervin', and was described as most dangerous to those strangers who desired to make the attempt; not one of the guides would have ventured on the pass alone with the traveller for all the money in the world; at least two were required to cross the glacier of 'La Rouièse', as they called it, and if the weather was not fine they would not start.

Brockedon was made aware of this when he was obliged, owing to a slight fall of snow, to stop two days and two nights in the inhospitable quarters of the 'Mont Jumont', because his guide, Jean Baptiste Pession, insisted on waiting for a caravan of mules to come up from Valtournanche, so that they might cross the pass together; and, as the muleteers failed to arrive, he finally procured a second guide.

On the way up to the pass Pession sought to hearten his weary traveller with these encouraging words: 'Be of good cheer, sir! No man can stop here and live'; a thing to make the bravest shudder. When they reached the pass the second guide, a Meynet (Pierre Antoine), to amuse him, told him that Hannibal had crossed the Mont Cervin; that the insignificant ruins they saw there were walls that the Carthaginian general had built; and in support of this he quoted Livy and Polybius! They must have been strange characters, these primitive guides! It seems to me that in their humble local pride they must have treated their 'Monsieur' with a certain rustic arrogance and with a simple familiarity which could not fail to recommend them to the traveller, and to afford the latter a store of interesting anecdotes.

To the men of Valtournanche all strangers, even Germans and French, were Englishmen; Quintino Sella himself, when he climbed the Breithorn in 1854, did not escape being taken for an Englishman. 'Fortunately for us', writes Gorret, 'he was an Englishman . . . from Biella.'[32]

John Ball, who crossed from Zermatt to Ayas in 1854, relates a very significant instance of the mountaineering usages of that time. His guide, on his way back to Zermatt alone, found on the glacier below the pass an English gentleman, also alone, and in a pitiful state of prostration and helplessness. It had happened shortly before that the Englishman's guide, a man from the lower part of the Val Tournanche, who had been preceding him, unroped, by a few steps, had suddenly disappeared in a deep, snow-covered crevasse. The arrival of the fresh guide removed the Englishman from his evil predicament, but as they were both without ropes, they were not able to succour the unfortunate victim, who was left in the abyss, while the Englishman was taken in safety to Zermatt. As it was understood there, from the lost guide's name, that he was not one of the three or four who made a profession of guiding travellers across the pass, but an interloper in the business, his fate roused no compassion; it was only when the Englishman said that his money was in the sack which had fallen in with the guide that active researches after the victim were set on foot.

This gloomy picture of times when it was customary to walk confidingly on the glaciers alone, unroped, without the most elementary precautions and with little or no experience, brings home to us the enormous difference there is between those who were called guides then and the guides of to-day. On the Zermatt side also the guides were most primitive. Peter Damatter, who accompanied Professor Forbes up to the pass in 1842, instead of taking with him a rope and a good iron-shod stick, had provided himself with nothing more than an umbrella; as soon as he came on to the glacier, he was so disturbed by the sight of a few crevasses that he begged for the loan of a stick, and it appears that he was incapable of handling even that with any skill. And it is related of two other guides that they refused to proceed unless the travellers would walk in front of them and cut steps in the ice.

The profession of a guide as it was understood in those days cannot have been a very difficult one: a pair of good shoulders, a certain amount of eloquence, and no more was needed! The sickle or the spade was laid aside, the cattle were entrusted to the better half, and the traveller was taken in charge.

The peaceful mountaineers of Paquier, seeing that travellers were beginning to arrive in considerable numbers, recollected that they too had known the pass, from father to son; they saw that there was money to be made, and they felt that they were guides. A real frenzy took possession of the inhabitants of the village; almost every family gave up one or two of its members to the new profession; but the daring, emulous, self-sacrificing ideals, the desire for conquest, the thirst for glory which are the essence of the modern guide were far removed from those patient, sturdy, and courteous men; they were excellent mountaineers, not guides.

It often happened that Chamonix guides, famous ones, on their way through this region with their employers, hired the men of Valtournanche to carry the baggage. They preferred them to the Zermatters because they spoke their language and were, perhaps, more easily satisfied in the matter of wages. It is probable that the Chamoniards did not treat their Valtornein colleagues very well either in respect of manners or of money; they undoubtedly considered them their inferiors.

In the hotel books, and particularly in that of the Theodul, I often find the names of these Chamonix guides written; they were Michel Payot, Jean Tairraz, Michel Charlet, Gédéon Balmat, J. P. Cachat, and more besides; and below these names are modestly inscribed those of their Valtournanche comrades.

The latter, who were not lacking in intelligence, gradually learnt from the others how to lead a party and how to behave to travellers; they found out how much a good guide's pay amounted to, and it occurred to them that if they made themselves independent of the tutelage of their Savoyard colleagues they would earn greater fame and keep all the profits to themselves.

After that the men of Valtournanche were seen to descend to Châtillon and offer themselves, with a persistence that was sometimes tiresome, to the travellers who came up the main valley in the diligence or in carriages; and they would spend whole days and weeks there, waiting for the English,[33] whom they would guide up the Cimes Blanches, to the Theodul, sometimes, but rarely, up the Breithorn.

In Nicolas Pession's little book I find, between 1857 and 1865, the ascent of the Theodulhorn mentioned three times, and that of the Breithorn twice only.

Certificates of competency were delivered by the customs officer at Valtournanche. I have seen one of these documents, which was given in 1855 to 'Messrs. Charles Gorret and Augustus Meynet', in which there is a declaration that 'to my personal knowledge these men have this year already crossed the Mont Cervin several times, and are the best known guides in the village and thoroughly familiar with the pass, and with other mountains as well, wherefore travellers have always expressed their complete satisfaction. I also certify that, considering the well-known honesty and trustworthiness of the aforesaid two guides, travellers may unhesitatingly entrust their lives and their money to them'.

They were very willing, these Valtorneins, who were awaking at the breath of the new pursuit of mountaineering! A self-written recommendation on the first page of the book of an ex-guide, about 1856, is not devoid of local colour, in the *naiveté* of its self-praise: 'The brothers Augustin and Gabriel Meynet, keepers of the inn on the Theodul Pass, opposite the Mont Cervin, with a well-furnished restaurant, offer their services to visitors, artists, and tourists! They have reliable guides to lead travellers to the finest view points, mountains, valleys, glaciers, and other beautiful spots near Valtournanche. They are proud of the confidence with which travellers have honoured them.'

Some of these guides must have been really good; even Wills, though expressing a preference for the men of Zermatt, adds nevertheless that Pierre and Charles Emmanuel Gorret were excellent guides; and Jean Tairraz, one of the best known Chamonix guides, who enjoyed the confidence of the mountaineers of that date, often sent them to Nicolas Pession, of whom the testimonials in his book all speak in terms of nothing but praise.[34]

The following must also have been good guides for that time: Joseph Bich, one of the oldest, who is said to have taken to the profession in 1845; Augustin Pelissier, known as Theodul, who was Barracco's and Benedetto Rignon's guide; Antoine Gorret, the Abbé Amé's father; Antoine and Charles Pession; Pierre and Gabriel Maquignaz, the latter of whom accompanied Mr. Jacomb in 1860; Augustin Perron; Solomon Meynet, who climbed the Cervin (Matterhorn) with Craufurd Grove in 1867, and others besides; and above all Jean Jacques Carrel, a mighty hunter, the future companion of Hawkins and Tyndall, an adventurous spirit, a daring mountaineer, who took part in the very earliest attempts on the Becca, and

OLD ZERMATT

LOUIS BURGENER
the famous Zermatt Bootmaker

Schwarzsee and Chapel

who had in him the stuff of which real guides are made. Carrel the Bersagliere, on his return from the Novara campaign, had turned his keen glance on the Cervin in the first half-hearted attempts, and had then gone back to fight on the San Martino hills. Jean Joseph Maquignaz was still working peacefully at his mason's trade.

Thus, while on the Valais side the local names of Johann Kronig, Biner, Franz and Alexander Lochmatter, and Joseph Moser were connected, even before 1860, with some of the first important ascents in that group of mountains, on our side there were as yet none but humble names; no great guide had yet arisen; opportunity was lacking.

If I may be allowed to compare a guide with a pilot, those of Zermatt seem to me like sailors already grown daring, who seek to be the first discoverers in the unknown seas of the Dom, the Dent Blanche, and Monte Rosa, while those of Valtournanche are still worthy boatmen who ferry the traveller from one bank to the other of their peaceful river, the Theodul.

But neither the Theodul nor the Breithorn could ever create great guides. It was the Matterhorn that saved these men from mediocrity. Till then the Cervin had not taken any part in the life of Valtournanche; a cloud of ancient and terrible traditions still enshrouded it. Men looked upon it with indifference as something not essential to their lives.

But a new breath came and blew that cloud away, and the Cervin was revealed in all its beauty, promising fame and riches to those unknown men. And they were not unworthy of the peak; unconsciously they had been trained by the whole course of their own and their fathers' lives, that had been spent among the rough rocks in the valley, on the steep, rocky hills that form the giant's spurs, working and hunting, with the Cervin ever before their eyes

Then a miracle was worked; a group of wonderful guides sprang up; it seemed as if a foot stamped upon the ground in Valtournanche and called forth these valiant men; and in a few years their names echoed far and wide. The demon that had so long dwelt among the rocks of the Becca vanished as if at the exorcism of a saint; thenceforward the demons of the Cervin were called Whymper and Carrel.

But how did it come to pass that those mountain folk, so tenacious of their ancient primitive ways, so slow to grasp new ideas, who but a few years before had looked with suspicion on the new visitors who came up their valley from the city, how did it come to pass that they were fired with such enthusiasm? Before that time they had been shepherds, hunters, muleteers, or smugglers, and had lived in the bondage of their narrowing egotism, of their miserable self-conceit. They now cast away their nets like the apostle and followed the Master; a new moral meaning of life displayed itself to their minds, a ray of idealism filtered through to their unenlightened souls, and their hearts seemed to grow greater and stronger.

Who was the fiery monk who first preached the new crusade, who incited them to attempt to scale that inaccessible mass which bounded the horizon of their valley and seemed to be the end of the earth, who stirred them and made them daringly attack the rocks of the peak, intoxicating them with a new enthusiasm? Who was the first pilgrim who came from afar to whisper in the ear of Carrel the magic name: the Cervin?

The humble in spirit feel instinctively the beauty of great objects; the noble frenzy that no other had understood seemed natural enough to these simple-minded men. Valtournanche was slowly awaking, and in its last sleep it had dreamt of the Cervin.

CHAPTER III

THE CONQUEROR S

'Cette noble folie et que nul ne comprît
Apparaît toute claire à ces simples d'esprit.'
E. ROSTAND, *La Princesse Lointaine*.

THEY had arranged to meet before dawn at Avouil, which consists of a group of isolated châlets at the lower end of the basin of Breuil; they were to arrive there separately, each by a different way, so as not to arouse suspicion.

They were punctual at the meeting-place; the last stars were growing dim in the sky, the valley was still shrouded in darkness when they all three left Avouil and stealthily made their way up towards the mountain. They had told the dwellers in the châlets that they were going after marmot, and, in order to give colour to their statement, they had with them their '*grafios*', ashen sticks with an iron hook at one end, which the mountain people use to pull the animals out of their holes.

They were a strange trio, differing much one from the other. One, Jean Jacques Carrel, who, as the oldest, seemed to be in command of the party, was a mighty hunter in the sight of the Lord; he had no equal in the whole valley as a hunter of the chamois on the steep slopes. His wrinkled and sunburnt face bore witness to the long hours he had spent up on the rocks, amid heat and cold, watching for his prey. He was a man inured to all kinds of exertion and ready for any daring venture. When poor Pierre Vallet, known as 'de la Dodet', had fallen into a crevasse on the Theodul glacier in the year 1842, and a large number of men, under the guidance of the priest, had started from Paquier to try and save him, Jean Jacques was the only one who dared go down into the crevasse on the rope to pull out the victim. The back pocket of his coat was bulging and heavy, for in it were concealed the day's provisions; a large piece of the six-months-old bread, a slice of cold polenta, and a small flask of grappa, the brandy of our mountain people; between his shirt and his waistcoat he carried, as wood-cutters are wont to do, a hatchet, to be used in the day's undertaking.

Another, Jean Antoine Carrel, was a man of about thirty, short of stature, thick-set but agile, with a vivacious eye and a martial cast of countenance, and wore a pair of brown moustaches and an 'imperial', as was customary with the soldiers of that date — an 1848 fellow, as they are called; he was a discharged soldier and had fought at Novara.

The third, one Aimé by name, the oddest of all, was in strange contrast with the others. He was a beardless lad of about twenty, something between a cleric and a shepherd, tall, bony, straight as a pine-tree, with a certain mixture of timidity and resolution in his bearing and gait; a cheerful companion withal, ready and quick in discourse, and endowed with a most serviceable pair of legs. His searching glance and his open and thoughtful brow bore witness in him to a habit of study and reflection that the other two did not share. His face was not bronzed like theirs, because he spent almost all the year at the seminary, and only came home for the holidays. But what grand expeditions he made then, during the bright days of the Alpine summer, through fields and meadows, up hill and down dale, from Paquier to Cignana, from Cheneil to Avouil, to recuperate after the nine months he had spent in study at Aosta!

Those solitary rambles of his were spent in prolonged contemplation of the summits of the mountains. They seemed to him more beautiful than when, as a child, he had left his village with eight sous in his pocket on his way down to the great city where they had shut him up in a school.

He now began to realize the feeling of freedom that they suggested, to understand their beauty, and he gazed upon them with an undefined sense of longing. He spent many hours alone in the upper pastures, comparing one peak with another, measuring them with his eye in order to learn which was the highest; they stood all round him and he did not even know their names; he knew of two only, the most conspicuous: that one was called the Tournalin, the other the Cervin. This was the highest of all, and his comrades called it the Becca. It filled him with curiosity and admiration.

To-day when it, and no other, was his goal — for they had set forth actually to attempt to climb the Becca itself — the young seminarist's heart was beating with impatience and with joy. It seemed to him too good to be true, and he besieged his sponsor, the hunter, with a hundred questions. But the sponsor himself knew not what to reply and just went on his way, chewing tobacco and frequently raising his eyes to the precipitous Becca, on whose summit the first rays of the rising sun had just lighted. No man knew what was to be found beyond on those mighty vertical walls, for no man had yet set foot there. Old men indeed remembered having heard, when they were children, of the two daring hunters who had reached the shoulder of the mountain many years before in their pursuit of chamois; and the names of these two, now forgotten, had even been mentioned; but the story has more legend than history. The event had happened in the previous century, and, on mature reflection, it seemed impossible, for chamois hardly ventured on the Becca; and the tale had left in the minds of the later inhabitants but a faint desire to emulate such prowess.

It was said that some Englishmen, who had lately passed through Valtournanche, had asked whether it were possible to climb those precipices, but no one, either native or foreigner, had ever thought of it seriously. Only Aimé's uncle, the chanoine, had once said to his relatives that if it were possible to ascend the Becca it would be a source of gain for the whole valley.[1]

The chanoine, who lived at Aosta, was a learned man, and his words carried great weight; even the English who came up to the Val d'Aosta, knowing him to be a great student and a lover of mountains, did not fail to visit and consult him, so much so that he was called in the neighbourhood 'the friend of the English'.[2]

By talking with them and hearing them express their curiosity concerning the Cervin and their admiration for it, he had perceived before anyone else that the mountain at whose foot he had been born might become the glory and the blessing of his valley, and he had imparted his opinion to his fellow-villagers, who were unaware of their hidden treasure.[3]

Our three friends, who were related to him, had listened to his words, and, after much discussion and much planning, had at last set forth to search for the way. On that morning the sun was shining brightly on the roseate rocks of the Becca, which was almost free from snow, for the season was midsummer; and in the bright morning air the peak seemed quite near. They were excellent walkers and they rose rapidly, their hearts full of hope.

At the châlets of Planet they found Gabriel Maquignaz and Carrel, 'the painter', and told them of their plan. They said that they had no objection to the idea, that they would not even have minded joining in, but having no real desire to follow three such madmen, they bade them farewell.

Higher up our friends met a shepherd, who was surprised to see them coming up that way. They showed him the '*grafios*'; it was to be a bad day for the marmots! The motionless cows watched them passing, fixing their stupid, large eyes upon them. On the highest pastures a few goats marched gracefully beside them for a short distance, regarding them with much curiosity and hoping for a pinch of salt. After that they were alone.

The marmots, having sallied forth at dawn for their first meal, hastened back into their holes, whistling with alarm at the approach of the party, but no one of the three gave them a thought.

They had no fixed plan. When they reached the moraine they made their way upwards by the rock-face which closes in the glacier on its left bank. This was the Keu de Tzarciglion, as it was called by the hunter who had been there on former occasions hunting chamois, and who knew the way.

For the time being everything was going well. They climbed up the enormous precipitous and riven face for three or four hours, but when they were nearing the top the hunter took to the glacier, while the other two continued on the rocks, thinking them safer. Shortly after they heard their companion shouting for help. They hastened towards the spot whence the cries came and saw their comrade motionless on the slope of the glacier, in such difficulties that he was unable to move a single step forwards or backwards. A single movement would have sent him rolling down to the bottom, for the slope of the glacier is very steep at that point, and he would have perished.

The soldier and the seminarist came to the hunter's assistance. With every precaution, holding on to one another by means of the marmot stick, they succeeded in approaching him, and, pulling out of his pocket the hatchet he had with him, they cut holes in the ice, which allowed all of them to return in safety to the rocks. They were exhausted and breathless. A few steps more brought them to the top of the wall where it comes to an end on the ridge which bounds it. This point, which lies between the Tête du Lion and the Dent d'Hérens, is now known as the Col Tournanche. At that time it had no name.

The opposite face, which falls precipitously for 1,600 feet to the Tiefenmatten glacier, is revealed at this point. To our three friends it was a completely new sight; they had heard confused accounts of how the pays d'Hérens lay behind the Cervin, and their wonder was great when they found instead a valley completely covered with ice, and enclosed by rocks of enormous height.

They stood there for a few moments speechless, almost terrified, at the sight of its savage beauty; it was so different from their native valley, all clothed in green! They sat down on the snow and broke their fast; then they began pushing rocks over into the abyss. They followed the course of the heavy blocks with childish delight as they struck the slope of the Col, throwing up clouds of powdery snow, and then rebounded and described huge parabolae, finally splitting in pieces in mid-air, or disappearing with a dull thud in the mysterious crevasses on the glacier below. They were in no hurry; like good hill-men they recked little of the time.

The Becca was now near at hand and would not move; if they did not reach it that year they would the next; they were masters of the peak, and no one would come and take it away from them. Thus thought our three heroes, with enviable sang-froid, and thus they continued to think in the following years, until there came another, more resolute and less of a hill-man, who bore off the prize.

After amusing themselves for a time they turned their thoughts to Cervin once more, and started to climb again. They found no difficulty in reaching the Tête du Lion, which they considered the first step of the pyramid, but when they arrived there they saw the wide gap which separated them from their peak, and beheld its precipitous face rising on the other side, far off, inaccessible.

They gave up the attempt, and, on the descent, they saw a ledge of rock on the face of the Tête du Lion, which seemed to afford easy access to the base of the Cervin. But it was growing late; they thought the way was found, and for that day they left the mountain in peace. They drank a glass at Breuil in the Saussure tavern, and slept the sleep of the just in the hayloft at Avouil.

Such was, in all its simplicity, the first attempt made to ascend the Cervin, and it took place in 1857. They started without provisions, without proper gear, naïvely unprepared. Reaching a spot which pleased them, they wasted several hours in throwing stones into a well like children; they mistook the way . . . No matter; this was the first occasion when man had set forth to climb to the summit, and in the mountain's history this moment is as fine as is the first word that comes from the halting lips of a babe, making all the household smile with joy.

In Valtournanche the attempt was much discussed. The majority declared that the three were madmen, that the Becca was unassailable; others expressed the opinion that 'the Cervin was only for the English'; some few approved and thought of renewing the attempt, and among them were those two who had refused to follow the three madmen at the châlets of Planet.

When the chanoine, their uncle, heard of it, he exclaimed that it was but a mad, ill-considered venture.[4] But in his heart of hearts he must have rejoiced, and I will wager that he would fain have been of the party.

At that time the good chanoine did not come often to Valtournanche; not, indeed, that the religious quiet of the cathedral stalls or peaceful siestas in the shade of the ancient willow in the chapter-house of Sant 'Orso had dulled his love of his native place, or his insatiable longing for the mountains. Other work kept him far from Valtournanche; the excursions on passes and peaks that he was making with famous men of science, such as Forbes, Sismonda, and Studer; the first small observatory which he had set up on the roof of his house in 1840, when as yet no one in the valley had thought of studying the phenomena of the Alps: there he assiduously added to his knowledge and his hopes. It was the little fortress, whence in the name of science he carried on alone his campaign for the glory of his mountains.

He fought against the indifference and the prejudices of his own fellow-countrymen, and his doggedness of purpose undoubtedly made men secretly suspect him of harmless insanity, before his ideal was understood, and the encouragement of sympathy and praise reached him from the cities.

The smiling slopes round Aosta, the châlets of Comboë and of Chamolé were more frequented by him during those years than his paternal cottage at Cheneil; the Becca di Nona and the Becca des-dix-heures (as the Mont Emilius was then called) seemed to attract him more than the precipices of his native Tournalin; but from those peaks he saw the Cervin, and during the long days he spent on the summit of the Nona drawing the panorama of the Pennine Alps, he had before his eyes and his mind the wondrous pyramid which, in his opinion, 'if it could not claim the glory of being the highest peak in Europe, was undeniably the most beautiful'. And when he spoke of it he was wont to say, 'my Cervin'; and even then he would affirm to his friends the probability of its being conquered, and would give utterance to his earnest hope of climbing it himself some day.[5]

The pleasant figure of the Chanoine Carrel appears in this history as that of the pioneer of mountaineering in his native valley, and I rejoice that the evidence of his co-dwellers in the valley agrees with that of his old friends in attributing to him a share in the honour of the first attempt. He was the spark which kindled a great fire; he was the creator of the idea, the others merely carried it out. No man could perceive better than he, so learned and so gifted, the beauty and the utility of the Cervin, that seemed so repulsive and so useless: none better than he could foresee how, thanks to that mass of rock, his fellow-Valtorneins would be inspired with a higher ideal of life, and his native valley enriched by the new influx of strangers. He deeply loved his church tower and that other lofty tower of rock which dominates the whole valley. The son of many generations that had lived at the mountain's foot, he was full of the pride of his race, and knew well its great strength and bravery.

A man of science, he was the first to feel an inclination for research. He had read in the books of strangers of the enthusiasm of the mountain's first worshippers, and he carefully followed the accounts of the expeditions which were taking place in the Alps, and, above all, of the attempts on Monte Rosa; and the victory of Gnifetti, likewise a priest and a son of the Alps, must have awakened in this worthy son of the Cervin a feeling of keen rivalry.

Perhaps, when he heard of the naïve attempt of the seminarist and his companions, he thought it a profanation of his beautiful mountain, and hence came, perhaps, the severity of his judgment.

But the first step had been taken: the idea of climbing the Becca had arisen in the village; men of Valtournanche had been the first to doubt its inaccessibility. And the matter was not to be allowed to end thus; the three who had reached the Tête du Lion were henceforward bound with indissoluble ties to the Cervin; the thought of climbing it was ever with them from that day forward.

When we think how long it was before the idea of mountaineering commended itself to the educated men in our cities, and with what difficulty a superstitious terror of the monster was converted in the minds of the mountain folk into a keen desire to attack it, we see that the first attempt was the decisive moment of a new era in the history of the valley.

It may be that others, among the distinguished foreigners who passed by and admired it, felt its immense fascination, but the mountain's tragic aspect must have set it above any hope of conquest. Thus Mr. King, a famous English mountaineer, in his book published in 1858,[6] declares that the Cervin is an absolutely inaccessible obelisk of rock. And if the bold thought flashed through the mind of any one of them, it would seem that none ventured to express it.

It is said that in the following years other attempts were made by men of Valtournanche.[7]

Of our three 'madmen' one was absent for some years from his native village, deep in his theological studies, and became the Abbé

Gorret; the second was recalled to the army, fought at San Martino, and won his sergeant's stripes, and he was Carrel the Bersagliere. The hunter, who remained at home, was left ready to accompany the first Englishman who came to attempt the ascent.

The English did not long delay their coming. These were exceptional years for the valley: a breath of progress was blowing up through it; it seemed as if something new and great were about to take place.

The fine church of Paquier was finished, and was smiling in its whiteness among the dark pines and the old grey cottages; the parish priest Bore was proud to see his work complete before he died. The Chanoine Carrel had published his *Panorama from the Becca di Nona*.

A painter from Paris, named Aubert, visited the Aosta valley and went up to Valtournanche in order to draw its picturesque landscapes and to collect notes on places and on their history. Drawings and notes were destined to proclaim in foreign lands the beauties of the valley.

The stream of visitors had swelled. Since the conquest of the highest peak of Monte Rosa had been effected (1855) from Zermatt, it was only natural that the thoughts of the boldest should turn at length towards the Matterhorn.

An English book, published in 1858, mentioned the first attempt of the Valtournanche hunters, and observed that the Mont Jumont (Jomein) would be thenceforth the starting-point for every daring mountaineer who should make the venture, and that if the mountain were to be climbed it would probably be from the Italian side.[8] This was the first published allusion to the possibility of the attempt being made. And so men were busy with the problem of the Matterhorn.

Kennedy, an excellent climber, prowled round the mountain in 1858, and considered that the ascent to the summit on the Breuil side was impossible.

Vaughan Hawkins (1859), after examining it on every side with the Swiss guide Bennen, was very nearly convinced that it was possible to conquer it; but he concluded that it would be no easy matter: 'Accessible or not,' he says, 'the Mont Cervin is assuredly a different sort of affair from Mont Blanc or Monte Rosa, or any other of the thousand and one summits which nature has kindly opened to man.'[9]

Hawkins and Bennen returned in 1860, and with them came Professor Tyndall, the famous scientist. They inquired at Breuil for a man to carry their sacks. Jean Jacques Carrel, he of the first attempt, was pointed out to them as the best mountaineer in the whole valley. 'Uncle Carrel' came forward; a rough, good-humoured fellow, an ordinary specimen of the peasant class. He is thus described by Hawkins in his narrative.

They set forth. Carrel was put last in the party; the guides from the other side of the Alps, who had already acquired greater skill, felt the profoundest contempt for our mountain guides. Bennen, as they made their way up to the Col du Lion, answered all Carrel's suggestions as to the choice of route with glances of mild pity, and kept muttering: 'Er weiss gar nichts' (He knows nothing about it).[10]

They reached the Col du Lion, proceeded as far as the spot to the east of the couloir, which was subsequently called the cheminée, crossed the gully, and climbed up about 300 feet. Carrel was left with Hawkins, while Bennen conducted Tyndall a short distance further; but they soon gave up the undertaking.[11]

Bennen returned from the attempt full of confidence in future success; but he had seen how long and difficult it would be.

Hawkins observed: 'The mountain, too, has a sort of prestige of invincibility which is not without its influence on the mind, and almost leads one to expect to encounter some new and unheard-of source of peril upon it. Hence I suppose it is that the dwellers at Zermatt and in Valtournanche have scarcely been willing to set foot upon the mountain, and have left the honour of doing so to a native of another district' (*Mountaineering in 1861*, pp. 86, 87). He was alluding to his guide Bennen, a native of Laax in the upper Rhone valley. But the eminent climber was wrong in so far as concerned the Valtournanche guides; and in our turn we may ask why Bennen himself, on returning to Breuil with Professor Tyndall for the third time in the following year, and making another attempt, should have been so inexplicably lacking in courage to go through with the undertaking, and should have answered the exhortations of his employer to attempt at least the ascent of the lower peak with the discouraging remark that the peak 'had neither name nor fame'.[12]

In the same year the Messrs. Parker made an attempt from Zermatt, by the Hörnli ridge. They tried again in the following year (1861), but only reached a height of about 11,000 feet.*

Now Edward Whymper came upon the scene. Into the bullring, under the burning sun, before thousands of eager spectators, the *espada* steps forth eager and brave; the eyes of all are fixed on him. The arena is now empty; the bull alone awaits him in the centre of the circus, motionless, with horns erect. The struggle is to be terrible, unceasing, full of daring stratagems; one of the two must fall. The *espada* scans the monster and strides up to him with resolute gait. Now is the critical moment.

In the same way Whymper appeared in the majestic amphitheatre of mountains, among which the Matterhorn rears his dark head aloft in sign of defiance. Here too, as in the arena at Seville, it is not the bull which seeks the encounter: the man attacks, the bull defends himself, dies or kills; and in the duel the Matterhorn had all the material advantages of its enormous strength, of its fits of brutal rage; the man's weapon was his iron will.

The history of the contest between this man, young, strong, and confident, and the hoary, cold, and unresponsive rock is perhaps one of the finest and most telling in the whole history of mountaineering, and, apart from mountaineering, it is a not unimportant episode in the hard-won conquest of unknown territory.

Whymper was at the outset of his Alpine career. He came to the Val Tournanche for the first time in 1860, and saw and desired the Matterhorn. In the following year he came again: two peaks, still virgin, drew him to the Alps – the Weisshorn and the Matterhorn. Rumours were current that the former was conquered at last, and the victor, Tyndall, was at Breuil to subdue the latter.

Whymper hastened up to Breuil and inquired for a man fit to be

* [This attempt on the Eastern Face, hitherto regarded as inaccessible, by three young amateurs *without guides* was one of the boldest adventures in the history of mountaineering. A height of about 11,500 feet was reached in the first attempt, about 200 feet higher in the second – R.L.G.I.].

his guide. All unanimously declared Jean Antoine Carrel to be the man for him. Jean Antoine, the cock of the valley, made an excellent impression on him; his determined look, the defiant expression on his face, pleased the Englishman, who immediately proposed to him that they should attempt the ascent. Carrel temporized, wished to take a friend, would not start without him. All this did not suit the Englishman; negotiations were broken off, and thus, at their very first meeting, the two revealed their obstinacy to one another.

Whymper had with him an unknown guide who had been given up to him at Châtillon by some other climbers. He made vain attempts to induce another to accompany him. There were at Breuil many famous Swiss guides, among them Mathias zum Taugwald, but they all refused to set forth; one of them, old Peter Taugwalder, was willing, but made exorbitant demands.[13] All of them, good and bad, brave and timid, displayed an invincible aversion to the Matterhorn.

'The men who went had no heart in the matter, and took the first opportunity to turn back. For they were, with the exception of one man . . . universally impressed with the belief that the summit was entirely inaccessible.'

This solitary one who had faith was Jean Antoine Carrel, known as the Bersagliere.[14]

Whymper was obliged to start alone with his chance guide. He spent the night in his tent on the Col du Lion, reached his chimney,[15] and climbed it, but his guide refusing to follow him any further, he was obliged to give up.

In the meantime Carrel had prepared one of those surprise tricks to which Whymper must later have become quite accustomed. Taking with him his uncle, Jean Jacques — the same who had been out with Bennen — he set forth, and, climbing in front of Whymper, he came to a point on the ridge that no other had yet reached, and there, on the rock man had not yet touched, cut out with the iron spike of his axe the date, a cross, his initials, and the rough design of a tiara.[16] It was his mark of ownership.

So Carrel had climbed about 300 feet higher than Tyndall the year before. He was content for that day with so much progress, proud in his heart at having taught the Englishman the Bersagliere's worth. For the first time he revealed his inmost thoughts; it is plain that he had hastened up thither to watch the invader's movements; he was an advance guard disputing the passage with the enemy, and undoubtedly, if Whymper had continued to ascend that day, Carrel would have climbed far ahead, from rock to rock, in the certainty of reaching the summit and of reaching it first. For Carrel considered the Matterhorn a thing of his own, and the attempts of others as an invasion of his own territory. This mighty jealousy of his, full of the impetuousness that was typical of him, explains his conduct in these transactions — conduct whose good faith has seemed to some most questionable; conduct which was swayed at one time by the desire for the Matterhorn to be conquered, at another by his selfish eagerness to keep it for himself.

A rich and powerful man is rarely inclined to admit that the poor and the ignorant may have wills of their own. Those who have wished to judge Carrel have not considered that he was rough and not servile; they thought that he was formed like so many others, to obey, whereas he was born to command. He was not the man passively to serve the ambition of another, because he had his own; and this it was, together with his profound conviction of his own worth, which clouded his judgment to the end and prevented his being the first to reach the summit.

The Matterhorn had the same fascination for Carrel that Mont Blanc formerly had for Jacques Balmat.* It was the aim and object of his life, and he wished to climb it from his native valley for the honour of the Valtorneins. And he did not see, he would not believe, that the mountain might be conquered from the other side; he wrapped about him the proud illusion that without him none could reach the summit, and he made no haste. He was forestalled, and no harder punishment could have befallen him. The discovery of the right way proceeded, almost foot by foot, slowly and painfully.

The Chanoine Carrel at Aosta eagerly followed the attempts. Seeing how the mountain repelled attacks time after time, he con-

*** Since Rey wrote, evidence has come to light which transfers most of the credit for initiative to Dr. F. Paccard.**

tinued to indulge his ardent dream that the glory and the profit of victory should go to his fellow-Valtorneins, and, early in 1862, he wrote to Mr. Tuckett, a distinguished English climber, and a friend of his, recalling how Saussure had offered a reward in 1760 to anyone who should find the way up Mont Blanc, and proposing that the same should be done for the Matterhorn. There was no lack, he said, of competent and willing men in the Val Tournanche; and he begged him to mention the matter to the president of the English Alpine Club. Tuckett then answered that he did not think it right to tempt poor men with promises of money to risk their lives on an expedition which was without any scientific aim; and the matter was dropped.

But the Matterhorn had never yet been in such danger as in that year 1862, when the contest for the great prize took place between Tyndall and Whymper.[17] Both arrived fully conscious of the difficulty of the undertaking.

Whymper came first. He had engaged the guides, J. zum Taugwald and J. König, at Zermatt, and was accompanied by Reginald Macdonald. Adding Luc Meynet, the hunchback, to his party, in the capacity of a porter, he set forth. He slept in a tent on the Col du Lion; the next morning he was repulsed by the cold and the wind. Returning to Breuil, he found Carrel there, the news of Whymper's presence having brought him up thither. Carrel agreed to accompany him, together with a Pession; the Swiss guides were dismissed.

The party started up and bivouacked beyond the pass at the foot of the famous cheminée; they reached the base of the Great Tower, but were then obliged, by an indisposition of Pession's, to return.

For the third time Whymper had made an unsuccessful attempt, and had not even passed the point his adversary had reached. Indefatigable as ever, he hastened to Zermatt and inspected the Hörnli route, which he judged to be impracticable. The want of guides at Zermatt drove him back to seek Carrel and Meynet again, but the exigencies of their trades prevented their accompanying him.

The conception of the professional duties of guides had not yet penetrated to the minds of the men of Valtournanche. Carrel practised guiding as an amateur, as we should say nowadays; he was a hunter, not a guide. The climbing of mountains was with him an

Michel Croz

D. R. Hadow

THE FOUR WHO FELL IN 1865

Rev. Charles Hudson

Lord Francis Douglas

The End of a Day

instinct, a pursuit to which he was passionately devoted, not a calling. Intolerant of the rules of war, he carried on his campaign with bold strokes, varying as the independence of his mind dictated; and though Tyndall was pleased to call his beloved Bennen 'a Garibaldi of guides', the honour of such a name more properly belonged to Carrel.

Whymper, impatient of delay, set forth without guides; the shepherds who saw him making his way thus, all alone, towards the mountain, marvelled greatly. By that time they must have known him as the Matterhorn's antagonist, and on that day more than ever he must have seemed to them a madman.

He safely reached the tent, which he had left on the site of his last bivouac, and he found it buried in snow. One of the fairest of the pages in Whymper's book is that in which he describes his daring climb, and tells of the lonely hours he spent on the threshold of his little tent at the height of about 12,000 feet, in view of the mighty circle of mountains, and in which he describes the wondrous sunset he beheld that evening, and the moonlight reflected from the icy walls of Monte Viso, a hundred miles away.

Next morning he continued his ascent, climbed the cheminée, reached the base of the Great Tower, attained a height of more than 4000 metres, or 13,200 feet, and returned to his bivouac well satisfied with the progress he had made by his own unaided efforts. But, on his descent towards Breuil the same evening, while he was traversing the rocks of the Tête du Lion, and was trying to punch steps in the hard snow with the point of his alpenstock — he had left his ice-axe in the tent — he slipped and fell.

Who, of all those who are familiar with Alpine books, does not remember Whymper's picture which portrays this incident? It shows a man falling through the air down the side of a horrible precipitous ice-slope. I saw that picture when I was ten years old, and I still remember the emotion it then aroused in me; to me that man flying headlong downwards seemed in a hopeless case. Whymper extricated himself from his predicament at the cost of a few scratches,* stopped

* [By a lucky chance his fall was arrested above a big drop; he was badly cut about the head and fainted from loss of blood, but managed to get down to the valley unaided—R.L.G.I].

seven or eight days at the Jomein with his head bandaged, thinking of the hardness of rocks and of man's comparative fragility; then he started once more for the Matterhorn.

This time Jean Antoine decided to accompany him. The proud hunter must have felt some admiration for the Englishman's perseverance and courage. They set forth with César Carrel and the porter Meynet, and climbed up past the Great Tower, but were overtaken by bad weather, and were again obliged to descend.

Whymper wished to try again the very next day; Jean Antoine, a past master in the art of procrastination, had disappeared with the other Carrel, leaving word that they had gone marmot shooting. Whymper started out with his trusty Meynet.

The figure of the poor hunchback of Breuil — for so Whymper is wont to call his porter — is one of the most pleasing and most interesting in the whole story. Always ready and willing to start, he was always excellent when at work, and his very deformity enabled him to carry the tent; in the bivouacs he was a useful and cheerful companion. Throughout Whymper speaks of him with sincere liking, whether it were when he saw him at the Col du Lion, full of humility and tact, contenting himself with the remains of his 'Monsieur's' meal, and showing gratitude at being granted a poor sleeping-place on the threshold of the tent; or when he saw him fall on his knees in adoration and weep with enthusiasm on the rocks of the Col, at the sight of the vast panorama that he then beheld for the first time.

It was vouchsafed to Luc Meynet to reach the summit some years later, and he is said to have exclaimed, on arriving there, that he could hear angels singing and that he could now die happy.[18] His was a pure and beautiful mountaineer's soul.

So Whymper and Meynet ascended to the Col du Lion, and thence to the foot of the Tower; they passed the furthest point Whymper had reached, but overcome by the difficulties, they then returned. This was Whymper's fifth attempt, and his last for that year.

Returning to the Jomein he found there, to his great surprise, his rival, John Tyndall, who had engaged Jean Antoine and César Carrel as porters, and had with him the guides Bennen and Walter. They formed a strong and determined party.

Whymper concealed his annoyance, re-ascended all alone as far as the tent which he had left at the Tower, and, having awaited Professor Tyndall there, he put the tent at his disposal; then he returned to Breuil and waited on events with anguish in his soul.

The next day he saw a flag fluttering on the peak which subsequently took Tyndall's name. The latter had succeeded in climbing higher than anyone else had yet done. A wooden ladder, which he had taken with him, had helped him over the most difficult passage, subsequently named the 'grande corde'; but he too was forced to retreat; at the 'enjambée'[19] — a cleft in the mountain which separates the Shoulder from the final peak — the Matterhorn shut its door in his face.

Bennen had made a mistake: when they reached the first peak he had said that in another hour the people of Zermatt would see the flag planted on the highest summit. By a strange delusion they thought they had reached one of the summits of the Matterhorn.

In his heart of hearts Carrel must have mocked at the mistake and have rejoiced at the failure. He perhaps felt that, had he wished, he could that day have guided Tyndall to the summit; but in his jealousy and pride he would not share the glory of the conquest with alien guides, who would too cheaply boast of it thereafter.

It is sad to think that Bennen and Carrel, fine men both, did not appreciate each other. On one side there was the deeply rooted, and at that time not altogether unreasonable, conviction that a Swiss guide was superior to an Italian one; on the other there was the antagonism felt by the mountaineers of Valtournanche against those strangers who invaded their territory and sought to deprive them of their gains and their glory. There was also the language difficulty between them, for Bennen only spoke German and Carrel only his own particular French; they did not understand one another. Finally there was Carrel's personal temperament, which was impatient of control and could not brook a superior. He meant to climb the Matterhorn in the position of leading guide, whilst on that day he was subordinate to others; and, at the enjambée passage, when asked by Tyndall to give an opinion as to the possibility of proceeding, he answered: 'Ask your guides; we are only porters.'

That answer embodied all Carrel's pride. His old comrades still remember having heard him declare many times when telling of that day: 'Si j'avais été moi chef, je lui aurais fait voir par où on passait pour arriver au sommet.' Bennen, being thus saddled with the sole responsibility as leader, was forced to accept defeat.

Tyndall subsequently affirmed that Carrel had not dared to proceed.[20] He wrote that 'Of the guides and porters, Bennen was the man who entertained a thought of going on, and both Walter and Carrel shrank from the danger of the last ascent'. No one who has known Jean Antoine can believe this statement: he was obstinate, easily offended, but not cowardly.

Whymper had anxiously waited for his rival's return; the account the latter gave of the difficulties of the undertaking was such that the former gave up hope and departed.

The mountain was left in peace for the rest of that year. The Matterhorn had fought and still held out. In this contest of mighty passions it was quickened into life; it became an essential personage in the drama, intimately connected with the thoughts of its antagonists; it was no longer a rock, but an ideal which spurred men on or filled them with fear. It had acquired an influence over men, and it shaped their ends; it conquered them and urged them on to further efforts.

Who can describe the anxieties, the strenuous efforts, the hardships and the emotions of those men who were enthralled and fascinated by the mountain? Who can tell of their sleepless nights, the snowstorms and tempests, the falling stones, the Matterhorn's fearful cannonade, the violent disputes with the guides, the mutual threats, the disappointments, the annoyances? Verily these adventures form one of the most life-like pages in the history of mountaineering.

In the preface to the first volume of the London *Alpine Journal*, which appeared in 1863, the editor, Mr. H. B. George, after remarking that nearly all the highest peaks in the Alps had by then been conquered, writes the following words, which sound an appeal to English climbers: 'While even if all other objects of interest in Switzerland should be exhausted, the Matterhorn remains (who shall say for how long?) unconquered and apparently invincible.' And at the same time as this public call rang out from the English Alpine Club, a conspiracy was going on in Italy. At Turin, in 1863, a few men of character and standing had met in the Valentino Castle, in order to discuss a project for the formation of an Alpine Society; and it was secretly proposed there to attempt at once some feat that should bring honour to the institution at its birth.

English climbers had deprived Italians of the first-fruits of the conquest of Monte Viso, the Piedmontese peak *par excellence;* the Matterhorn remained, and this was the victim that was chosen. They were full of ardour, those *carbonari* of Italian mountaineering. They were young scientists of great genius and noble character — Quintino Sella, Bartolomeo Gastaldi, Felice Giordano, and beside them Benedetto Rignon, Perrone di San Martino, Di Saint-Robert, Rimini, and a few more.

They knew of the attempts that had been secretly made by the guides of Valtournanche; the soil seemed to be well prepared. Neither Gastaldi, owing to his temperament, nor Sella, because of the important occupations which kept him a prisoner in the sub-Alpine capital, could undertake the work of studying and fitting out the expedition; the honour of the arduous task was offered to Giordano, who accepted it.

Meanwhile Whymper had returned to the foot of his beloved mountain. He was not the man to give up the Matterhorn, or to bear Carrel malice; he had need of him. 'With him I had hopes, without him none'; thus he wrote, and he added that Carrel knew he was indispensable to him, and that he did not conceal the fact from him.

When he arrived at Valtournanche, he re-engaged him, made an excursion round the Matterhorn, by Zermatt and the Valpelline, and then started from the Jomein for his sixth attempt.[21] Besides Jean Antoine, he had with him César Carrel, Luc Meynet, and two other Valtournanche porters.

At the foot of the Great Tower he was overtaken by a violent snowstorm, that forced him to halt and spend a terrible night in his little tent, which was buffeted by the wind, while outside the Matterhorn was wondrously illuminated by lightning, and the rumblings of thunder were hurled back in mighty echoes from the rocks of the neighbouring Dent d'Hérens. In the morning the snow ceased to fall, they set forth again immediately, and climbed for two hours up the rocks, which had become most difficult; then the snowstorm began again and Whymper was vanquished once more.

When he returned to the Jomein and told of those twenty-six hours of storm, Favre, the landlord, answered in surprise that the weather had been quite fine down below, and that only a small cloud had been seen on the mountain.

'Ah! that small cloud!' exclaimed Whymper. That was the last time he attempted the Breuil arête.

In the following year (1864), it seemed as if there were a truce between the Matterhorn and mankind. But whilst the mountain rested, man was preparing his weapons.

Giordano, returning from an ascent of Mont Blanc, came to Zermatt, and stood for the first time face to face with the mighty Matterhorn. He filled his travelling note-book with sketches of the beautiful pyramid, and among his numerous notes and barometrical and geological observations the mountaineer's interest stands out most prominently. He writes that 'The Matterhorn is a magnificent sight from this point; it is an irregular but real obelisk, which seems to threaten the beholder'.

Beside a sketch of the mountain taken from the Riffel is a note, which in the sketch corresponds with the height of the Shoulder, to the effect that: 'This is the highest point which has hitherto been reached on the other side'; and further on is this observation: 'From information received, we gather that the western face has been ascended to within about five hundred feet of the summit. In order to complete the ascent it would be necessary to cut steps and do other work in the rock for a height of about a hundred feet; eight or ten days, and three or four stone-cutters at twenty francs a day would be required.' I quote these notes in the simple form in which they are hastily jotted down in pencil, because when I found them in that note-book I was filled with a deep emotion of which I will not deprive the reader.

Giordano came to the Jomein over the Theodul Pass. 'On the

Col,' he says, 'I met Carrel, a Valtournanche guide, who had attempted the Matterhorn and had spoken with Sella.' We see here the sequel to the conspiracy of 1863: the chief of the conspirators had summoned Carrel to him.

Sella had, in fact, charged his friend, Giuseppe Torelli, who was going to Breuil towards the end of July, to seek out Jean Antoine and to send him to Biella. Giuseppe Torelli, a politician and an elegant writer, well known under the pseudonym of 'Ciro d'Arco', inquired for Carrel, found him out, was filled with admiration for him, and after an hour's conversation with him induced him to accede to his request to go and meet Sella in accordance with the latter's wish. He also gave Carrel thirty francs for his journey from Breuil to Biella, which sum, as the jovial writer is careful to point out, was afterwards scrupulously returned to him by the future minister of the Italian kingdom.

Returning to Giordano's note-book, I find in it the following note, which seems to me significant: 'Spent a whole evening at the Jomein with Carrel and the Chanoine Carrel.' Of what can those three great men have talked but of the Matterhorn, the thought of which lay so close to the heart of each of them?

A few days later Giordano was at Biella, in order to attend the meeting of the Italian Society of Natural Sciences, and stopped, as was his custom, at Quintino Sella's hospitable house. There is no doubt that the ascent of the Matterhorn was the subject of conversation between the two great geologists. Giordano's laconic notes do not affirm it, but some who were intimate with Sella have told us how he did not desist from talking of that plan, amid the mass of labour which politics had laid upon his shoulders during those years.

He knew of all Tyndall's and Whymper's attempts, and a patriotic feeling of rivalry urged him to emulate those foreign champions, whom he greatly admired, and by whose example he wished young Italians to benefit.

He had chosen Giordano, a devoted and well-tried friend, who was at once young, adventurous, and confident, and a serious man of science, to make all preparations and to lead the daring expedition; for these were the qualities which Sella considered necessary to the mountaineer, because he had in his mind, besides the difficulties in the projected conquest of the mountain, a high scientific ideal.[22]

1865

We now come to the last act. Tyndall and Bennen have retired from the contest; Whymper and Carrel remain on the stage, and a new personage comes upon the scene — Giordano, whose presence hastens the dénouement of the drama.

Whymper, weary of the defeats he has sustained on the Breuil arête, tries new ways. The stratification of the rocks on the east face seems to him favourable, and the slope not excessive. His plan of attack is very complicated: a huge rock couloir, the base of which lies on the Italian side below the Breuiljoch, on the little Matterhorn glacier, is to take him to a point high up on the Furggen arête; from there, traversing the east face of the mountain, he means to reach the Hörnli ridge, and by it the summit.

A mad plan; we may call it so after Whymper's own and Mummery's subsequent experience of it. Michel Croz, the famous Chamonix guide who had accompanied Whymper in the difficult first ascent of the Barre des Écrins, thought the route practicable, and agreed to try it.

They started from Breuil together with the Bernese guides, Almer and Biener, and the faithful porter, Luc Meynet. They had reached a certain height in the rock couloir when the Matterhorn discharged such an avalanche of stones upon them as nearly to sweep them all away. They descended disheartened. Whymper would have attempted the Hörnli ridge with the same guides. They refused, however. Biener repeatedly pronounced the word 'impossible!' 'Any ascent you please, my dear sir, but the Matterhorn,' was the reply of Almer, who sarcastically added, 'Why do you not attempt a mountain that can be ascended?' Croz had an engagement at Chamonix; the party broke up, and Whymper once more looked out for Carrel.

From time to time he returned to him who was alternately his friend and his adversary, who one day appeared to be the good genius of his undertaking, the next its evil genius. But Carrel alone had understood him when all others thought him mad; Carrel alone had shared his faith; therefore Whymper based his hopes on him.

The Englishman's tenacity throughout all these difficulties was indeed admirable. Though repulsed by the dangers, warned to desist, and abandoned by the most able guides, he persevered and made fresh attempts, each more vigorous than the last; each repulse seemed to harden his iron will the more.

Tyndall, who had listened to his guides, was forced to desist; Whymper knew how to persevere, and he succeeded. Although we are not impartial judges of this contest, we cannot but admire this man and his passionate admiration of the mountain as of a noble ideal. It is a contest which reminds us of old-time jousts, when men would risk their lives for the sake of a flower.

Our friend Giordano appeared upon the scene. He had made serious preparations for the enterprise, and had made calculations and experiments concerning the strength of ropes, and provided himself with barometers and tents. On July 8th he went up to Valtournanche, and there met Carrel, who had just returned with some other men (C. Carrel, C. E. Gorret, and J. J. Maquignaz) from reconnoitring the Matterhorn in his (Giordano's) interests. They had come down because the weather was misty, and they had not been able to see very much.

In the meantime Carrel had spoken with Whymper and had engaged himself to him for an attempt on the Swiss side. 'Carrel was engaged to the Englishman till Tuesday, the 11th, inclusive, if the weather were fine; but the weather being bad he was free, and he stopped with me.' This statement appears dated Monday, the 10th, in Giordano's note-book. I quote the lines because they clearly and loyally explain a circumstance which was made use of to accuse Carrel of breaking his word to Whymper.

On the morning of the 9th Whymper, as he was descending to Valtournanche, was surprised to meet Carrel with a traveller, who was coming up with a great deal of baggage. He questioned Carrel, and was told that the latter would be unable to serve him after the

11th, because he had an engagement with a 'family of distinction'; and when Whymper reproached him for not having told him so before, he replied frankly that the engagement dated from a long time back, and that till then the day had not been fixed. The Englishman was unable to find any fault with the answer.

This is Whymper's own account, and, although he was vexed at being left again without guides, he was not angry with Jean Antoine. He said to him, 'Well, it is no fault of yours', and that same evening they drank together like good friends in the hotel at Valtournanche and talked over their old adventures.

Whymper had as yet no suspicion that the 'distinguished family' was Giordano himself; he became aware of it at the Jomein on the morning of the 11th, when the guides had already started to reconnoitre, and he learnt that everything had been made ready long before for the expedition which was to prepare the way for Quintino Sella. His annoyance was unbounded, and he gave vent to it in bitter words. He considered that he had been shamefully deceived; but, even if his resentment and his grievous disappointment were natural enough, it does not seem to us that he ought to blame Carrel and his companions for concealing Giordano's name and intentions from him, or accuse the Italians of bad faith.

Whymper afterwards forgave Carrel, and when Professor Tyndall, writing in defence of Bennen, attempted to belittle our guide's merits and the importance of the Italian victory by declaring that Carrel benefited by Bennen's experience, and that, without the latter's example, Carrel would perhaps never have set foot upon the Matterhorn, Whymper nobly and vigorously took up the cudgels in his defence.[23] In the heat of the contest men's passions break out with greater violence.

Giordano alone, ignorant as yet of the surprises the Matterhorn had in reserve, was calmly awaiting his victory. Here I will let the letters which he wrote during those days to Sella[24] speak in their frank simplicity. They are pages thrilling with energy and hope, and they reveal fully the intimacy subsisting between the two friends, who completely trusted one another and who throbbed with the same passion.

'TURIN, *July 7th*, 1865.

'DEAR QUINTINO, — I am starting off, heavily armed, for the destination you wot of. I sent off the day before yesterday the first tent, 300 metres of rope, and some iron hoops and rings, besides various kinds of provisions for ourselves, a spirit-lamp for heating water, tea, etc. All these things together weigh about 100 kilos. I have also sent Carrel 200 fcs., in order that he may meet these articles at Châtillon and transport them to Valtournanche and Breuil at once. I shall be up there myself to-morrow evening, to superintend the work.

'I am taking with me a second tent, three barometers, your own among them, and the *Annuaire du Bureau des Longitudes.* As soon as I reach the scene of operations I will write to you again.

'You need only trouble about your own personal requirements, viz., your headgear, a few rugs, etc., and — some good cigars; if possible, also a little good wine and a few shekels, because I have only been able to bring about 3000 fcs. with me.

'Let us, then, set out to attack this Devil's mountain, and let us see that we succeed, if only Whymper has not been beforehand with us.'

'BREUIL HOTEL, AT THE FOOT OF THE THEODUL.
'*July 11th, evening.*

'DEAR QUINTINO, — It is high time for me to send you news from here. I reached Valtournanche on Saturday at midday. There I found Carrel, who had just returned from a reconnoitring expedition on the Matterhorn, which had proved a failure, owing to bad weather.

'Whymper had arrived two or three days before; as usual, he wished to make the ascent, and had engaged Carrel, who, not having yet had my letters, had agreed, but for a few days only. Fortunately the weather turned bad. Whymper was unable to make his fresh attempt, and Carrel left him and came with me, together with five other picked men who are the best guides in the valley.[25] We immediately sent off our advance guard, with Carrel at its head. In order not to excite remark we took the rope and other materials to

Avouil, a hamlet which is very remote and close to the Matterhorn, and this is to be our lower base. Out of six men, four are to work up above, and two will act continuously as porters, a task which is at least as difficult as the other.

'I have taken up my quarters at Breuil for the time being. The weather, the god whom we fear and on whom all will depend, has been hitherto very changeable and rather bad. As lately as yesterday morning it was snowing on the Matterhorn, but yesterday evening it cleared. In the night (10th-11th) the men started with the tents, and I hope that by this time they will have reached a great height; but the weather is turning misty again, and the Matterhorn is still covered; I hope the mists will soon disperse. Weather permitting, I hope in three or four days to know how I stand. Carrel told me not to come up yet, until he should send me word; naturally he wishes personally to make sure of the last bits. As seen from here they do not seem to me to be absolutely inaccessible, but before saying that one must try them; and it is also necessary to ascertain whether we can bivouac at a point much higher than Whymper's highest. As soon as I have any good news I will send a message to St. Vincent, the nearest telegraph office, with a telegram containing a few words; and do you then come at once. Meanwhile, on receipt of the present, please send me a few lines in reply, with some advice, because I am head over ears in difficulty here, what with the weather, the expense, and Whymper.

'I have tried to keep everything secret, but that fellow, whose life seems to depend on the Matterhorn, is here, suspiciously prying into everything. I have taken all the competent men away from him, and yet he is so enamoured of this mountain that he may go up with others and make a scene. He is here, in this hotel, and I try to avoid speaking to him.

'In short, I will do my best to succeed, and I have hopes. Provided Æolus be on our side!

'I will write no more at present, hoping soon to send you a favourable sign. I trust this news from the Alps will refresh you somewhat in the heat of Turin and the oppression of ministerial affairs.'[26]

While Whymper was restlessly prowling about the Jomein, watching Carrel's movements with a telescope, and meditating a counterstroke, Giordano was calmly spending his time in study and in excursions; he had met up there the Abbé Gorret, the young and sturdy curate of Cogne, who had ardently desired to join the exploring party, but had not been included. Together they ascended the Theodul Pass, the Mont Pileur, the Pointe de Plété; they conversed, sketched, made barometrical observations, and continually gazed upon the Matterhorn.

Whymper, deprived of Carrel, had been left like a general without an army; his plans were frustrated, and his only comfort lay in the thought that Carrel and his men would lengthen out the work of preparing the route, in order to consume the large stock of provisions, and he rejoiced because the bad weather would delay them. Having rolled up his tent and packed his luggage, he wished to hasten to Zermatt and attempt to reach the summit from that side, but he could find no porters; even the hunchback of Breuil refused this time.

A young Englishman arrived with a guide. Whymper made himself known to him, and learnt that he was Lord Francis Douglas, who had lately ascended the Gabelhorn; he told him the whole story, and confided his plans to him. Douglas, declaring himself in his turn most anxious to ascend the Matterhorn, agreed to give him his porter, and on the morning of the 12th they started together for Zermatt. Whymper is said to have been weeping with anxiety and vexation as he set out.

This day and the next one were spent in quiet expectation at the Jomein. Giordano descended (on the 12th) to Carrel's châlet at Avouil, and was told there that two of his men had come down thither the evening before to get provisions, and had already returned to the mountain; they had reported that their four comrades had gone to pitch the tent very high up, below the Shoulder. On the 13th enormous icicles were seen through the telescope hanging from the rocks of the Matterhorn; Luc Meynet said he had seen the guides at work below the Shoulder. The evening was beautiful, and the stars shone most brightly; Giordano's hopes ran high. On the following day he wrote as follows:

'BREUIL HOTEL, *July 14th.*

'DEAR QUINTINO, — I am sending a telegram for you by express[27] to St. Vincent, seven hours' walk from here; at the same time, to make assurance doubly sure, I send you this letter.

'At 2 p.m. to-day I saw Carrel and Co. on the top peak of the Matterhorn; many others saw them as well as I; so success seems certain, notwithstanding that the day before yesterday the weather was very bad, so that the mountain was covered with snow. So start at once if you can, or else telegraph to me at St. Vincent. Fancy, I do not even know whether you are at Turin! I have had no news from there for a week; so I am just writing on the chance. If you do not come or telegraph by to-morrow evening I shall go and plant our flag up there, that it may be the first. This is essential. I will, however, do all I can to wait for you, so that you may come yourself. Whymper has gone off to make an attempt on the other side, but I think in vain.'

I have this letter here, and I gaze upon it with respect. I think of the quiet joy the writing of it gave Giordano: his emotion is betrayed by these few words: these few disconnected lines, meandering over pages, speak of this haste to send his friend the good news: we no longer trace the steady hand of the engineer, but a hand trembling with enthusiasm. I seem to see Sella's stern countenance relax into a smile when he received the letter; and then my heart aches when I think that all this was but an illusion!

'BREUIL, *July 15th.*

'DEAR QUINTINO, — Yesterday was a bad day, and Whymper, after all, gained the victory over the unfortunate Carrel. Whymper, as I told you, was desperate, and seeing Carrel climbing the mountain, tried his fortune on the Zermatt slope. Everyone here, and Carrel above all, considered the ascent absolutely impossible on that side; so we were all easy in our minds. On the 11th Carrel was at work on the mountain, and pitched his tent at a certain height. On the night between the 11th and 12th, and the whole of the 12th, the weather was horrible, and snow on the Matterhorn; on the 13th weather fair, and yesterday, the 14th, fine. On the 13th little work was done, and yesterday Carrel might have reached the top, and was perhaps only about 500 or 600 feet below, when suddenly, at about 2 p.m., he saw Whymper and the others already on the summit. Whymper must have promised a considerable sum to various Swiss guides if they could take him up, and having been favoured with an exceptionally fine day, he succeeded. I had, it is true, sent Carrel word of Whymper's proposed attempt, and had enjoined on him to get up at any cost, without loss of time to prepare the way, but my warning did not reach him in time, and moreover Carrel did not believe the ascent from the north to be possible. However, yesterday, as I saw some men on the Matterhorn, and was assured by everyone that they were our party, I sent off the telegram to you, bidding you come up. Poor Carrel, when he saw that he had been forestalled, had not the courage to proceed, and beat a retreat with his weapons and his baggage. He arrived here late this morning, and it was then that I sent off another telegram by express to stop you from coming. As you see, although every man did his duty, it is a lost battle, and I am in great grief.

'I think, however, that we can play a counter-stroke by someone's making the ascent at once on this side, thus proving at any rate that the ascent is feasible this way; Carrel still thinks it possible. I was only vexed with him for bringing down the tents, the ropes, and all the other things that had been carried up with so much labour to a point so near the summit. He puts the blame on the party, who had completely lost heart, and on his fear that I should be unwilling to go to any further expense.

'At any rate, in order not to return ridiculous as well as unsuccessful, I think that we ought at least to plant our flag on the summit. I at once tried to organize a fresh expedition, but hitherto, with the exception of Carrel and another, I have not found any men of courage whom I can trust. Some others might, perhaps, be found if I paid them extravagantly, but I do not think it wise to go to such expense; and then, if their courage is deficient, there would be no certainty of success.

'I am therefore trying to fit out the expedition cheaply and will only give up if this one is unsuccessful. Now I shall not even have the satisfaction of going up myself, because Carrel says that, for the sake of quickness and in order to make the best of the short time we have at our disposal, it will be better that they should not have any traveller with them.

'We must also remember that we are threatened by the weather, which is doubtful.

'Just see how annoying it all is!

'Yesterday the Val Tournanche was already *en fête* thinking that we were victorious; to-day we were disillusioned. Poor Carrel is to be pitied, the more so as part of the delay was due to his idea that Whymper would not be able to ascend from Zermatt. I am trying to act like Terentius Varro after the battle of Cannae.

'PS. — Notwithstanding what has happened, you might still make the first ascent from the Italian side, if you had the time; but till now Carrel has not assured me that the way is feasible right to the top. That is why I have not telegraphed to you again; perhaps I shall come to Turin myself in a couple of days.'

So the men who had been seen on the summit were the Englishmen. Carrel, who with his companions was on the Shoulder not far from Tyndall's flagstaff, heard Croz's shouts of victory,[28] and the crash of the stones which the Chamoniard hurled down from the summit to attract the Italians' attention; raising his eyes he recognized Mr. Whymper's white trousers.

Whymper in that moment wished that he had by his side, sharing his joy, that brave man who, far below, was leading the little party of vanquished Italians; but assuredly he did not realize that his shouts of victory cruelly sounded the knell of the hopes and aims of that man's whole life.

The feelings of Carrel and his companions may be imagined but not easily described. Many suppositions were formed as to the reason why they did not continue the ascent: was Carrel not quite sure of his comrades? Had discord broken out between the members of the little party? It was said that Carrel and Maquignaz wished to proceed, whilst the others thought it useless to do so; that Carrel then cried out, 'All or none', and that they thereupon descended.[29] But how

The Italian Hut (12,560 ft.)

INITIALS ON THE ROCKS

The photograph shows the initials of Luc Meynet and Edward Whymper (Alone!)

The complete lettering is
M. LUC E.W.A.L

1861
C. + J.A
(Jean-Antoine Carrel with Cross)

can it be that Jean Antoine's influence over the others, which was absolute, was not able to drag them to the goal?

Carrel's judgment failed him at this critical point. He did not see what a fine *rôle* was still within his reach: namely, to proceed at all costs, to reach the summit a few hours after his rival, and, having solved the problem of the Italian ascent of the Matterhorn, to bring it as a gift to Giordano. It would have been a victory far more hardly won than the Englishman's! How came it to pass that Carrel did not see this was his duty?

But no man can answer these questions, and perhaps Carrel himself could not answer, if he were alive. Only he who has been in places of great difficulty, a prey to doubts and fears, in face of the unknown, can know how under such circumstances a moral shock can paralyse in an instant all the energy that has been hoarded for years.

Carrol, vanquished, descended and hastened to hide himself in his own hamlet of Avouil; only on the following day did he dare to show himself to Giordano.

'An evil day!' wrote the latter in his diary, dating the entry the 15th. 'Early in the morning Carrel, more dead than alive, came to tell me he had been forestalled. He had reckoned on climbing to the top to-day, and expected to be able to force a passage not by the highest tower, which he considers impossible, but on the Z'Mutt side, where the snow is. I have decided that he and others shall at least try and ascend and plant our flag.'

So we see Giordano, with renewed vigour, intent on hastily recruiting an army after the defeat. He was in a most unfavourable position: he was at any rate uncertain whether the last bit were passable. The men who had been with Carrel steadily refused to try again, as if they were overcome with terror of the mountain. It was in vain that Giordano attempted to rouse them out of their depression, and explained to them that till that day he had expended money and labour for himself, with the object of being the first to reach the top; but that now, such good fortune being denied to him, he was only acting for the honour and in the interests of the guides of Valtournanche.

The guides' replies were most discouraging. Amé Gorret came forward and offered to accompany Carrel; the fire of the former seminarist was not quenched in the priest; his early love of the mountain had been rekindled. Carrel accepted the sturdy volunteer, and thus two of those who, eight years before, had taken the first steps towards climbing the Matterhorn, were together in the last attempt.

The others round them went about saying ironically, 'Oh! if the abbé is in it success is assured!'

J. Augustin Meynet and J. Baptiste Bich, servants of Favre the innkeeper, and two porters were added to the party, and the attacking force was ready to start. Giordano would fain have joined them, but Carrel refused absolutely to take him with them; he said he would not have the strength to guide a traveller, and could neither answer for the result nor for anyone's life. Giordano, for his own credit, desired Carrel to state as much in writing.

At the end of that stormy day he makes the following note in his pocket-book: 'Walked a mile, suffering the pangs of disappointment. A very bad night with fever. Only one barometrical observation.'

On Sunday, the 16th, after hearing Mass at the chapel of Breuil, the little party started. Giordano was left sad and lonely at the Jomein.

'I have once more made the great sacrifice of waiting at the foot of the peak instead of climbing it,' he writes in another letter to Sella, 'and I assure you that this has been most painful to me.'

He saw them through his telescope pitching their tent at the customary bivouac at the foot of the Tower at 2 p.m. Amé Gorret has described this ascent with youthful enthusiasm: 'At last we crossed the Col du Lion and set foot upon the pyramid of the Matterhorn!' On the following day they continued the ascent and reached Tyndall's flagstaff. 'We were about to enter unknown country,' writes Gorret, 'for no man had gone beyond this point.' Here opinions were divided; Gorret suggested ascending by the ridge and scaling the last tower[30] straight up. Carrel was inclined to traverse to the west of the peak, and thence go up on the Z'Mutt side. Naturally the wish of Carrel prevailed, for he was the leader and had not lost the habit of command, notwithstanding his defeat.

They made the passage of the enjambée, and traversed the giddy slope to reach the Z'Mutt ridge. A false step made by one of the party and a fall of icicles from above warned them to return to the direct line of ascent, and the traverse back to the Breuil ridge was one of the greatest difficulty. A falling stone wounded Gorret in the arm.

At last they reached the base of the final tower. 'We stood,' writes Gorret, 'in a place that was almost comfortable. Although it was not more than two yards wide, and the slope was one of 75 per cent, we gave it all kinds of pleasant names: the corridor, the gallery, the railroad, etc. etc.'

They imagined all difficulties were at an end; but a rock couloir, which they had hitherto not observed, lay between them and the final bit of ridge, where progress would be perfectly easy.

It would have been unwise for all four to descend into the couloir, because they did not know where to fix the rope that would be needed on their return. Time pressed: it was necessary to reduce the numbers of the party; Gorret sacrificed himself, and Meynet stopped with him. Very soon afterwards Carrel and Bich were on the top, 'and as for me', writes Gorret, 'in order not to be overcome by sleep, I pointed out to Meynet the beauty of the mountains and of the meadows in the valley'.[31]

Meanwhile Giordano at the Jomein was writing in his diary as follows: 'Splendid weather; at 9.30 saw Carrel and his men on the Shoulder, after that saw nothing more of them. Then much mist about the summit. Lifted a bit about 3.30, and we saw our flag on the western summit of the Matterhorn. The English flag looked like a black shawl lying on the snow, in the centre.' After these words in the note-book comes a sketch of the summit with the two flags, and beside one of them is written the word 'Italy!'

On the following day at noon the victors were back, safe and sound. During the descent they had seen the flags waving over the Jomein as a sign of rejoicing; fatigue, the strain of the struggle, the excitement of danger — all these were past. Their arrival was a triumph. Giordano's pocket-book mentions 'Great hilarity all day at the hotel and at Breuil, bonfires and songs. Amid the rejoicing I alone was sad; I had not personally climbed the Matterhorn'.

At Valtournanche, amid the dancing and wine-drinking, they composed a little song, whose chorus was somewhat as follows:

'Vive le Monsieur Italien Qui a vaincu le Mont Cervin!'	'Hurrah for the hero, Italian born, Who has conquered the mighty Matterhorn!'

Giordano, sad at heart, fled from these festivities. Important business called him back to Turin; the weather had turned bad. Yet he wrote to Sella from Turin, saying: 'I wished to tell you that, if you wish, you may still climb the Matterhorn and gain some honour as the first "Monsieur" to do it from the Italian side.[32] So I have had the tent and some ropes left up there.

'Although we have been forestalled by Whymper, the victory from a practical point of view is ours, because we have now proved that the peak is accessible on our side, while it does not seem as if any other ascent would be attempted in a hurry from Zermatt. Poor Whymper is overcome by his ephemeral victory, while the Val Tournanche is full of joy at the sight of the three-coloured flag calmly waving on the lofty peak. You could still make scientific geological and barometrical observations up there; the peak might still be considered as virgin from this point of view, and we should thus give a solemn proof of the feasibility of the route on the Italian side, and of our calm perseverance in the face of the tragic upshot of the Zermatt ascent.'

> 'What next? If any one of the links of this fatal chain of circumstances had been omitted, what a different story I should have to tell!'—
> E. WHYMPER

Zermatt was in tears. The black flag seen by Giordano on the snow at the top was at that very time a signal of misfortune. An unheard-of disaster had stained the fair record of the Englishman's victory with an indelible blot of sorrow.

How this happened is well known: Whymper had left the Jomein in a very excited state; his repeated failures on the mountain, the remembrance perchance of the day on which the Matterhorn had chastised him even to drawing his blood, the fear lest all his efforts were soon to prove fruitless — all these things agitated him. The thought that Carrel was up aloft, approaching the summit step by step, and his anger at that which he considered a betrayal, committed him heart and soul to the struggle from which he meant to issue the victor at any cost.

He had thought himself the Matterhorn's master; thenceforth the Matterhorn was master of him.

The first link in the fatal chain of circumstances which were to lead him up to the catastrophe was the arrival of Douglas; when he reached Zermatt fate willed that he should find Michel Croz there, on the point of attempting the ascent; with the latter were Messrs. Hudson and Hadow. Whymper, content if only he might have Croz with him, admitted them all to a share in his expedition, as he had already admitted Douglas; and so these four brave men, who were all nearly unknown to one another, were joined together to attempt to conquer one of the hardest peaks in the Alps.

That same evening everything was settled; they were to start immediately, the very next day. Croz and old Peter Taugwalder and his son were to be the guides; and Whymper, during a sleepless night, marvelled at the strange fate which had brought him once more into the company of his faithful Michel Croz, and at the hasty march of events, from Carrel's desertion to the meeting with Hudson and the others, and perchance he asked himself in the night how it would all end.

Two days after they had conquered the Matterhorn, and on the summit, where no man had yet stood, the brave Croz's blue shirt waved, a modest but glorious standard. The victory had not been a difficult one; but, on the descent, when they were barely an hour from the summit and were all on the rope, Hadow slipped and fell on Croz, who was in front of him. Croz, who was unprepared, was unable to withstand the shock; they both fell and pulled down Hudson and Douglas.

On hearing Croz's shout Whymper and Taugwalder clasped the rocks; they stood firm, perhaps they might have held up their companions, but the rope broke. Whymper saw them slide down the slope, trying with convulsive hands to stop themselves, and then falling from rock to rock and finally disappearing over the edge of the precipice.

It was all over in a second! The great victory was turned into an overwhelming disaster.[33] The torn and mangled bodies were soon after picked up at the foot of the mountain, on the Matterhorn glacier, 4000 feet below the spot from which they fell, and buried in a small tomb in the Zermatt cemetery. Douglas alone was never found. His body remained up on the mountain, mysteriously hidden among the mighty rocks.

The news of the catastrophe gave rise to a universal cry of horror. Of all Alpine disasters, not one, not even of those which had a larger number of victims, ever moved men's minds as this one did. The whole of Europe talked of it; the English papers discussed it with bitter words of blame; Italian papers invented a tale of a rock detaching itself from the summit, and sweeping the helpless victims to destruction, or of a hidden crevasse opening wide its terrible jaws to swallow them. An intelligent German published to the world a newspaper article in which Whymper was accused of cutting the rope between Douglas and Taugwalder, at the critical moment, to save his own life. Gustave Doré made a fantastic, terrible drawing to illustrate the catastrophe. The superstitious mountain folk whispered among themselves, foolishly reminding one another of the unlucky dates of the enterprise: the 13th for the start, a Friday for the victory.

Whymper had then to answer grave charges of responsibility and the aforesaid absurd accusation of having betrayed his companions. Under the influence of passion men are wont to allow themselves to make cruel and unjust statements. Whymper cleared himself by the simple narrative of his misfortune. Taugwalder was accused, tried, and acquitted; but all his life he lay under the burden of the shameful, unjust suspicion.

Perhaps some of the old men of Zermatt may have exclaimed that time as the mountain dweller cried to Manfred:

> 'Hold, madman,
> Stain not our pure vales with thy guilty blood.'[34]

It occurs to us, even now, so long after the sad event, to ask, with all respect due from us to the illustrious name of the conqueror of the Matterhorn, how he, who had almost always attacked the mountain alone, refusing all company, ever agreed to give battle at the last with a large party, collected at haphazard, made up of people who were unknown to him, among them being a youth who was quite devoid of mountaineering experience;[35] how he, who knew so well the difficulties of the mountain, ever put himself at the head of a party containing only two guides to four amateurs.*

The terrible mistake he was led to make by his feverish anxiety to reach the summit before his rival cost Whymper many a bitter pang of grief. At the conclusion of his sad narrative he wrote these words, which sound a solemn note of warning to Alpine climbers:

'There have been joys too great to be described in words, and there have been griefs upon which I have not dared to dwell; and with these in mind I say: Climb if you will, but remember that courage and strength are nought without prudence, and that a momentary negligence may destroy the happiness of a lifetime. Do nothing in haste; look well to each step; and from the beginning think what may be the end.'

There is something of ancient tragedy in this story, which shows us weak mortals revolving in grief and in joy about a mute, inexorable Destiny, the Matterhorn, which sets their valour at nought. But, amid the tumultuous passions, amid the shouts of triumph and the lamentations of misfortune, amid the curses and the accusations, the voice of those who know how to suffer and to hope rises calm and full of human dignity. On the tomb of Hadow, the youthful victim, his parents, with admirable resignation, wrote this verse from the Gospel: 'Ita, Pater, quoniam sic fuit placitum ante te.'

The people of Zermatt had taken no interest in Whymper's victory; its terrible sequel made it appear a defeat, a blot which

* [Hudson was one of the best, if not the best, amateur climber of the day; Douglas had proved his capacity just before on the Gabelhorn. If Croz had been behind Hadow, the accident might not have happened, for guides, at any rate in those days, were accustomed, as amateurs were not, to keep an ever-vigilant eye on the *herr* in front of them and check the slightest slip. Hudson was perfectly competent to lead down; he had led up a considerable part of the East Ridge. There is a particularly sound judgment on the matter by Captain J. P. Farrar in *Alpine Journal*, vol. XXXII, pp. 28-31 – R.L.G.I.].

time alone could wash away. That is why Zermatt did not at once see what great material profit would follow the event.

On our side it was different; Carrel's victory was considered a most fortunate occurrence, as a local triumph for the valley. The feat had been performed by one of its inhabitants, and, as is the case in all popular successes, it was bound to make a deep impression on men's hearts and to excite enthusiasm and ambition.

Giordano modestly disappeared behind Carrel; the Alpine Club's work was not seen; the sons of the Matterhorn had conquered alone.

A new era seemed to be dawning for the valley, and I think that thenceforth the Valtorneins looked upon their mountain in the same way as medieval artists and burghers viewed with a new sense of life the Gothic cathedral that their labour and their faith had built.

Our fellow-countrymen had conquered where the best strangers, amateurs and guides, had tried in vain for five years. Some foreigners wished to explain the Italian victory by alleging that the Matterhorn had presented fewer difficulties that summer than in the foregoing years; but Giordano's observations tell us that the weather was bad during those days, that fresh snow had fallen on the mountain, and that huge icicles were hanging from all the rocks.

In Italy they let men talk and they held high festival. Not, by Heaven! that there were many in our land who were interested in that victory. They were few indeed: Giordano, the Chanoine Carrel, Quintino Sella and his friends, and the members, as yet far from numerous, of the Alpine Club.

But these few were ardent; the new-born Club rejoiced as one man at the triumph which heralded a happy future; the pages of the *Bollettini* of those years are full of the note of victory, and active, vigorous steps were taken to profit by it.

A project was formed to facilitate future ascents, by fixing ropes in the most difficult places, and setting up a refuge on the mountain, in which the night might be passed. A subscription was started for 'hollowing out a cave on the Matterhorn', and in a short time a sum of 1400 francs was collected. The hut was to be built on the Cravate at a height of about 4000 metres (13,200 feet *circa*), in a spot where the overhanging rock formed a natural roof, which with very little labour could be made into a rudimentary refuge, by means of a little blasting, and a small dry stone wall. The climbers of that period were easily satisfied.

An Aosta paper observed: 'If a safe and comfortable refuge be built four hours' climb below the summit, the ascent will be accomplished without difficulty. On the second day it will be possible to be on the top by eight or nine in the morning; five or six hours may then be spent there, if the weather be good, in sublime meditation; return to the cave before nightfall. On the following day it will be merely a delightful stroll back to the hotel.' So the former fears were replaced by over-weening confidence, and the Matterhorn, which had been so lately reputed invincible, was brought down by foolish enthusiasts to the status of a delightful stroll.

After the double conquest opinions were divided concerning the relative difficulty of each of the two slopes of the mountain; but the prevalent idea, due to the terror excited by the catastrophe on the Zermatt side, was that the Swiss slope was the more dangerous.[36] The London *Alpine Journal* at that time pointed out that it was natural for Italians to consider their own side less difficult and dangerous than the northern route, and that the question would perhaps be decided in the following summer. It added, however, that it was doubtful whether the Matterhorn would attract so many climbers as before, now that it no longer possessed the prestige of inaccessibility. No one foresaw in the least at that period to what lengths we should be led by 'cervinomania', to use an expression of the Abbé Gorret's.

In the year following that of the conquest, no foreigner appeared to attack the Matterhorn. Giordano alone returned, being impatient to finish the work he had begun, and to fulfil the vows he had made to the cause of Italian mountaineering. He wished to complete a geological study of the mountain, and personally to inspect the spot where it was intended to erect the refuge which the Alpine Club had sanctioned; and, indeed, Carrel, Bich, and Meynet went up as far as the Cravate, towards the end of June, for the same purpose.

The fact that Italy was then at war allowed Giordano very little leisure; but one day in July he left Sella, Perazzi, and Brin in the capital, and flew off to his beloved Alps.

At this point I am helped by another of his diaries, which is full of valuable and accurate notes, and when I read those pages, so rich in memoranda and in calculations, in practical observations and in curious anecdotes, with occasional mention of names illustrious then or subsequently to become so, I seem to see again that strange man, who was at once a dreamer and a scientist, absent-minded as a poet and accurate as a mathematician, an acute observer and a naïve enthusiast, with a mind both gentle and strong, and capable of the most delicate sensibility and of the boldest deeds. I seem to see his tall, slender figure, such as I knew it in my early youth; I feel his grey eyes fixed on me, through the searching lenses of his glasses; I fancy that his gentle, kindly smile comforts me when I halt in my work and tells me that I do well to recount to the youth of to-day the noble enthusiasms of the youth of that past time.

No desire for popular applause urged them on, but the conviction that they were doing a fine and useful work. By climbing mountains they honoured their country; for us, their successors, they opened out a path, which following, we found great joy of the noblest kind.

The feats which to them appeared arduous and glorious may seem easy and modest to us; but now that almost all the actors in that story have disappeared it is well to recall their memories and to cultivate once more those early ideals. It is our duty to preserve the poetic worship of the past history of mountaineering. Craufurd Grove, the second amateur who climbed the Matterhorn, wrote the following:

'. . . But let not the younger generation of mountaineers, exulting in easy victories over the once dreaded Cervin, look with scorn on the slow progress of the pioneers of civilization.'

Giordano, on his arrival at Aosta, went to see the Chanoine Carrel and his observatory, which had now been enriched with instruments provided by the Government, and from which an account of the observations was sent off every day to the Capital. On his way up the Val Tournanche he visited with much interest the gorge of Busserailles, lately discovered and made accessible by J. Joseph Maquignaz. At the Jomein he summoned his guides for the ascent of the peak: they were Carrel, Bich, and Meynet, with the porters Pierre, J. Joseph, and Aimé Maquignaz, and Solomon and Gabriel Meynet. After three days' doubtful weather, spent by him in continual observations, he started on July 22nd, before daylight. He went up by the glacier almost to the Col du Lion, and there he set up a barometric station. When he reached the spot where Whymper had been wont to pitch his tent, he left his porters there with the tent, and made his way up beyond the Vallon des Glaçons, to a point on the ridge 300 feet above the tent; and there on a tiny plateau, on the buttress which separates Breuil from Z'Mutt, at a height of about 12,500 feet, he spent the first night. On the second day he climbed up to the Cravate and took up his position there.

At that point Giordano took notes like a peaceful burgess visiting a farm with a view to building a villa on it. 'In order to reach the balma, or natural grotto, where it is proposed to construct the hut, we cross a very steep snow slope (35° to 40°) which forms the Cravate. The passage is somewhat blocked with snow, and when it is thawing icicles fall there, and perhaps even a few stones; but, as the lofty rock is perpendicular, they fall a good way off. The guides say there is very little danger.' A sketch of the place follows, with a section of the grotto, showing the height and depth (4 yds. by 2½ yds.), and a little plan of the proposed hut.

'The place is very suitable for the hut. Altogether there is clear space for walking about twenty yards long; it faces due south, and looks towards M. Viso; it gets the sun from about 9.30 a.m. till 5 p.m. — a very quiet spot and sheltered from the north wind. Water boils at 86° C.; barometer (mean), 462 mm.'[37]

In this lovely spot, facing south and very sheltered, at a height of 13,596 feet, Giordano lay encamped for five days and five nights, alone with his three guides, with a single rug for all of them, and with a temperature that sank as low as — 9° C. inside the tent.

The weather was stormy, the mountain in bad condition; three inches of snow lay on the tent on the first morning; the choughs that had their nests close by hovered round restlessly and cawed — a bad sign. High up the struggling winds whirled the powdery snow in eddies round the top of the Matterhorn; down below was a mass of mighty clouds, which seemed to rise from all the surrounding valleys.

Brandy and wine were running short, and Giordano, strong in the faith of a man of science, observed his barometer, and found on the third day that it had risen slightly. The following day dawned cold and clear. Giordano was left alone with one guide; the two others had gone down to the lower tent to fetch rugs and provisions. He contemplates and describes the wondrous panorama which the clearness of the atmosphere at last presented to his admiring gaze. In the evening the two guides returned. The fourth night was passed amid fearful cold, the morning was clear and mild. Giordano and the guides attempted the ascent; they reached Tyndall's flagstaff, and proceeded along the whole arête of the Shoulder.

'We reached in this manner,' says the note-book, 'the foot of the final peak, and I saw the route we must follow to the summit; but there was much fresh snow, and Carrel thought it dangerous to proceed. The guides decided to go no further. I was forced to obey, much to my regret. I was very well and in excellent condition that day, and I should certainly have reached the top if they would have come. I could already see our last year's flag on the summit.'

They turned back; they spent the fifth night under the rock of the Cravate, whither the porters had brought Giordano papers, letters, and telegrams that summoned him in all haste back to the town. Never did the post come up so high, nor a telegram arrive so inopportunely!

It was already the seventh day Giordano had spent on the mountain; the bad weather induced him at last to renounce the undertaking. The descent was tedious and difficult, but was at length accomplished. It had been thought that he had died of cold and hunger, and he was received with joy. 'At the Jomein rejoicings, which I did not appreciate,' says his note-book. 'I had not reached the summit.'

His perseverance deserved success. Never, to my knowledge, had any man showed such strength and self-denial in an Alpine enterprise.

Giordano's equanimity and iron will were needed to withstand such discomfort and such prolonged failure; all the influence of a strong and good man was needed to keep his guides with him for so long a time.

Nevertheless, the attempt was rich in scientific results. Giordano, during those days, by his copious observations, started his geological and orographical study of the mountain, which he subsequently completed with the observations he made during his ascent in 1868. These researches, whose results were first communicated by him to the Natural Science Congress at Vicenza in 1868, redounded to the honour of Italian science and of the Alpine Club. They are preserved in the Minutes of the Italian Society of Natural Sciences in Milan (vol. XI), which contain his excellent geological sketch of the Matterhorn, that Whymper subsequently used to embellish his own book.

In the following year (1867) the Valtournanche guides began to derive benefit from Carrel's victory; indeed, the names of these Italian guides are associated with almost all the events which followed the conquest.

J. A. Carrel, J. Bich, and S. Meynet guided Mr. Florence Craufurd Grove to the summit; it was Carrel who had persuaded him to prefer the route on the Italian side. Grove was delighted with Carrel, and gave him a most flattering testimonial;[38] and in his report to the English Alpine Club he praised the almost excessive energy of the Valtournanche guides, whom he found wonderful mountaineers, and the zeal with which they had made easy almost all the awkward bits of the ascent.

'... The comparative ease', he writes, 'with which it is now traversed is due to the Valtournanche guides, who, with a zeal for which the traveller does not feel unmixed gratitude, have put a ring in the nostrils of the leviathan, or, to change the metaphor, have bound their captive with cords.'

When Grove made the ascent there were no ropes above the Shoulder; from there up to the top he followed Carrel's original route.

A month later, J. Joseph Maquignaz and J. Pierre, accompanied by Victor Maquignaz, César and J. B. Carrel, started for the Matterhorn, without amateurs. The enterprising spirit of the men of Valtournanche did not belie itself.[39] J. Joseph meant to find a new route, shorter and more direct, to the summit, surmounting the final tower by the ridge facing Breuil, without traversing over to the Z'Mutt face on the Swiss side. This line of ascent had already been traced out by the Abbé Gorret in 1865, and Giordano, looking at the summit from the Shoulder, had made the following note in his diary in 1866: 'I do not see why one should not go straight up by the ridge. Perhaps it may be very difficult, because the first part seems to be perpendicular, nay, even overhanging.'

Jean Joseph may have thought the Italian victory incomplete until the top had been reached without any point of foreign territory being touched — in fact, he was subsequently wont to call his 'the first completely Italian ascent of the Matterhorn'. He was certainly moved by a feeling of rivalry with Carrel, who had till then held a monopoly of the mountain. J. Joseph and J. Pierre reached the summit, not without great difficulty, by the way the former had marked out, which was subsequently always followed. Their companions were left about 300 feet below the top. With them was a brave girl, called Felicita, a daughter of J. B. Carrel. The spot was thenceforth called by the happy name of Col Félicité.

J. Joseph Maquignaz, the humble porter who had been enrolled by Carrel in 1865 to work as a stone-cutter, had suddenly become a great guide. That was the heroic age, when men lay down to sleep as private soldiers and awoke as field-marshals. Directly afterwards he found himself at the head of Mr. Leighton Jordan's party, guiding it to the summit by the recently discovered route, which shortened the ascent by about an hour.

In the following year (1868) John Tyndall had the pleasure and the honour (style of the period) of climbing the Matterhorn; he also had J. Joseph as a guide, and he wrote of him, happily enumerating all the qualities which go to make a first rate guide, that he was an excellent companion, calm in perilous places, and strong wherever strength was needed. In his opinion a better guide for the Matterhorn could not be desired.

Tyndall was the first to accomplish what in Alpine slang is called the traverse of the Matterhorn — that is, the ascent from one (the Breuil) side and the descent by the other. *Á propos* of this expedition, I may remark that Tyndall's party unroped on the descent towards Zermatt, before reaching the site of the Alte Hütte, and I do not think that Maquignaz, when I knew him in his old age, would ever have allowed me to do such a thing, but would have rightly considered it most imprudent. But times had changed; Mummery, the valiant explorer of the Matterhorn, has pointed out with the incisiveness that was peculiar to him, the apparent falling off in the quality of climbers:

'The Matterhorn,' he writes, 'gives a curious illustration of the way in which the modern amateur is deteriorating. The early climbers roped at the "Shoulder". In 1873 they roped at the old hut. In 1886 they roped some distance below the old hut. Now they rope at the new hut, and the exploits of a gentleman in 1893 render it not impossible that future climbers will rope at the Hörnli.'

Again, in 1868, Messrs. Thioly and Hoiler crossed the Matterhorn from Zermatt to Breuil, and M. Sauzet climbed it from the Italian side, and they all had Italian guides. Giordano came and reached at last the summit he had so long yearned to attain; and his guides, as was fitting, were the champions of the Matterhorn — Carrel and Maquignaz.

In the same year the Swiss guides awoke, and the first ascent on the north side, after the catastrophe, was accomplished by the Rev. J. M. Elliott, with the guides J. M. Lochmatter and Peter Knubel, and other ascents followed immediately afterwards. Thus we have four ascents from the Italian side and seven from the Swiss. The rush to the Matterhorn had begun.

I end this list by the mention of one of the ascents in 1869, that of Mr. R. B. Heathcote, with the guides Joseph, Pierre and Emmanuel Maquignaz and B. Bich; it was on this occasion that the guides fixed at the last bit the rope ladder which was called the Echelle Jordan, from the name of its donor. Let everyone who is responsive to the influence of memories, when he passes Busserailles, make his way into the wooden shed which forms the entrance to the gorge; he will see there Jordan's old ladder nailed to the small, dark wall. The first of the Matterhorn ladders, which stood in its lofty perch for nearly twenty years, exposed to the sun at 14,500 feet above the sea, a target for stones and buffeted by storms, is now at peace, a white and worn-out relic, kept with veneration by the grandchildren of old Maquignaz.

The spell of the Matterhorn was gone, but yet its great name for difficulties and peril still endured. The writings of that time bear witness to the fear inspired by the avalanches which fell on both sides of the mountain. Whymper wrote that rocks and stones rained day and night from the Matterhorn. The *Alpine Journal* (vol. ii) called attention to this danger on the Italian side, and Giordano mentioned it on the Swiss.

He wrote as follows to Tyndall after his ascent: 'As for me, I may say that I found the peak fairly difficult this time. . . . On the descent to Zermatt I was exposed to real danger by the avalanches of stones; one of my guides had his sack cut in two by a rock, and I was somewhat bruised myself.' It is strange to notice that for many years after this danger was no longer mentioned, either because the disintegration of the mountain was really checked by special climatic conditions or because experience of the route had taught how the line of falling stones might be avoided; and no accident due to this cause happened to any of the innumerable parties which used the two ordinary routes, excepting, I think, the case of the guide who was hit in 1900 by a stone on the Swiss side.

I have gone over the Zermatt arête four times, up or down, at different hours of the day, and the Breuil arête three times, without ever noticing any falling stones, except those started by the parties themselves; but it is not to be supposed that climbers' footsteps have sent down all the movable material on the mighty peak. The mountain is alive with a life that is gradually wearing itself out, and from time to time it gives dangerous proofs of this living state.

The Matterhorn became a field for rival feats of daring. In 1871 came the first ascent by a lady, Miss Walker; in 1876 the first by amateurs without guides, Messrs. Cust, Colgrove, and Cawood. There followed a man who dared to climb the mountain alone, and then those who made the ascent on their honeymoon. Lord Wentworth spent the night on the summit, and remained there fully seven-

THE CORDE TYNDALL
leading up to the ridge above the Grande Tour

NEAR THE TOP OF THE CORDE TYNDALL

teen hours; Mr. Jackson (1872) ascended from Breuil and descended to Zermatt in a continuous day of eighteen hours. This was the first time such a speed was attained.

Vittorio Sella (1882) reached the summit, after two attempts, in the winter season. Such an undertaking as this required, owing to the danger of iced rocks, the shortness of the days, and the intense cold, unshakable courage, great skill, and exceptional powers of endurance; and it was rightly considered one of the boldest feats of mountaineering known. Once more did the annals of the Matterhorn ring gloriously with an Italian name — the name of Sella.[40]

Finally, in 1902, the guides of Valtournanche carried to the summit a cross, as a symbol of their faith and their love, and on September 24th a priest said Mass there. This was the Abbé A. Carrel, great-nephew of the famous guide.

Whilst the zeal of the boldest thus incites them to seek on the Matterhorn new and thrilling emotions, the common herd, attracted by the mountain's fame, climbs in crowds from Zermatt, hauled by guides up the route which is now made easy by numerous stout ropes, to the very summit of the Matterhorn, which seems to have been tamed. On a fine day in 1892 the top was seen to be crowded with at least twenty-three people and their numerous guides.

The sad result of this overwhelming number of ascents, by men among whom there were weaklings, novices, and reckless climbers, was the accidents. The Zermatt side is responsible, up to 1900, for six victims, besides those of the first disaster; the Breuil slope, a more difficult one, for only two.

But fortune was evidently inclining towards the Zermatt side; statistics in 1880 show approximately, out of 159 ascents, 132 on the Swiss side, and only 27 on the Italian. Fortunately for us, the Italian side of the Matterhorn kept up its name for difficulty. Emile Javelle, a famous Swiss climber, one of those who knew the Matterhorn best, and who idealized it most in writing,[41] has left us this statement: 'When the Zermatt Matterhorn has become as commonplace a mountain as the Faulhorn or the Brévent those tourists who wish to see it in all its pristine ruggedness, and to realize the difference between a common ascent and a serious expedition, need only descend it on the Italian side' (1875). The Matterhorn was now reckoned among the wonders of the world; its photograph was on show in shops in capital cities, side by side with those of great monarchs; the cosmopolitan travellers who, under the spell of an insatiable curiosity, rushed about the globe in all directions, told one another how they had 'done' the Matterhorn, as if they were talking of having gone up to the propylaea of the Acropolis or the dome of St. Peter's in Rome. Telegraphs and railways were brought to its foot, and threatened to storm its very summit.[42]

The first intense enthusiasm of the few was spread out among the many, and lost in depth what it gained in breadth. Thousands came and gave expression in ten different languages to their wonder at the mighty monument, but it may well be that the primitive, simple desire of the Valtournanche mountaineer and the deep feeling and the suffering of the ambitious Englishman were a purer offering to the giant on his throne than the chorus of the many-headed throng. It seemed as if, by degrees, the best climbers abandoned the mountain to the mediocrities. Real mountaineers now go far afield, seeking new and profitable glories, aiming at the summits of the Caucasus, the Andes, the New Zealand Alps, the Himalayas, and continue thus to contribute to the discovery of the unknown corners of the earth. Yet from time to time a few idealists still prowled mysteriously about the mountain, scanning with eager eye its huge faces bristling with difficulties, and as yet unexplored. They were ardent worshippers of the Matterhorn, alone amid the crowd which had invaded the temple and they strove to lift the last folds of the veil which still covered the idol, hoping thereby to set free the rays of some new bright light. They thought in their hearts that the mountain was still, in spite of all, the mysterious mountain of the past, and they yearned to feel for themselves the emotions of the first discoverers. The dark and awful chimneys on the Zmutt arête gave Mummery and Penhall scope for fresh victories; and the knife-edged ridge of Furggen, which rises in a few aerial leaps to the summit, afforded the brave Mummery, and after him another, an obscure enthusiast, indescribable emotions. But these were the last idealists of the Matterhorn.

The common herd will continue to climb the mountain, unmindful of the sacrifices that have been made for it, perchance unconscious of the nobility of the feat that they are performing, ignorant of the value of the prize, because it is so lightly won.*

The Matterhorn, for a short hour the goal of ardent desire, echoing with cries of grief and of victory, will pass away, as other ideals have passed. The chains with which man has bound it will fall; the ancient monument will be broken to fragments by slow disintegration and perchance, many centuries hence, men passing by its foot will turn their eyes upon the ruins of the mountain, standing alone in the desert waste of snow, as upon a mysterious menhir, inscrutable symbol of an ancient and forgotten religion.

* [Generalizations about other persons' attitude to mountains are likely to be incorrect. I have, it is true, myself heard a member of a party discussing future plans say: 'I suppose we must do the Matterhorn.' But, quite apart from the adventurous ascents recorded at the end of this volume, there are, and always will be, many climbers whose emotions will be deeply stirred by this unique mountain—R.L.G.I.].

CHAPTER IV

MY FIRST SIGHT OF THE MATTERHORN

'To climb steep hills
Requires slow pace at first. Anger is like
A full-hot horse who being allow'd his way,
Self-mettle tires him.'
SHAKESPEARE, *Henry VIII.*

MY first sight of the Matterhorn . . . ! When I think of it I seem to grow young again; a host of memories crowd into my mind and strive to free themselves as if each one desired to be the first to find an issue, and I must needs throw the door wide open and let them force their way out *en masse*, singing and laughing, like boys issuing from school, and rejoicing to be once more in the sunshine and to breathe the fresh, pure air.

The first time I saw the Matterhorn I was thirteen years old, a pleasant age when everything is new. I was making my first Alpine ascent. From the modest summit of a mountain 6600 feet high, in the clear dawn of a summer's day, a great man pointed out to me and my companions a mighty dark blue pyramid in the far distance. No cloud darkened the horizon of the view and of our own hearts. 'That is the Matterhorn,' he told us, and a tremor of admiration filled our young minds at the sight of that wondrous pointed shape rearing itself aloft amid the vast sea of other mountains.

That great man was Quintino Sella, and he was worthy to point out that mountain and to tell us of its charm. We stood round him, a group of eight or ten boys, awestruck, and intent upon the novel spectacle, whose beauty was not as yet entirely comprehensible to us, in the same way as we did not yet completely realize the nobility of soul of him who was interpreting it all to us, and who earnestly desired that we should admire and learn.[1] Later I learnt to appreciate the greatness and nobility of the mountain and the man, and they have held a place together in my mind, equal in greatness, because the concrete form of the one seems to me to illustrate the moral virtues of the other; and to both I am deeply grateful for the good they have done me.

But the impression, though unconscious, must needs have been a deep one for the image of that first view to have remained so clearly stamped upon my mind after so many years. Perhaps it was at that instant, in view of the distant Matterhorn, during those first happy hours of life when the simple aims are born which shape our future, that that ideal was first formed which was destined to fill so large and so worthy a part of my life, and 'which, as you see, has not yet left me' ('e chè, come vedi, ancor non m'abbandona').

But on that day I thought I had climbed up to heaven in that I had reached a height of 6600 feet. I was tired, and I had no wish whatever to climb any higher. And when I looked at that summit, which I knew must be so difficult, and so much higher than the point where we stood, when I heard Sella talking of over 14,000 feet, and tell of Whymper and how he had lost four of his companions on that peak, and of Giordano, and how he spent five days and five nights up there, methought these were superhuman deeds and tales of fabulous heroes.

No, indeed, I did not then aspire to ascend the Matterhorn; I little thought that I should attain its summit many times. We eight or ten boys who stood round Sella on that morning in 1874 have all more or less been lovers of the mountains. He wished that all Italians might be climbers, and in the meantime he made climbers of his sons and nephews. With this object he opened before our eager eyes the first pages of the great book of the mountains, which is so full of wondrous tales, and which we have read and re-read again and again with such keen zest; he expounded it to us, and commented on it with great wisdom and with a lofty and untroubled faith, and we, before believing in the mountains, believed in him.

Those early expeditions have left a strange impression on my mind. We would leave our uncle's hospitable house, a numerous party, very early in the morning. For me, a son of the town, to rise before the sun was a great sacrifice, but in that dear house all woke early, even to Quintino's venerable mother, who would always bid her son and her grandsons farewell before they started. My cousins, although they were about the same age as myself, were more accustomed to Alpine excursions. I, a novice, and often the youngest of the party — which is nowadays no longer the case — felt very insignificant beside them. They had real alpenstocks, that excited my envy and my admiration, and round which were burned in small letters the names of passes and peaks they had ascended, strange names like Betta-Furka, Weissthor, Lysjoch, Breithorn. They had already been on glaciers, and this fact filled me with respect for them. Ah! how I too yearned to see how a glacier was made, and to climb one of those peaks whose name ends in 'horn'! Now that those days are so long past, it seems to me that one's first love of the mountains is largely the fruit of a sense of rivalry.

At that time I knew the mountains by having seen them from the far distant hills of my native place, or by having studied a few coloured prints, of the most primitive description, which came to us in those days from Switzerland. I had formed in my own mind visions of imaginary mountains, like those which children make at Christmas for the crèche. And the first time I was taken among the real mountains I was, I confess, somewhat disillusioned. I did not recognize the beautiful blue peaks I had gazed at from afar; here there was only an oppressive, melancholy, and massive heap of ruins. I sought in vain for the Alpine landscape such as it had been portrayed in the romantic vignettes, in which every scene is symmetrically drawn, with a background of peaceful and harmless glaciers, encased amid thick pine forests; a path edged with flowers winding along the bottom of the valley; at intervals a neat and picturesque chalet; the tiny cascade which falls down the well-proportioned mountainside, and in the centre of the picture the silver torrent flowing under the little wooden bridge.

I did not then find this Arcadia in the Alps. The mountainsides, bare and stony, seemed hideous to me. Instead of the poetical wooden chalets I was confronted with wretched stone hovels, filthy dark lairs, which, when approached, exhaled an acrid smell of smoke and dung; instead of the flower-decked path, a track bristling with rocks and stones, a way of dreadful steepness, which wearied my small lungs; and in my heart of hearts I thought the mountains as described in books or painted in pictures were more beautiful than those of reality.

During these first attempts I suffered at times from the strange disease that is known as mountain-sickness, and, had it not been for the presence of my cousins, to whom I would not for all the world confess my condition, I should have allowed myself to fall to the ground. The feeling of self-respect is a mighty factor in the formation of the climber. And when our leader asked if I was tired, I lied bravely, and my little legs, weak as yet, performed prodigious feats of energy, so that I might not fall behind the others on the ascent.

I remember still certain springs at which we halted. Sella allowed us to drink but sparingly, for he said cold water, drunk on the ascent, was harmful, and he was quite right; but I felt a burning in my throat and a shortness of breath which I thought water would have cured.

The first steps in the mountains are wearisome, as our uncle, who knew his Dante by heart, often told us—

'Questa montagna è tale,
Che sempre il cominciar di sotto è grave
E quant'uom più va sù, e men fa male.'

This peak is toilsome in its lower part, but as one rises, so the way grows easier.

At that time I should have liked much better than Dante's lines another draught of the cool water which gurgled so temptingly close at hand, but Sella was not to be disobeyed. But when we reached the ridges, high up near the summit, and saw the valleys far below at our feet, and the glaciers and distant ranges and the boundless horizon were revealed to us, then I understood that he was right.

I saw the mountains as none had ever painted them, as no book had ever described them to me; full of new wonders that no fairy-tale had ever shown me even in dreams. I knew sensations that nothing had ever afforded me till then—the instinctive pleasure of rising above the plain, the delight of great exertion, and of complete repose that followed. The bread I ate so hungrily up there had a sweet savour hitherto unknown to me, and I tasted the fresh, ineffable joy of reaching the highest point—the summit; the spot where the mountain ceases to rise and man's soul to yearn. It is an almost perfect form of spiritual satisfaction, such as is perhaps attained by the philosopher who has at last discovered a truth that contents and rests his mind.

On my return home, and after I had slept fifteen hours at a stretch, I would awake with an infinite number of new ideas and aspirations, and with a mad desire to return to the heights, to climb higher still, and to attempt more difficult ascents. The mountains must possess some secret fascination to lead us on to seek greater and greater difficulties and fatigue, and to make us love them more in proportion to the sacrifices we have made for them. But these are secrets that the mind of youth does not analyse; it rushes headlong towards that which attracts it, without asking why.

One fine day, many years afterwards, I came to see the Matterhorn quite close. Imagine my eagerness in approaching that mysterious, cruel mountain, after all I had heard about it; imagine my earnest desire to know the men of the Matterhorn, those famous guides of whom Englishmen and Italians had written with such respect and such affection!

Alexander Sella, one of the companions of my earliest expeditions, had done me the honour to take me with him, promising me an ascent with J. Joseph Maquignaz. I did not care what the ascent might be; it was enough for me to know that I was to climb beside a great mountaineer, behind a famous guide; I had risen greatly in my own esteem. Till that season I had modestly used an alpenstock, but on that occasion I thought my dignity required that I should exchange it for an axe, such as real climbers had.

The young men of the present day carry an axe from the very beginning of their Alpine career, and they do right, for in this way they learn quite early to handle the weapon of the Alps; but for a climber in 1883, the day on which he was promoted from the alpenstock to the axe was as solemn as that on which the youth of Rome assumed the *toga virilis*.

They had given me a heavy, solid, somewhat ill-balanced instrument, too long in the spike, and studded with nails which wounded the hand that grasped it. I did not know how to handle it; it was much in my way, but it was my first axe, and I looked upon it with pride and clasped it tenderly.

The lapse of years will change what was then a childish delight in a new toy into a kind of friendship. We shall find in the axe something more than a material support; it will be bound up with our Alpine memories, and habit will unite its humble existence with our own. When we find some weak point in it, some split in the wood that was once so smooth and fine, some crack in the iron which has lost its temper, it will be as painful to us as the sight of the first wrinkle on our brow, or the first white hair on our head. When its defects make it useless, we shall part from it unwillingly. We will give it a successor — a fine, new, bright axe, better made, more slender. But the old one, which has served us in our youth, will continue to be dearest of all to us.

I religiously preserve my own first axe, which shared so many keen delights with me. One day, when I was descending the ice-slope on the Barre des Ecrins, and was on the edge of the great *bergschrund*, in a most difficult place, it gave under my weight, but, although cracked, it supported me. Since then it has lain in honoured repose in a corner of my room, beside another axe, broken also and less fortunate than mine, for the climber who owned it fell with it and lost his life.

But to return to 1883. Besides the axe, I had provided myself, for the solemn occasion, with a pair of boots as much like Sella's as was possible, a mighty pair and bristling with nails, like those which Teja had at that time made famous in his caricatures of Father Quintino. I thought I had donned the famous seven-league boots.

I was going up the path in the Val Tournanche — the carriage road was not yet built — full of modesty, but full of pride as I walked by my companion's side, regulating my steps by his. I listened eagerly to the tales of his Alpine adventures, which he told me as we went along. One among them has remained in my memory.

I must premise that Alexander had a thick black beard, a keen cast of countenance, a fine pair of shoulders, and was wont to dress very carelessly in the mountains, eschewing those typical garments which at first sight denote the climber. One day, as he was walking up this valley all alone, with his axe under his arm and his pipe in his mouth, he came up with a German gentleman who mistook him for a guide, and asked him to carry his knapsack. The black-bearded man took the sack, a very heavy one, lifted it on to his shoulders, and, followed by the German, carried it as far as the hotel, which was a long way off. When they reached the hotel, the landlord, who knew Alexander very well, came out to meet him with much *empressement*, and hastened to relieve him of the sack, and altogether to make much of him, whilst the German gentleman waited in astonishment, and learnt to his great surprise that his porter was the son of the Finance Minister of the kingdom of Italy. How Alexander laughed as he related this anecdote! And, above all, he rejoiced at having been mistaken for a guide.

Meanwhile we drew near to the turning of the Grands-Moulins, and my companion said, 'Prepare yourself; in two minutes' time you will see the Matterhorn'. My heart beat fast. No pilgrim, full of faith, before whose eyes the dome of St. Peter's suddenly appeared in all its grandeur, after his long journey, ever felt his heart palpitate more violently than did I when I saw the Matterhorn rising, huge amid the mist, and framed by the two green sides of the valley. I was utterly fascinated; it was loftier and grander than I had fancied. At the same time I felt deep discouragement, together with a great longing to reach the summit myself, at some far distant date, when I should be worthy. And even to-day, whenever I see it again, I am seized once more with this feeling of uneasiness and of desire, a feeling which is perhaps only known to those whose minds are bewitched by this noble passion of mountain climbing.

I think that few Alpine peaks can create so sublime, so stern an impression as this one does, when it is seen from this point, at certain hours, at sunrise or at sunset, when the walls of the valley which frame it are sunk in shadow, and the whole towering pyramid is wrapped about with light and seems to shine in glory. At such times we have before our eyes no reality, but an apparition. No other mountain is revealed in so personal a manner to our gaze; we are tempted to expect to find it has a countenance, like a man or a monster, to believe that head contains a conscious thought, to read upon its stony brow the expression of its pride and its strength; and if the clouds, chasing one another round it, assist the optical illusion ever so slightly, our fancy seems to see it move, bending its head in sorrow, or raising it with a Titan's pride, and we think with terror what its power would be if it moved indeed.

Every time the Matterhorn appears upon the landscape it is wise for the writer to cease his description, and to refer the reader to — the Matterhorn. If the reader has already seen it, even once, he will not have forgotten it; while, for him who has not seen it, no words can describe the magnificence of the rock which rises perpendicularly towards the sky for 9000 feet from the bottom of the valley, an ever-changing apparition which fascinates and threatens by turns, and appears at one time to be the product of a tremendous cataclysm, at another a mighty work of peaceful nature, given to man to ennoble his mind.

As we made our way up the valley the ghostly Matterhorn disappeared from view, and was not seen again till some hours afterwards, when we had reached its foot. After a short halt at the village of Valtournanche, we walked up to Crépin, a picturesque little hamlet, where Maquignaz's house stands. Alexander inquired for his guide, and was told that he had gone up to await us at the Jomein. We pushed on the quicker; we were anxious to meet him, and to hear what plans he had made for us.

Half way between Valtournanche and the Jomein, where the valley narrows and seems to come to an end, there stands a plain little white church, built on the rock at the edge of the cliff of Busserailles. The path winds steeply up the rocks and passes in front of the church before entering the dark gorge, vertically above the ravine. It is the only way up the valley — the way which leads to the Matterhorn.

Two mountaineers were coming down, and, as they passed the church, they devoutly uncovered their heads. It is the chapel of Our Lady of La Garde; when I came up to it I read an inscription on the door: '*Iter para tutum*'. I thought then, as ever after, that pious line was wonderfully appropriate to the place. It is the hasty prayer of all those who go to brave the dangers of the mountains; it seems as if the good priest of Valtournanche, who built the chapel in 1679, had the future climbers of the Matterhorn in his mind as he wrote that simple poetic prayer.

In the presence of the majesty of the high mountains, man, who has never yet grown accustomed to the terrors of primitive nature, is assailed by unwonted fears; he becomes vaguely conscious of a trace of that instinct which he has inherited in a modified form from his remotest ancestors, who used to struggle unarmed with the invincible forces of Nature. He shudders like a child left alone in a great forest full of strange sounds, and is overwhelmed by some secret sense of the infinite powers of the unknown which surround our life, like the '*timor panicus*' of the ancients. In this place, where mountains rise threateningly on all sides, and the great voice of Nature is heard close at hand in the rumbling of the stone avalanches that fall 3000 feet from the Becca di Créton down in the valley — in the roar of the falls of Marmore, which, hidden in a chasm, seem to make the ground tremble under our feet — in this place our instinctive feeling of weakness is renewed; we feel insignificant and once more like little children. Ah blessed mountains! Here the scoffer is silent, and the sceptic does not laugh if he sees a guide drop his obol into the alms-box and uncover his head as he passes before the little statue of the Madonna.

I was beginning to be aware of the neighbourhood of the vision hidden behind the rocks that was about to be revealed to me once more. At last we reached the basin of Breuil. The Matterhorn was before us; we could scan the whole of it with one glance from head to foot. We were in its dominions.

Le Breuil is a large space, 500 yards broad and 2000 long, and it abuts on the base of the Matterhorn. Down its centre winds the Marmore, a small torrent whose waters come down grey from the glaciers, amid meadows and heaps of stones; on the left, as one goes up the valley, stretches a curtain of steep battlemented mountains which runs from the Château des Dames to the Dent d'Hérens, a wall of rock whose mean height is about 12,500 feet.[2] Fragments of glaciers break off and fall from its steep, smooth sides. Only a marvellous balance keeps the glaciers in place, for at any moment they seem as if they must rush down into the valley. The wall falls rapidly to the Col du Lion, and thence rises in one last leap to the culminating point, the Matterhorn, which lifts its cone, 'lonely as a noble thought', to heaven amid the savage architecture of its rocks and glaciers. Then the mountain rests, as if tired of rising, and the background on the right of the scene consists of a peaceful mass of white, undulating summits; Nature seems to have exhausted all her ferocity on the other side of the valley. I remember that from that point the Matterhorn seemed to me squat and unimposing. It was no longer the same vision which had appeared to me but a few hours before at the Grands-Moulins. The monster appeared to have squatted as the gentle dromedary kneels to put his swelling hump within reach of the traveller in the desert.

I confessed my feeling to my companion. Alexander was almost displeased, and answered with some severity that in order to judge the mountain it was necessary to have been on it. 'Look at the Great Tower', he said to me; 'you would think you could reach it with your hand, but six hours are required to reach the foot of it. Those small needles which stand out against the sky are gigantic rock teeth. The nearer summit, which seems to be joined on to the Matterhorn, and to be almost as high, is separated from it by a long ridge, from which to the summit there is still a climb of 1000 feet.' Then he pointed out the Jomein Hotel, a tiny white spot, a mere point on the highest pastures, at the foot of the Matterhorn. I began to be convinced, because comparison with the insignificant work of man is the only means of realizing the vastness of nature.

In three-quarters of an hour we reached the hotel, near which was seated on a low wall, with his legs crossed, and smoking a pipe, a tall, thin man, red-haired, hooked-nosed, with a small, eagle eye and a somewhat contemptuous cast of countenance. 'This is Joseph Maquignaz,' said Alexander in a tone of great respect; 'say How do you do? to him.' Maquignaz seemed to me like a strict guardian of the Matterhorn, and when I perceived Alexander's respectful affection for the brave companion of his ascent of the Dent du Géant, I became more deferential still to the great guide, and presented myself to him with increasing awe.

'I have brought you a pupil,' said Alexander; and knowing

Maquignaz's natural distrust of novices, he at once gave him a list of my expeditions. They were not much — the Grand Combin, the Bessanese, the Ciamarella, the Pelvoux; but my legs were good, and I was full of zeal. Alexander knew it, and made himself responsible for me. 'We will see about that to-morrow,' was Maquignaz's laconic reply, as he surveyed me from head to foot; and on the morrow we all made a long and difficult expedition together. We climbed the Punta dei Cors, which stands right opposite the Matterhorn. For fourteen hours I had the latter before my eyes, and I understood he was really great. It appears that I acquitted myself well; I saw that Maquignaz was pleased with me; he took good care not to tell me so, but in the following years he accompanied me in the mountains often and willingly.

The confidence with which guides at that time inspired me was boundless. I was convinced that when I was with them no mishap could befall me. And this trust, though weakened by the fatal experience of others, is still with me, and continual comparison of my own ability with theirs, which was infinitely superior in the contest with the mountains, has always prevented me from being self-reliant.

Jean Joseph seemed to me invincible; if anyone had at that time predicted his death on Mont Blanc I should have laughed heartily. Maquignaz would have contemptuously shrugged his shoulders, while Alexander would have taken the insult to himself, and threatened the rash prophet with his stick.

I think that Alexander was jealous of his guide. He would have no other guide but J. Joseph, and perhaps he wished the latter to have no other amateur but himself; a naïve jealousy that is rarely met with in our day, and that shows plainly what the relations between a climber and his guide were at that time.

Alexander's was an excellent school; modest himself, he taught modesty, which is a fine thing in mountaineering, as in everything else. By precept and example he discountenanced all stage effects and all useless paraphernalia. 'Knickerbockers be hanged!' he was wont to say at that time, 'take the most ragged suit in your wardrobe and start for the mountains in it.' His was a school of prudence and moderation; in his opinion ten years' practice was required to fit a man to attempt the Matterhorn. He firmly believed that the climber's first steps in the Alps should be taken under the aegis of a good guide; in the same way, he said, as the weakly child of a rich family would be given to a sturdy peasant woman to suckle. He continually urged me to watch how guides placed their feet, if I wished to learn to walk properly; he insisted on my going slowly uphill; on the way down the valleys he rebuked me if I walked carelessly and did not admire all the beautiful objects that we passed on the road.

As I recall these memories, I see the dear form of my former comrade take shape before me, as in a distant mirage of my youth. At that time I loved the mountains and trusted them blindly; I enjoyed them with all the abandonment of a first love. Perhaps I looked about me but little and thought less. I was satisfied with the delight of moving my legs, climbing, reaching the summit, and, after devouring the provisions, rushing down the slope to find a good dinner and a bed below. And yet I can still see and hear what was then revealed to me — the important incidents in an ascent, the guides' movements, and even the words they said to me at certain given moments. I can see and hear them almost more clearly and sharply than things seen and heard last year; and the smell of the smoke of Alpine chalets always reawakens in me a great longing for those evenings of long ago, which I spent in haylofts, planning and laughing with my friends, whilst the bells of the herd rang their chime in the stable below. I had a respect for the mountains, but I had not yet learnt to fear them. Until misfortune has fallen close to us, we do not believe in misfortune; but the fatal stroke that falls near to us wounds us deeply.

One day — eighteen years have gone by since then, and I still grieve at the thought — I was induced by some friends, bolder than myself, to attempt the Matterhorn without guides. The undertaking seemed to me a glorious and difficult one, but I had no fear of it. When I think it over now I feel I was ill-prepared, and that I made a great mistake in giving way to temptation, but I confess that at the time I agreed with enthusiasm. We were ready; only a few days separated us from the date of our departure, when a terrible warning

On the Crête du Coq

THE FINAL PEAK
from Pic Tyndall

came to me from the mountains: a youth who was very dear to me, one full of strength and intelligence, had met with his death by falling from a rock as he was ascending to the Col du Géant alone with a young friend. I did not climb the Matterhorn that year, and as to doing so without guides, I have never thought of it again.

From that day forward I have looked upon the mountains with different feelings. They have appeared to me stronger and more cruel; I have seen that the way I tread is more difficult, and my love has become deeper and more serious. I had learned in sorrow how mountains should be loved.

In 1893 I came up to climb the Matterhorn. These were the happiest days in my Alpine career. Why, I do not know. There are days on which we chance to awake in a happy humour, when we feel healthier and stronger and more sure of ourselves, when the most difficult things appear easy, and when we almost long to meet with obstacles for the pleasure of overcoming them. These are exceptional days, but they certainly recur more frequently in the mountains than in cities.

The Matterhorn, too, was in an excellent humour and looked very handsome and clean; the summer sun had divested it of its cold mantle of snow, and had melted the formidable necklaces of icicles which at times encircle its neck. The ancient rock, bare and gilded, burnt by the suns of centuries, and eaten away by the elements, seemed to be alive, and to be enjoying one of those rare moments of peace and joy that the short summer season vouchsafes to it. The Matterhorn, like Dante's monster, 'had the just man's face' during those days. Since my first sight of it, I had year by year passed my examinations, each one more difficult than the last, in mountaineering. I felt specially competent in the matter of rock climbing, and I was ready to undergo with honour this last test.

We who stand between the old and the new generation of climbers, approach the Matterhorn respectfully and realize its prestige to an extent unknown to the younger members of our fraternity. The legend, still recent, of its inaccessibility, is yet present in our minds, as is the story of the noble efforts men made to ascend it — men some of whom we have known and heard speak;

there still rings in our ears the joyous echo of the first victory, 'which stirred our hearts as children'.

It was a Sunday. The guides, as is their custom, wished to hear Mass before starting. I also went down to the little church, which stands not far from the hotel at Breuil. It is an unpretending structure of stone, built with rough mortar and flanked by a slender tower. The priest who was to celebrate Mass had arrived; he had had a two hours' walk and an ascent of 1500 feet to reach the place. I looked through the bars at the interior of the chapel: its walls were all denuded of their plaster, and spotted with the damp; an old altar occupied almost the whole space; there were no ornaments except two wooden candlesticks and a white cloth. It was a poor and simple place, such as many an early Christian temple must have been. Four or five women from the neighbouring hamlets were kneeling on the boards, their faces hidden by their white handkerchiefs; outside, near the threshold, under the overhanging roof, stood a group of guides and shepherds; a short way off a few cows were grazing, the little stream was gently murmuring, and from the glacier of Montabel, as the rising sun struck it, the avalanches began to thunder. My guides knelt down and bared their heads. The young wife of one of them had arrived from Crépin to greet him, and she prayed by his side.

I alternately looked upon this group and upon the Matterhorn which rose above the heads of the worshippers: a deep harmony reigned between them and the mountain. The priest as he prayed was to them a divine messenger who scattered the hostile forces of the mountain with unintelligible words, as St. Theodul had in days gone by cast out the demon and the serpents from these places. And when the priest's strong voice pronounced the '*Ite missa est*' it seemed to me that he was saying to the guides: 'Go, climb the Matterhorn, now that you have done your duty.'

I deeply regret that I did not take any notes or write any account of that ascent. The pleasure of climbing the Matterhorn was enough for me; it did not seem to me that there was any need for relating the ascent. We are silent concerning certain things that are infinitely dear to us; it is only later, when we begin to live in memories, that we regret the gap that those too happy hours has left in our minds. In order to realize exactly what are the first sensations that the Matterhorn creates in the youthful mind, I should wish to climb it with a youth who had never yet ascended it, and to read in his eyes and hear from his mouth his impressions at every step on the ascent. But perhaps the youth would prefer to climb alone and to enjoy in silence the intimacy of his first meeting with the beautiful mountains, as I myself did on that occasion.

The first violent emotion I underwent was at the Col du Lion.[3] This is a place of tragic splendour and vastly horrible. That narrow tongue of snow that stretches from the rocks of the Tête du Lion to those of the Matterhorn, like a bridge hanging over an abyss, gives us our first impression of the mountain's vastness. Being now close to it we see it as an enormous heap of broken rocks, of walls furrowed with cracks, of crumbling towers, of torn lace-work, like a tower of Babel destroyed by lightning and by time. It is only now that we realize the inclination of its walls; the lines that fall headlong from the top down those mighty precipices give the eye an impression of a whole that is continually moving, that is unceasingly falling into ruin, stone by stone and fragment by fragment.

The thought of the struggles of the first climbers for victory over this first part increases the natural fascination of the place. The stretch which lies before us is the most famous in the Alps; in this stone staircase, three thousand feet high and more, every step has its history. Here, on the Col, Whymper's first tent was pitched; below there is the ice-slope on which he slipped and fell in a solitary attempt; a little higher up on the right-hand side was the base of the celebrated Chimney: now no recognizable trace of it is left, for it has been destroyed by continuous disintegration. Thus does the aspect of the mountain change in its details from time to time, its destruction goes slowly on; but the Matterhorn is so huge that thousands of years will be required to change its general appearance and to spoil the beauty of its form.[4]*

The first few steps on the ridge above the Col du Lion are easy,

* [This is reassuring after the somewhat gloomy prophecy that concludes the preceding chapter.—R.L.G.I.].

and one immediately inclines to think that all the accounts have exaggerated the difficulties of the mountain, and that what seemed stiff to a climber in 1865 is all plain sailing to the *fin de siècle* climber. The sight of a rope attached to the rocks comes opportunely to remind us that difficulties do exist, and that the first climbers, who ascended when there were as yet no ropes, were not devoid of skill and courage. At first these ropes, which curve in a white line among the rocks, inspire the inexperienced climber with a sense of distrust: they appear slender, frayed, and insecure, and he can hardly bring himself to trust to them, suspecting as he does that they may break or become detached. It is only when he sees the guides using them confidently, that he also gains assurance. But it is not as easy as it might appear to profit by these ropes: the weight of the body pulls them out of place, and they give unexpected jerks which threaten one's already precarious balance and paralyse one's movements and one's efforts: long practice is required to know the caprices of the ropes and to learn how to watch them and to make use of them.

There is only one case on record of one of the Matterhorn ropes breaking during an ascent, and that occurred on the occasion of Quintino Sella's climbing the mountain; but at heart we still have a certain instinctive dislike for this way of climbing, a feeling that it is not natural, and every time we come to the end of a pitch that is roped, it is with delight and with a feeling of greater security that we once more entrust ourselves to the rock alone.[5]

On the ascent between the Col and the hut there is an angle of rock about thirty feet high, and formed by two perfectly smooth walls. Down this a rope hangs vertically. Here is the first trial for novices on the Matterhorn. It has happened that inexperienced travellers have stopped short at this obstacle, not daring to proceed, even though the guides have urged them to ascend, and have pointed out to them the hut close above. After surmounting this place by sheer strength of arm, one reaches a small, flat space; this is the site of Whymper's second camp, a stage in his long and weary contest. I saw there a gang of about ten men; they were the workmen who were building the new hut that was to take its name from Luigi Amedeo di Savoia.

In that year the Prince had begun his Alpine expeditions, and the report of them already rang gloriously and joyfully in the ears of Italian mountaineers. It was such a strange thing to find at that height and in so rude a place these artisans, quietly busied with their work, to see huge beams and tools scattered about on the rocks, and it made a most extraordinary impression on me. The Matterhorn seemed to me to have become a familiar and a tame mountain, in touch with civilization, and the small wooden skeleton whose outline had begun to take shape was like the first house that industrious colonists build on the border of the desert. Those men were in pleasant harmony with the tamed Matterhorn. But when one looked at their faces, lean, dark, and wrinkled as the surrounding rocks, and at their ragged clothes, when one heard them tell how slow and toilsome a work it was to carry up the materials, and how much inferior their capacity for labour was at this height compared with the lower levels, one understood how painful and grievous a task it was to erect that little hut on the great mountain.

Some of these men had seen the fatal fall of young Seiler and his guide Biener, which had occurred a few days before not far from the hut. They told us that the spot whence those poor victims had fallen was one which they themselves had passed time after time, with their loads on their shoulders, handling and lifting the beams for the hut, and they could not understand how the accident had happened. It had occurred with lightning rapidity: not a cry; the pair had disappeared, roped together; a crash of falling stones had been heard far below.

They told me all this quite calmly, with the fatalism of rough, uncultured men, who are ever impassive in the face of destiny. I stopped a while among them. I should have wished to offer them a drink; I said so to Ansermin, the guide who was carrying our wine-flask. Ansermin, who is a philosopher, replied that I might give them all my money, if I so pleased, for money would be of no use to me on the Matterhorn, but that I must keep the wine. He was right: he was unconsciously pointing the ancient moral of the fable of the man who was dying of thirst in the desert and would willingly have exchanged his sack of precious stones for a draught of water.

The men had finished their day's work; they roped, and started downwards towards their bivouac, which was almost two hours lower down. We continued our ascent as far as the Great Tower hut. Thence I looked downwards: the men had reached the Col, and were traversing in shadow under the Tête du Lion; I saw their line moving among the dark rocks; I shouted a greeting to them, and they answered several times; Ansermin let them have one of his best jodels. Great gaiety, it seemed to me, prevailed all over the mountain: they were going down to their polenta; I was making for the summit of the Matterhorn.

The arrival at a high mountain refuge affords one of the pleasantest experiences in all mountaineering; the sight of its thin walls and its fragile roof among the hard rocks fills us with a deep feeling of security and peace; the terrors of the ascent are stilled, and anxiety concerning the following day ceases for the time being: our hearts are invaded by tenderness, as when we set foot safely upon our own threshold after a long journey, and they overflow with gratitude towards the builders of the refuge. When the mountain is deserted, the little hut remains to testify to man's possession of the mountain. It is wrapped in mist, and covered with ice throughout the long winter, it creaks and shakes under the onslaught of the winds like a little ship among the perilous waves, and then when the bad season has passed, it once more smiles gaily and hospitably in that region of terror, an emblem of our weakness and our perseverance.

From the hut there is a marvellous view. Immediately below is a mighty precipice — the Tiefenmatten gulf; beyond that a few sharply defined, imposing shapes rise heavenwards — the Weisshorn, the Gabelhorn, the Dent Blanche, in a line, regular and symmetrical as the three Egyptian pyramids; then the jagged, ice-clad Valpelline and Hérens groups, and the black, rocky summits of Valtournanche. Next, a deep green basin — the valley. In the distance is the softly undulating chain of our Italian Alps from Mont Blanc to the Maritimes. Far away to the south-east we see the blue outline of Monte Viso, and at its foot a long, low, misty line, which is the plain of Piedmont.

Evening comes. The sunset is one of indescribable magnificence:

rocks and glaciers are suffused with a universal flush of pink, beneath a clear sky of green, streaked with slender bars of orange. The sun has gone down behind the further peaks, whose outlines stand out blue and clear against the sky; a few of the highest points glow for a short time longer, like brands amid the ashy grey of the snows; a little cloud, floating alone in the sky, is flushed with a last gleam of light, like a flame that burns and flickers out. Now all light fades, and night falls, first transparent and then black.

I had promised my friend Vaccarone, who was at the Jomein, to burn some magnesium wire at a given hour: the small space before the hut glowed with the dazzling light for a few seconds, and then returned to darkness blacker than before. But down below in the valley a distant point of light appeared. It was my friend's reply to my greeting; I re-entered the lonely hut full of the pleasant thought that someone was thinking of me down on earth. . . .

The alarum sounded in the hut; the guides had been up for more than an hour, busied about the stove, and talking softly among themselves. Between sleeping and waking one was dimly aware of what they were doing. I asked what time it was, but before they answered I was asleep once more. The light of the lantern was thrown strangely round on the walls of the hut, and the men's shadows, enormously magnified, were outlined there likewise. A voice informed me that the coffee was ready; more than half asleep I descended from my couch, my guide put on my boots and laced up my gaiters, I submitting like a weak, unresisting child. Seated on the bench near the stove I gazed uncomprehendingly at the preparations for departure, as at something that did not concern me, and unwillingly swallowed the black decoction which the guide handed me in an iron cup. My legs ached and felt as if they would be too weak to carry me. My keen desire was quenched; I should have been almost glad if the weather had been threatening and prevented us from starting. I instinctively asked what the weather was like. Fine! answered the guide. I at once woke up and grew impatient to start, chafing at the time the guides were taking to set the hut in order. We roped because the bad bits begin immediately outside the hut; we went outside.

Ah! that first mouthful of pure, fresh air, how it penetrates to the very base of the lungs! We revive, we feel that our legs are equal to their task, that our hearts are stout and gay. It is a real transformation. At last I was about to ascend the Matterhorn!

'E vidi cose chè ridire Nè sa nè può qual di lassù discende; Perchè, appressando sè al suo disire, Nostro intelletto si profonda tanto, Che retro la memoria non può ire.' *Paradiso*, I.	'And have seen things which whoso descendeth from up there hath nor knowledge nor power to re-tell; because, as it draweth nigh to its desire, our intellect sinketh so deep, that memory cannot go back along the track.'

Between the moment when I entered the dark Vallon des Glaçons and first began to face the mysteries of the Matterhorn in the uncertain light of dawn, and the moment when I emerged on the glorious summit, there lies the gap which I mentioned above. My memory is a blank concerning those hours; a veil has descended upon it, through which I dimly see fearful chimneys, where an icy cold reigns as in a deep crypt, lofty walls down which hangs a single rope; narrow, jagged ridges rising skywards. I see a white peak glistening close at hand, as it is kissed by the first rays of the rising sun, and a long ridge, the only level stretch among the vertical lines, leading up to the base of the topmost buttress; then a deep cleft that seems to divide one peak from the other, and again vertical walls and crags and ridges, and finally near the summit a lofty, slender, aerial ladder swinging over an enormous precipice.

As I worked my way upwards amid the rocky labyrinth, every detail seemed to be largely magnified. The celebrated places went by rapidly as in a dream: the Mauvais Pas, the Linceul, a patch of snow lost among the infinite mass of rock, the Grande Corde, the Crête du Coq, which resembles the battlemented curtain of a great fortress, and the Cravate, a white ribbon that encircles the neck of the mountain. The givers of these names were poets, though uncultured ones. I remember certain insignificant details: a few barely visible initials, with a date and a cross, which the first explorers had rudely scratched upon a rock, just as lovers cut their names and a transfixed heart on the rough bark of an oak. On the snow of the Pic Tyndall was planted a small black stick, the Englishman's ancient mark. From that point I had my first near view of the top of the Matterhorn; it reminded me of the wondrous cherub of the Babylonian temples, that had the body of a bull and the bearded and mitred head of a man, at once monstrous and serene. On the Shoulder, where we halted for breakfast, I smoked a pipe astride the ridge, with one foot over the Valtournanche precipice, and the other over that of Tienfenmatten; then there came the Enjambée, that great swallower of ice-axes, which slip from the climber's arm as he takes the long step. I remember that the Matterhorn exhaled a good smell of rock under the hot sun; the light of heaven streamed vertically down upon us, barely touching the lofty walls: our voices sounded muffled, as in a subterranean place. Ansermin now and then broke the wonderful stillness of the air with a jodel in the Swiss guide's style. Ah! how the plain golden rings he wore in his ears glistened against his skin, that was brown as any corsair's! Our little party, compact and well chosen, brought its gay humour with it up the Matterhorn. It was a happy journey; I did not seem to walk, but to fly that day. At such times our minds are assuredly in a rare state of happiness; we carry with us no weight of mundane cares, we are untouched by any saddening thought; we make our way wrapped in glamour to the supreme good, the summit; when we reach it, we are not yet in heaven, but we are no longer of the earth.

When the guides told me we were on the top of the Matterhorn, I said: 'Already!' and I ought to have exclaimed: 'At last!' But if they had asked me at that instant whether the Matterhorn were easy or difficult, I could not have answered. The Matterhorn was as I had imagined it to be, and God knows I had imagined it to be beautiful! We shook hands, and sat down side by side on the snow on the summit, at nine in the morning. Still wrapped in the stupor produced by the rapid ascent, I saw the guides get out the provisions; the bread was still warm from the heat of the sack, the meat wrapped up in paper was beaten soft by the blows it had received; the wine, which had acquired a rough taste of iron from the vessel that contained it, was thick and bubbly. We had but frugal fare, but up there it seemed a banquet; the meal did not appear commonplace; it was a solemn function, a reward. I lifted my little cup towards my guides, to thank them for the victory; but Ansermin, who is a believer, notwithstanding his barbarous appearance, said, as he lit his pipe: 'Do not thank us, thank Him who gives little birds their tails.' He meant Almighty God.

The sudden thought that Vaccarone at the Jomein was probably just then searching for me with a telescope among the rocks of the Matterhorn, made me start to my feet, and raise my arms above my head, waving a handkerchief and shouting, as if my invisible friend, 8000 feet below me, could hear my voice. Perhaps a wave of sympathy did reach him from me at that instant, spreading through the thin air, just as the mysterious influence had come to me shortly before and made me jump up and send him my greeting. My guides lay in peace and smiled: they too were happy, though they had been up so many times before. The infinite horizon was free from cloud; I thought I was on the uttermost point of the earth on the shore of an endless sea. One object alone was higher than we: the sun which shone above us, hurling down cascades of light on all sides. It was the light that fell from heaven, and rose again from below as if strongly reflected by crystal prisms; our eyelids closed to shut out the glare; the whole atmosphere shivered with heat; we were on ice and our faces burned.

Round about us lay one of the most sublime panoramas in the world. Almost the whole range of the Alps was grouped around us, from Monte Viso to the Monte Disgrazia, and stood out as clearly as the figures in a raised model, painted in conventional colours, the snows in white, the rocks in purple, the valleys in dark green. One could mark the divisions of the chief Alpine groups: close at hand the chain of Monte Rosa, beyond the Oberland, and then Mont Blanc, which looked like a small, snowy hump and is yet the highest of all; to the north a deep furrow indicates the Valais, on the opposite side another furrow, almost parallel to the other, marks the Aosta Valley.

We stood on the boundary between two great tribes of mountains: on one side were the Alphubel, the Finsteraarhorn, and the Jungfrau; on the other the Diablerets, the Combin, the Jorasses, then the Gran Paradiso, the Grivola and Monte Viso; and the names the guide pronounced reminded us that our eyes were sweeping from Teutonic away to Latin lands and were freely leaping over the irksome barriers that lie between the nations. I instinctively sought among the numerous peaks the familiar outlines of the few I had ascended, and when found, I recognized them with joy; but when I thought of the time needed to ascend them all, I began to pant like a man who has an enormous amount of work to finish in a very short time. This is the real incubus of the mountaineer.

Experience has taught me that the view forms only a small fraction of the delights of climbing. On subsequent occasions, when I have again been on the top of the Matterhorn, in thick mist, in threatening weather, in fear of not being able to descend safely, my emotions have been just as strong as on that bright, still day. This explains how the blind climber who ascended the Matterhorn was filled with intense delight when his guides told him he had reached the summit. Like us, he must have smiled, as he had smiled but rarely in his life. Would that I had seen his poor, sightless eyes light up with an internal vision of a wondrous panorama. Like us, he experienced that sweet, wholesome fatigue, which is one of the keenest delights that the mountains can afford us, and he felt the unwontedly hot sun kiss his forehead, and a delicious breath of wind caress his cheek; he breathed the pure, fine air at 14,000 feet above the sea, the air which is so light, which tastes so sweet, which cools the burning chest like pure water, and is invigorating as a generous wine. Like us, he revelled in the eternal silence of those lofty regions; no one was about him, except his simple, friendly guides, who had helped him to ascend; and he groped for their rough hands and pressed them in token of his joy.

We all resemble that blind man. It is no blasphemy to say that one does not climb the Matterhorn for the view; Emille Javelle, an ardent worshipper of the mountain, has said so. It is not, as the vulgar think, the desire simply to admire a material spectacle, that attracts us to the summit; it is not a passing momentary impression that we bring down with us, but a memory that lasts a lifetime. I wish that all the youths in Italy, who are mentally and physically fit, would ascend the Matterhorn once at least, so that their unknown powers of mind might be revealed to them, and that a noble pride in their physical feat might purify them and make them more capable of high resolves, and more sincere lovers of their beautiful country.

I spent on the summit one hour of joy and infinite peace, feeling as proud as a conqueror of the world, indifferent as an ascetic to all human affairs. The hour passed as all the good things of life must pass; the guides said it was time to start. I put in my pocket a stone I had picked up on the summit, and we started.

The Matterhorn has no real top; it may have had one in past ages, but it must be in ruins below, and undoubtedly it fell on the Italian side, leaving on the brow of the mountain that sharp outline which is typical of its shape. The huts which appear below, tiny dots in the green basin of Breuil, are perhaps built with pieces of the ancient top of the Matterhorn. Anyone looking up from the Theodul glacier, whence the summit looks like the peak of a friar's hood, would never think that the mountain ends in a long ridge on which half a company of an Alpine regiment could sit almost in comfort in a row. The eastern extremity of the ridge forms the Swiss summit, the western the Italian. We crossed from one to the other, from the Cervin to the Matterhorn. The Matterhorn was deserted also; a party from Zermatt had already commenced the descent, and I could see their track in the snow on the upper part of the slope. The crows had been left in possession of the summit for the rest of the day, for it is very rarely that anyone reaches the top after the early hours of the morning.

The crows of the Matterhorn are strange, large birds with jet-black, shiny feathers, with long bills and with beautiful blood-red claws. They are a strange tribe, who live up in the heights in the summer, concealed in unexplored recesses on the inaccessible precipices of the Z'Mutt and Furggen faces. They are well disposed towards the few men who climb the mountain; they know they are harmless folk, and much too busy with other matters to wish to go after them. When the weather is fine, they watch from above parties of climbers as they make the toilsome ascent; they fly down to meet them and circle about them, as dolphins in the sea swim about in the wake of a ship, expectant of its refuse. If the weather be threatening, they utter their sad, unpleasing cry, as if to tell men of the coming tempest. They restlessly come and go and beat up against the wind with their strong wings, sometimes hovering almost motionless in the air; then they dash headlong into the mist with folded wings, dropping down like stones, to flee the storm.

The gilded St. Mark's at Venice has its emerald-winged pigeons, which build their nests among its pink marble capitals, and coo gently in the sunshine, and peck at the grain in a child's tiny hands. The Matterhorn has its black crows which nest in the cracks of its iron-hard rocks; they settle for an instant on the snow, quarrelling over their scanty food, and hurling their hoarse cry up to the clouds, in unceasing strife with the wind and the hawk. The pigeons of St. Mark are fair and lovable, but the savage crows of the Matterhorn teach us more of the realities of life.

Once more the guides warned me that the way was long, and that it was time to start. I there and then silently and fervently vowed to return once more. The descent on the Swiss side appeared to me as long as the ascent on the Italian had seemed short. I descended and descended, and the horizon continued to be boundless, and the bottom of the valley, though it looked close enough, never seemed to come any nearer. On the Zermatt side the Matterhorn is a regular pyramid, grand yet simple in outline;[6] it is this formation which renders the climb there more monotonous than that on the Valtournanche side, where the lines are broken, and where the aspect of the mountain changes every moment. May the Matterhorn forgive me! The descent seemed to me never-ending and most wearisome. Perhaps I myself was weary: as long as one ascends, one's mind aspires, one's body makes vigorous efforts; but once one has attained the goal and tasted a moment's ideal joy, the mind is sated and desires no more, and the body, now weary, goes listlessly on its downward way. To this lack of energy, to this relaxation of tension in the muscles and the mind on the descent, may be attributed some of the most serious accidents that have occurred in the Alps.

If there is a place where the greatest care is necessary both for amateurs and guides, it is just here, where peril is hidden under an appearance of safety. The stage between the summit and the Alte Hütte — the old Swiss hut — has witnessed the occurrence of catastrophes whose horror has only been equalled on the tragic theatre of Mont Blanc. The fame of the Matterhorn is not due merely to its beauty. Ruskin and the others who admired it before Whymper's conquest, saw the mountain in the guise of a pagan god, majestic and impassive; but when trodden by man, the god-like mountain roused itself in anger, and retaliated by causing suffering to men and taking their lives; then the Matterhorn awoke in us that essentially human feeling of terror and of wonder which makes it the object of our fear and our desire.

I neither asked my guides, nor did they offer to show me as we passed them, the places made famous by accidents, and I was grateful to them for their reticence on a day when I wished to taste nought but joy; but memories of the sad stories I had read kept recurring to my mind against my will, during the long descent; I was unable to resist the curiosity that led me to observe carefully these places where it was so easy to be killed, and I kept furtively on the lookout for them. There, on the ridge to the left, where the slope drops down sheer towards Z'Mutt, that must be where the fatal rope broke and Croz and his employers fell. Down below there, that small, flat space overhanging the precipice, was the deathbed of poor Borckhardt, who, after a terrible night, abandoned by his friend and his guides, died of weakness in the morning, while the snowflakes gradually covered up his body.

Great catastrophes seem to stamp the places where they have occurred with the impression of their own solemnity and gloom. As I passed those spots, I was filled with a sense of awe which I have felt nowhere else, almost as if I were on sacred ground, and as if the ghosts of the victims were hovering round me among the bare rocks; and the guide who followed me did not cease to urge me to be careful, and I felt him holding me by the rope even in places where it seemed to me unnecessary. The guides do not forget that the Matterhorn is dangerous even in its easy places, and I think they are less anxious on the other more difficult side than on this — they know that the amateur is more careful in the harder places.

Every year an increasing number of parties climbs to the top on fine days, but the Matterhorn will never be a vulgar mountain. Though tamed by mankind, who in their fear have fettered its flanks with ropes and chains, it still rebels from time to time, and the scale of its vengeance terrifies us; and if the chains were removed, and all its pristine power were restored to it, then the mountain would become once more the most worthy of human desire and effort.’

Compared with the hempen ropes on the Italian side, I found the iron cables which are fixed near the summit of the Matterhorn on the Swiss side most strong and secure. One slides quickly down them, then one climbs more carefully down the broken rocks of the Shoulder and over a small, very steep strip of glacier, which overhangs the edge of the precipitous Furggen face, and is the most delightful part of the descent. The way leads down the monotonous slope, which is already easier, to the old hut that for many years harboured the climbers of the Matterhorn; it is now half in ruins, and full of ice, and looks like a deserted nest. And so for hours and hours we thread our way among the deep wrinkles of the mountain to the Hörnli buttress, where the new hut stands. Here the Matterhorn ends.

The hut was already filling with other parties, who would ascend the following day. Not all of them would reach the summit: some would suffer by the way from the horrors of mountain-sickness and would spend some of the most painful moments in their lives; and when they came down, they would say it was not worth while; others would calmly enjoy the delights of the summit, and sound the praises of the Matterhorn on their return.

I did not stop at the Hörnli; I cast one glance from there at the lonely, romantic Schwarzsee, which seems to have collected in its deep basin at the foot of the Matterhorn the tears of sorrow and of joy that the mountain has caused to flow; then I hastily turned my steps towards Italy. I crossed the Furggenjoch, and reached the Jomein, late in the evening. Vaccarone was expecting me; he had followed me on my ascent with his telescope, and had looked long at me while I was on the summit. I saw on his face the reflection of the joy that shone on my own; he pressed my hand, as if to say that he esteemed me more than before, now that I had 'done' the Matterhorn.

The Jomein is the furthest point to which platonic lovers of the mountains venture. Some come up to see the Matterhorn and return leaving their names inscribed in the hotel register, as in the hall of a prince's palace. Others come back every year for the fresh, health-giving air and for the untrammelled freedom of the place. Once here they too fall under the giant's spell; they witness the departure of parties of climbers, they follow their vicissitudes with the telescope, they thrill with emotion as they make out tiny men climbing at an enormous altitude, on the rope ladder; and seeing that they look so small and proceed so slowly, they understand that the mountain is vast and the way difficult; when the climbers return they crowd round them with curiosity and respect, and listen with pleasure to the narrative of those who have trodden every stone on the mysterious mountain which they contemplate all day from below, and which has at last cast its spell about them. All honour to these honest pagans who do not mock at mountain worship.

Only once did I happen to meet at the Jomein with a gentleman, an educated and otherwise right-thinking citizen, who had brought with him in his luggage, among his bundles of newspapers, that cordial dislike for climbers which is current coin in our cities. He gave vent to his antipathy in the following remarks, which were full of practical common sense. He liked the mountains as far as one could go in a carriage, or at most with a mule; all the rest was vanity or lunacy. He said that for the last twenty years he had spent the summer in the mountains, at the best hotels, admiring Alpine scenery at his ease. That this was much better than our plan of starting off for our climb directly after arriving at the hotel, even by night in the dark. That when climbing we pay much more attention to the place where we are to put our feet than to admiring the view.

The Echelle Jordan
(a more elaborate ladder than the original one destroyed by a fall of rock)

Zermatt in Winter

That on the top we are so tired that we can think of nothing but our food, and that as soon as we get there we are already thinking of the descent. The day slips by, we slide down the ropes, we plunge panting and trembling down the steep rocks, and do not pause until we are in safety once more. 'You have performed marvellous feats of endurance,' he said, 'you can boast of having done the Matterhorn, but in what way have you appreciated its wondrous beauty, or heard the mysterious voice of Nature on those heights?' And he ended by declaring that he was familiar with the beauties of the mountains without having ever risked his neck. In my heart of hearts I pitied that gentleman. I likened him to one who fancies himself a sailor though he has never left the beach, or believes he has possessed a woman when he has only serenaded her under her windows.

But the mountains are so kindly and so great that they reject none of those who turn to them, and they are good to all: to the men of science who come to study them; to the painters and the poets who seek an inspiration in them; to the sturdy climbers who zealously seek violent exercise, and to the weary who flee from the heat and the turmoil of the city to refresh themselves at this pure source of physical and moral health. Mountaineering is merely a more vigorous, more complete form of this health.

I wish the idea, according to which climbers are a small company of conceited individuals, who are jealous of their mountains, and who live in a selfish atmosphere of petty vanities, could be set aside. I wish it were possible to break up once for all the ring of distrust and indifference which still surrounds them. Mountaineering is a human pursuit, which is as natural as walking, seeing and thinking; as human as all passions are, with its weaknesses, its enthusiasms, its joys, and its disillusions, and like all other passions, it exalts and matures the human mind. I would that I could reduce to its proper terms the conception of our ideals, which do not differ from those which impel men to seek the nobler and loftier things of life; that I could show climbers to be neither wiser nor more foolish than other men. The only difference is that where others believe the limit of the habitable world to lie, climbers find the gates of a marvellous region, that is full of charming visions, and in which hours pass like minutes, and days are as long and complete as a year; and that they take with them through those gates only the better part of themselves, wherefore life there appears to them purer and more full of beauty. They wish that all men could share their dreams, and by bivouacking high up on the rocks they seek to induce others to endure to sleep on the hay in a chalet or on the planks of a hut. By climbing to a height of 13,000 feet they try to lead others to go to 7000 or 8000. They surmount a hundred difficulties that others may be tempted to surmount one.

I wish that sceptics could experience the good effects that a great ascent produces in us. The vanities which filled our minds before we started now seem trivial to us. Now we appreciate the comforts to which use had made us indifferent. We feel a greater love for our home and our family which awaits us there. For we climbers also have our affections, and they are much more vividly present in our minds in moments of danger than to others who are leading their customary lives; and when we come down from the mountains we rejoice to bring back and display to our dear ones the equanimity we have acquired in the heights, and to see them smiling upon us because the mountain has restored to them a healthier, stronger, more affectionate son, brother, or friend.

The climbing is a means, not an end in life: a means to temper the character of youth for the coming struggle, to preserve the vigour of manhood, to check the flight of years, and to prepare for old age a treasury of memories that shall be untroubled and free from remorse. I have seen white-haired men deeply moved at the thought of their early ascents. Happy are those simple minds that retain their capacity to thrill as on the first day in the presence of the beauties of the mountains! My heart goes out in intimate fellow-feeling to those who return year by year to some familiar corner of the Alps and climb ten times over, as long as their legs will carry them, the same peak which was their first Alpine love.

I found one of these sublimely obstinate veterans one fine day at the foot of the Matterhorn.

'Intanto voce fu per me udita:
Onorate l'altissimo poeta
L'ombra sua torna ch'erasi partita.'

'A voice called me, saying: Honour the great poet, whose shadow was hidden from us for a time, but has come again.'

I was descending from the Theodul. Half-way between the Col and the Jomein I saw coming slowly up towards me a fine, tall old man, with a ruddy countenance, clean-shaven, clear-eyed, and with snow-white hair. His face bore the impress of an iron will; his body straight as a dart notwithstanding his years, was full of vigour; his long, rhythmical gait testified to his familiarity with mountains. As I passed him I took off my hat to him, as is the polite custom of those who meet in the mountains. He returned my bow and passed on. My guide had stopped to talk to his. When he rejoined me he whispered, 'Do you know who that is?' I answered that I did not. 'Monsieur Whymper!' And he pronounced the name in a tone of respect. I was as much moved as if I were in the presence of a ghost. I had never seen Whymper except in photographs. I at once turned round to look at him. He had stopped too and was looking at the Matterhorn, whose aspect was one of marvellous grandeur from this point.

I cannot describe how much I was impressed by that meeting in that spot. It was not a man I saw, but the idealized image of the perfect mountaineer, whom I and others have so often dreamed of imitating. They were there, the Matterhorn and Whymper, the two great rivals, and the sight of them in each other's presence brought home to one the superiority of the tiny conqueror to the conquered giant. He had come back after thirty years to see once more the mountain that had made him famous. He found none of his former comrades there. Croz lay at Zermatt, Carrel at Valtournanche; only the Matterhorn stood unchangeable, everlasting. He was looking at it, and was perhaps recalling the deeds of daring he had performed on the stubborn peak in the vigour of his youthful years.

I watched, without his noticing it, and with a kind of veneration, that man who had not feared the Matterhorn when the Matterhorn was a mystery, and who loved it still though the crowd had made it commonplace. I saw his snow-white hair flowing beneath the brim of his grey felt hat, and it seemed to me that it must have begun to turn white on the terrible day of victory and disaster. I myself was harrowed by the thought of what he must have suffered on that day and afterwards. The Matterhorn had cost him dear! It was not, however, the struggle with the mountain that had saddened him, but the contest with his fellow-men which followed his victory.

I would fain have made some sign, have shown him some act of reverence, some proof of my sympathetic interest; have told him that I had read his book again and again, that it had done me good, because it had brought me also up into these places. I would have told him that I understood and shared his passion; that I also, though speaking a different language from his, was a worshipper of the mountain for which he had done and suffered so much; have cried out to him that I too had attempted new ways up the mountain, and that I had not succeeded; have asked him for his iron will that I might try again some day and be successful, and be able to write and tell him that I also had in some measure conquered the Matterhorn.

Whymper started again and slowly continued his ascent, and I was left with my wish unsatisfied. But I too shall return in my old age to the foot of the Matterhorn. I shall struggle up step by step, leaning on my now useless axe, to these dear haunts, seeking comfort in the contemplation of the familiar peaks. I shall enjoy the final pleasures of Alpine life, the cool spring that quenches thirst, the refreshing cup of warm milk, the colour of a little flower, a breath of the wholesome odour of pines wafted up by the winds from the neighbouring forest, the silvery sound of bells which rises in the evening from the peaceful pastures. On the way I shall find my old guides, once my companions in the happy days of strenuous effort, and I shall stop to talk with them, and to recall old memories. Seated on the hotel terrace in the pleasant mountain sunshine I shall look out down the valley, over the long basin of the Breuil, for the arrival of parties of climbers. Young men will appear, full of courage and hope. Perhaps Fasano, the faithful waiter at the Jomein, will point me out to them, and say: 'That gentleman over there was a great climber in his day; he has passed many a night up on the mountain here.' The young men will look at me incredulously while I shall straighten my bent back, at the prompting of my last shreds of vanity; and I shall take aside those who are kind enough to listen to me, and bare my arm like a veteran of many battles, to show them secretly an old wound received up in the mountains, and shall encourage them to make attempts and exhort them to be prudent. Then I shall be content if I note in them traces of the emotion I felt the first time I saw the Matterhorn.

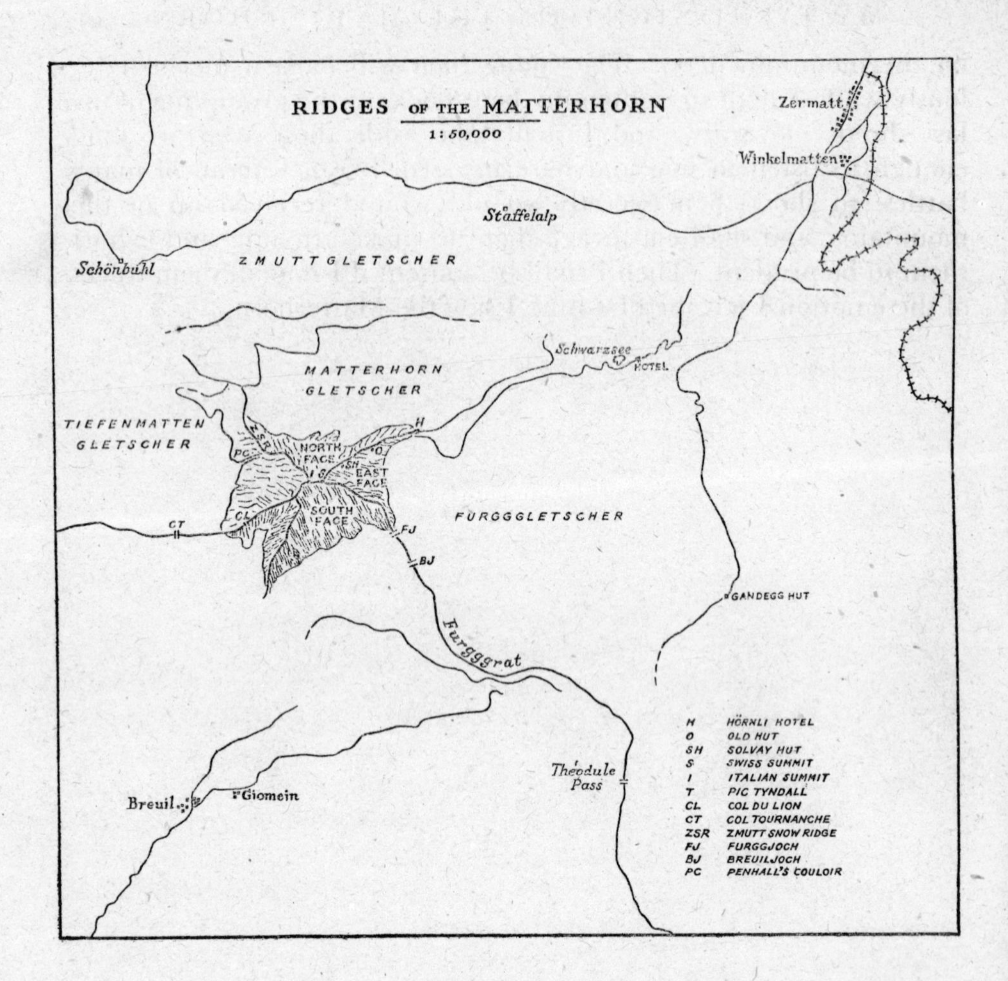

RIDGES OF THE MATTERHORN
1: 50,000
Zermatt
Winkelmatten
Staffelalp
Schönbühl
ZMUTTGLETSCHER
MATTERHORN
GLETSCHER
Schwarzsee
HOTEL
TIEFENMATTEN
GLETSCHER
H
NORTH FACE
EAST FACE
SOUTH FACE
SH
PC
CL
CT
FJ
BJ
FURGGGLETSCHER
GANDEGG HUT
Furgggrat
Théodule
Pass
Breuil
Giomein
H HÖRNLI HOTEL
O OLD HUT
SH SOLVAY HUT
S SWISS SUMMIT
I ITALIAN SUMMIT
T PIC TYNDALL
CL COL DU LION
CT COL TOURNANCHE
ZSR ZMUTT SNOW RIDGE
FJ FURGGJOCH
BJ BREUILJOCH
PC PENHALL'S COULOIR

CHAPTER V

THE Z'MUTT RIDGE OF THE MATTERHORN

'Von Zeit zu Zeit seh' ich den Alten gern
Und hüte mich mit ihm zu brechen.'
GOETHE, *Faust*.

A CLEAR September day in the Visp valley . . . At the station of Randa, the last on the railway below Zermatt, the little train is boarded by four individuals whose appearance is not at all in keeping with the smart car that the guard has allowed them to enter. Their chapped hands, their brown faces, would lead one to think they had been working at lime kilns; their clothes show signs of long ill-usage; they are carrying canvas sacks like emigrants, they are smoking like sailors, and they reek like peasants; they are very silent, their faces look tired, like those of men who have been hunted far over the mountains. One might suspect them to be smugglers or deserters, did not the ropes and axes they have with them betray their true identity.

They are climbers and guides; which of them are the former, and which the latter, is not easy to decide, for nowadays guides dress like their employers, and the latter do their best to look like guides. The car, which is full of clean people, is thrown into a great commotion by this sudden invasion. Little gloved hands are seen nervously pulling skirts aside to avoid contact with the newcomers, uneasy glances are cast at one of them who sits down close to one of the occupants; persons who find themselves obliged to move are heard grumbling, a little foot feels the weight of an iron-shod boot, but a little room is made at last; the rough canvas sacks are put up among the brand new luggage, the axes are deposited in the rack on the top of the little silk sunshades, and the four men manage to find a place to sit. They seem glad to sit down.

When the confusion has quieted down, the small collection of people contained in the handsome car begins to examine them with curiosity as if they were beings fallen from the moon; while they, with their somewhat tired eyes, look sleepily round at the new company in which they find themselves. It is the usual cosmopolitan collection typical of Alpine railways: there is a couple of very smart Parisian honeymooners; some British spinsters, proper and courteous, who travel about the world collecting flowers, admiring, sketching, writing letters to their absent friends, and devouring ten volumes of the Tauchnitz edition in a month; grave, broad-shouldered, gold-spectacled Germans, with field-glasses strapped on to them, and a little Tyrolese felt hat, bedecked with feathers and flowers, balanced on the back of their ponderous heads; whole families of Americans with children, nurses, and Kodak cameras, who photograph all that can be photographed. There are light summer suits and heavy winter shawls, straw bonnets and fur caps.

This strange, mixed crowd now begins to substitute a lively interest in their new travelling companions for the distrust it felt at first. They have real ropes and real axes, they bear on their faces and on certain parts of their clothes evident traces of high mountaineering, and it has become known that they come from the Weisshorn. A Randa guide has told the guard so, and has added that they have spent a whole night up there in the open, on the glacier.

In an instant the magic word Weisshorn! is in every mouth. Baedekers are consulted for the height of the mountain; heads are put out of the window to try and see the peak, and then all look at those who have been up the Weisshorn, to see how they are made. An observer of the moral influences of mountain railways, which are anathema to the climber, is somewhat comforted to perceive that people who come up for the first time feel a certain amount of good-will for the mountaineer. In a mountain landscape the climber is a suitable detail; the mountain appears the stronger by comparison with the weak man who ascends it; in the same way the sea looks more vast if a tiny white sail goes past in the distance. The traveller's own eyes convince him that those strange men really do exist, of whom he has occasionally read in a paper in the city that they have performed some daring ascent or met with some frightful disaster.

On this wondrous stage, before an audience which has come

to the theatre in search of amusement and emotion, the climber acts the part of the hero in the play, who makes sensitive hearts beat quicker; the guides' parts are secondary ones, those of indispensable, well-paid, competent actors who have taught the hero, and who modestly retire behind the wings when he is called before the curtain. On the Zermatt stage the drama of the Matterhorn has been played more than once, a masterpiece which seems to have lost much of its poetry nowadays. Between present-day ascents of the Matterhorn and former ones there is a difference in depth of faith and enthusiasm as there may be between the Mystery as represented by the peasants of to-day at Oberammergau and that of their modest and unknown ancestors. Here at Zermatt, as there in the picturesque Upper-Bavarian village, the spectacle, which in old days attracted only a few single devout spectators, now brings together, assisted by clever advertisement, an inquisitive crowd from all parts of the world. The plot and the personages of the play are not changed; it is the minds of the actors and the spectators which are changed. One essential difference does, however, exist between the two spectacles: in the sacred play at Oberammergau the hero is sure that at the end he can come down from Calvary and go and enjoy the toothsome sausage and the good beer of Bavaria, whereas not all the actors who have departed to climb the Matterhorn have returned to Mr. Seiler's *tables-d'hôte*. In these cases make-believe ceases, and the noble and terrible poetry of the old drama is renewed in all its sadness, and a real emotion is generated in the mind of the spectator. In these cases the ascent of the Matterhorn ceases to be a comedy.

The light train runs up the valley amid forests of beech and pine; the attention of the passengers is now claimed by the changing scenes that every curve of the boldly conceived line brings into view, by the torrent foaming furiously down the ravine, by the groups of picturesque chalets, by the miniature waterfalls which resemble the tails of long comets, as they are blown to and fro by the wind; and at the last corner, when the engine whistles gaily to announce the arrival at Zermatt, the final scene appears so fair a one that no other Alpine theatre can show its like. It is the Matterhorn which reveals itself at last to the eager eyes of those who have crossed the sea to come and admire it, and the reality surpasses the most fantastic expectation.

Inside the car everyone seems to have gone mad. They rise to their feet, they push one another aside to look out of the windows, and in many languages a cry is heard: 'Cervino! Matterhorn! Mont Cervin!' Even our Weisshorn friends have opened their eyes, and their faces brighten, but they speak no word. This outburst of enthusiasm is renewed every day, at the arrival of every train. And there are some who think that men's enthusiasm for the Matterhorn, an enthusiasm a century old, has died out! No: every year a new generation is born which, at its proper time, will be brought by the railway to the base of the great mountain, and which will kindle with renewed admiration. And from this point of view the high mountain railways will have conferred a benefit on mankind.

From the window of my room in the Monte Rosa Hotel at Zermatt I can see the Matterhorn. Lightly veiled by the mists which rise from the valley in the afternoon heat, the mountain takes on so aerial an appearance, so transparent a tint, that it looks unnaturally high and distant; it resembles a cloud, or a cone of light smoke, rather than a rock. My glance descends upon the modest tower of the church near the hotel, the old tower with its pointed gable and its cleft wooden top, through which one can see the little bells. It was they that rang for the funeral of Croz. Croz lies in the peaceful cemetery in the shadow of the church. 'He lost his life not far from this spot', says the inscription carved on a headstone; 'he died like a brave man and a faithful guide.' Not far from him lie side by side two of his employers, Hudson and Hadow.

That little plot of soil which contains, together with other victims of the mountains, the first victims of the Matterhorn, fills me with deep emotion every time I visit it; I think of the eternal peace which has followed upon the hours of fierce struggle; I grieve for those young men torn so early in their lives from the enjoyment of their noble pleasures, and then I wonder whether it were not a blessed thing to die as they died, quickly, unexpectedly, painlessly, in a moment of perfect peace, when life seemed full of beauty, and the mind was purified by passion and by joy.

In the village round about the smoke rises peacefully from the old chalets; down the narrow street pass the cows with their jangling bells, returning from the pastures; a sledge laden with hay slides silently down the hillside, and a little old woman, seated on a neighbouring knoll and wearing the black headdress of the Valais, is watching two goats while she knits a stocking.

Suddenly a strident sound strikes upon the peaceful atmosphere, a discord which offends my ears and my inmost feeling; it is music, but its intrusion upon the heavenly peace I was enjoying annoys me. I rush out of the hotel and see a regular orchestra of ten musicians, solemnly seated before their scores in a little wooden kiosk, and determined to work through the whole of their days' programme. A few children are playing with hoops round the orchestra; the tourists, stretched out in their comfortable basket-chairs in front of the neighbouring hotels, have not ceased to read the *Times*; a few ladies are writing letters in the open air, or sipping their afternoon tea; disengaged guides are chatting on the low wall that bounds the road, and smoking their pipes; no one listens to the concert or seems to desire it. For whose benefit does the band play, then? For that of the Matterhorn, towering up to the sky, or for that of the poor victims lying in the sacred churchyard, only a few feet from the bandstand? What barbarian brought the band up here, to break the harmonious silence of the mountains?

For the little village of Zermatt the harmony of the winds and the torrents, the sound of the bells of its cattle, the primitive songs of its inhabitants were sufficient. Zermatt is a discordant medley of the old and the new; the splendid hotels overwhelm the little chalets of former days, and the white plaster of the new buildings gives a dirty appearance to the beautiful brown wood of the chalets that have been washed by the rains and warmly tinted by the sun. The omnibuses which go down to the station to meet travellers block up the village street and throw the peaceful flocks into confusion as they drive past them; the new Anglican church, neat and severe, contrasts strangely with the old parish church with its many coloured altar and its baroque statues, and seems like an emblem of the new civilization that has invaded this remote corner of a Catholic canton, bringing wealth in its train and seeking romantic beauty in exchange.

Along the single street of the village innumerable booths full of Alpine trifles are built up against the houses, and the little open-air tables, lined with red as in a fair, display among illustrated postcards and photographs of the Matterhorn, wooden chamois carved in the Oberland, shell boxes made at Sorrento, Florentine mosaics and German ornaments. The fair lasts only for the summer months; after the September feast of the Madonna the shopkeepers pack up their wares and flit away to the lakes or the seaside; the band put up their instruments and take their repertoire elsewhere; the hotels close; Zermatt rests for eight months, and dreams that it is again the peaceful little village of Praborne.* It seems once more to see Saussure as he came down from the Theodul one day in 1789; he was the first mountaineer to visit that rude tribe, and he was received with distrust. Lord Minto seems to come again to climb the Breithorn, as in 1830, escorted by ten Chamonix guides. Lord Minto was the guest of the priest, for there were no hotels, and his reverence's housekeeper kept saying to him, by way of apology for the plainness of their hospitality: 'Prenez patience avec nous; pauvre pays, pauvres gens'; and the mountain folk grieved to see his lordship's sixteen-year-old son start with him up to the mountain; it seemed to them 'a monstrous thing that so young a lad should be taken up to perish thus miserably'.

These times were far remote and differed much from our own. Herr Lauber next opened his house to visitors to Zermatt; at that time they were few in number, and Desor, who was one of them, exclaimed, 'Heaven grant that the valley of St. Nicholas may be long preserved from tourists!' The cry of a noble egoism! but it was a vain one. In 1854 Mr. Seiler's hotel, the Monte Rosa, which has thenceforth harboured the pick of climbers of all nations, was grafted on to the doctor's wooden house.[1] Jost, the old porter of the hotel, convinced me by tapping a wall in the passage that the wood of Dr. Lauber's house still echoes under the new wall. Those who know its history can perceive a fragrance of the past still rising from

* [Zermatt has now become a winter sports resort—R.L.G.I.].

the little village; under the modern plaster they can still trace the romance of the early days of mountaineering.

The railway arrived, and soon it was carried up to a height of ten thousand feet, as far as the Gornergrat. At the present day Zermatt possesses eleven hotels, a little museum, a public garden, a tourist office, a bank, and a florist. Is this development a blessing or a curse? The old Swiss, who dearly love their country, have wept for the lost romance of their beautiful valleys, and have bemoaned the disappearance of the former simple habits of the natives. From Rudolph Töpffer to Edouard Rod a continual protest has arisen against the vulgarization of the mountains. 'Switzerland', wrote the gifted author of the *Voyages en Zig-Zag*, 'was formerly a chaste and beauteous virgin, wild and lonely, whose charms were unknown to the common herd, and made the hearts of a few real lovers beat. Foolish babblers, who had not the wit to keep silent concerning the secret favours vouchsafed to them! They talked, they made them known, and behold, all the scum of the Continent, and every Englishman who was suffering from boredom, arrived in a never ending stream, so that the chaste virgin was exposed to the glances of all, and preserved her beauty, but lost all her charm.' And Rod, who wrote at the time of the construction of the high Alpine railways, gives utterance to this cry of alarm: 'They are busy spoiling the mountains for us! Can nothing be done to protect them?' In his opinion the invasion and violation of the small valleys by the ruthless upheaval of modern progress is just as detrimental to the inhabitants as to the beauty of the scenery; the railway is a source of demoralization; the lust for easy gain spreads like the foul smoke of the engine, and in a short time the so-called 'Fremden Industrie' supplants the heavy but health-giving labour of their ancestors, which consisted in the cultivation of the soil, that, stiff, rough, and sterile though it was, was capable none the less of abundantly rewarding the toil expended upon it.

At every fresh proposal for a high mountain railway the Alpine and non-Alpine papers received the protests of those who, inspired by their long experience and their deep love of the mountains, considered that the beauty of the Alps should be left unsullied, and their difficulties intact, if they were to continue to be a cradle of energy and enthusiasm. Their cries were futile; the days of aristocracies, when only the few had a right to enjoyment, are past; Alpine solitudes exist now only in the vain dreams of poets.*

Prometheus, if he were still chained to his rock in the Caucasus, would see Cook's parties coming up to him; the nine Furies would cease to wreak their ancient vengeance on him; the vulture would fly away in terror, but the Titan's torture would be more fearful than before.

It is of no use to bemoan nowadays the profanation of sublime things. If Piranesi were again to sketch the ruins of Rome, he would see their magnificent perspective lines interrupted by electric wires and by the trollies of the tramway; and the brush would fall from Guardi's hands among the waters of Canalazzo, if the painter, come to life again, were to see a little steamer pass whistling and belching smoke under the arch of the Rialto which he so loved. We must hope for a future generation, more refined, more appreciative of beauty than our own, less nervous, and stronger, that shall do away with all the exaggerations which an eager curiosity and an unbridled commercialism have led us to mistake for progress. Then the Eiffel Tower and the Jungfrau railway shall fall together; the beautiful waterfalls which have been enclosed in iron pipes shall once more foam freely in the sunlight, amid the green foliage of the pines; and, thanks to the genius of the latest inventor, the telegraph wires and posts shall cease to intersect the view of the white peaks surrounding the Matterhorn and of the columns in Trajan's forum.

I started off on foot for the Staffel Alp, which is two hours' walk from Zermatt. The Staffel Alp is situated at the boundary of a beautiful forest and of a huge glacier. The forest, thick and luxuriant, consists entirely of pines, of the kind commonly called Arolla, with reddish trunks and dark, horizontal leaves, giving to these icy regions the appearance of a landscape on the Mediterranean coast; the glacier is known by the barbarous name of Z'Mutt, which Ruskin thought so ugly that he wished it exchanged for the more picturesque appellation of the Red Glacier, from the colour of the rocks that

* [There are still unspoiled solitudes for those who look for them—R.L.G.I.].

enclose its flanks. The highest growing pines are scattered on the moraines; the beautiful southern tree seems as if planted on the ice itself.

At that uttermost limit of the inhabited world there stands a lonely little hotel, far from the sight and the noise of Zermatt; there the tender care of the international travelling agencies ceases, and the traveller, left to himself, drinks a hot grog, his shivering person wrapped in a shawl, glances at the unknown waste stretched out before him, and at the dark Matterhorn towering above him, and hastily returns to Zermatt, where he feels safer.

The Matterhorn, as seen from the Staffel Alp, is quite unrecognizable; it is no longer the sharp, bright knife-edge that is visible from the Gornergrat, nor the severe, symmetrical pyramid that is seen from the Theodul, nor the mighty bull as it appears from the Jomein; it is a grotesque monster, deformed by an enormous hump that seems to overwhelm it by sheer weight. It is a sinister caricature of the Matterhorn, a Rigoletto who laughs and slays. It was down the great wall that hangs above the Staffel Alp that Croz, Hudson, Hadow, and Douglas fell. Douglas's bones are still up there, bleaching in some cleft in the rock, lying in the mountain's arms, but only the crows and the eagles which circle round the Matterhorn know where the young Lord Francis lies. This is the most savage of all the faces of the Matterhorn; turned to the north-west, it enjoys the sunshine only for a few hours late in the day; only on a very few days in the year does the sun strike it obliquely in the morning, afterwards disappearing only to return late in the afternoon. It seems as if the light were unwilling to remain there.

I was the only guest at the Staffel Alp. I spent the evening in freedom with my guides, and, tired of the *table-d'hôte*, I supped with them in the kitchen; with these silent men there is always so much to talk about. The next morning I started at four.

A start at night in the high mountains is always full of poetry; the unwonted hour, the uncertainty of the way, the strange light that envelopes, even in the dead of night, the mountains near great glaciers, fill our minds with a sense of mystery, as if we were passing through a world other than our own. We intended to climb the

Matterhorn by the Z'Mutt ridge. The way was known only to one of the four of us, but he was Daniel Maquignaz, and therefore I was easy in my mind. Nevertheless I was filled with intense curiosity. I had read the whole history of this side of the mountain — a short one, but full of bold deeds. Whymper had merely said that the fearful precipices that overhang the Z'Mutt glacier had deterred him from making any attempt on that side. Since the time when Whymper had written this, the art of discovering new ways up mountains had been much improved, and the climber's eye had grown sharper. The year 1879 marked the fall of the fortress of Z'Mutt; on the same date — September 3rd — two strong parties had set forth to the attack, and both had conquered. At the head of one was Mummery, and with him his followers, the Valaisans Burgener, Petrus, and Gentinetta; the leader of the other was Penhall, who had with him two Macugnaga guides — Ferdinand Imseng and Louis Zurbriggen. They followed different routes; Mummery was more fortunate or wiser — the two words are often synonymous in mountaineering, as in war — and was the first to reach the summit.[2]

Three days later Mr. Baumann, with the guides J. Petrus (Swiss) and Emile Rey (Italian), made the ascent with incredible speed, by Mummery's route, and arrived at the top at 8.45 a.m. So in one season, and within a few days, nine people had climbed the Matterhorn by its Z'Mutt ridge, till then reputed inaccessible. They were all, amateurs and guides, men of exceptional experience, strength, and daring; but when we recall their names, a disturbing thought presents itself — of these nine, six have since lost their lives in the mountains: Imseng in 1881, on Monte Rosa; Petrus in 1882, on the Aiguille Blanche de Péteret; in 1882 Penhall was killed by an avalanche on one of the Grindewald mountains; in 1890 or 1891 Baumann disappeared in Africa; in 1895 Mummery was lost on Nanga-Parbat; and our own Emile Rey slipped and was killed on the Dent du Géant.* A sad record, that gives rise in our minds to a host of troublesome questions: Were these disasters accidental, not to be foreseen? Was it those men's own exceptional daring which made them less careful? Did their overweening confidence in their

*[Alexander Burgener was killed by a great ice avalanche below the Bergli Hut in 1910 — R.L.G.I.].

THE MATTERHORN
from the Dent Blanche

The West Face
Tiefenmatten Glacier below

own ability impel them to undertake tasks that were beyond the strength of man? If we look into them carefully, each of these cases, as far as they are known to us, is capable of explanation, and an answer can be given to each of these questions; but those who propose to perform a difficult Alpine feat never remember such occurrences; the fate of others does not affect them; like Napoleon the Great, every climber is prone to think that the bullet that is to slay him has not yet been moulded.

As I drew nigh to that wall I was chiefly busy with the thought of the last fair page of its history: the quick and daring ascent made by Prince Louis Amadeus of Savoy, the only Italian climber who had as yet ascended the mountain by that route. A veteran mountaineer myself, I was anxious to grapple with those difficulties which he had found easy in the daring and energy of his vigorous youth, though he was only at the threshold of his climbing career.[3]

We descended on to the Z'Mutt glacier at that uncertain hour when the moon has ceased to shine and the light of dawn has not yet appeared. Before us lay a huge, undefined, flat way, whose surface was white as marble and broad enough for an army to march over in line of battle, and for a whole nation to pass along. On either side it was bounded by granite walls of enormous height; innumerable blocks, fallen down the mountainside and deeply imbedded in the ice, had the appearance of sphinxes half buried in the sand along the route of a Pharaoh's triumph.

The white pavement on which we walked was scarred with symmetrical clefts like the ruts that the iron-tyred wheels of a cart have worn on an ancient road. By day these clefts flow with impetuous rivulets of crystal-clear green water; by night they are hidden by a thin coating of ice which deceives the eye and does not support the foot, so that some of us incautiously let a leg go through and drew it out all dripping with icy water.

The royal road is not so smooth as it appeared from a distance. It is a road fit for giants; the network of ice-blocks which form the pavement is constructed in such a way that wide and deep clefts are left between the blocks. A giant could cross these at a stride, but the climber takes ten minutes to turn them and reach the other side.

Leaping from block to block, slipping sometimes, and helping one another, we were on the look out, as we skirted the base of the mighty buttress which juts out and separates the Matterhorn glacier from that of Tiefenmatten, for a place that should give us access to the rocks of the Matterhorn. An open schrund yawned between these rocks and the glacier, and defended them on all sides from attack. But at one point a tongue of ice shot up and crossed the schrund, like a half-raised drawbridge. One by one, treading carefully so as not to break down our tiny bridge, we climbed up over it, and at the end a long stride took us on to the rocks, which we grasped, and then climbed with hands and feet on to the buttress. This we found covered with *débris* of rocks of all colours and shapes, bearing witness to the continual disintegration and destruction of the rocks above.

We had reached the outer edge of the Tiefenmatten gulf, a huge chasm bounded on three sides by the precipitous rocks of the Matterhorn and faced on the fourth by the ice walls of the Col Tournanche and the Dent d'Hérens; a place shut off from the rest of the world, from the sight of any green valley, and darkened still more by the ever-present shadow of the mountain towering above it. I do not know any other scene in the Alps that gives expression to so sublime a melancholy; it is one of those spots which God has only passed by night, to use the poetical Provençal expression. There is a silence in it such as must have brooded over the earth during the first days of the creation. It was eight o'clock in the morning and still dark. We sat down to breakfast. A few paces away I noticed a few stones built up against a great tower with a certain symmetry which was in contrast with the confusion of the *débris* round about. This was not the work of Nature; the tiny hand of man had laboured at it. It immediately occurred to me, not without some emotion, that here was the trace of a bivouac, perhaps Mummery's bivouac, and I do not think I was wrong. I gazed with respect at the ruined wall, and my eyes instinctively sought among the ruins some object that might have been forgotten there and might have belonged to the first explorer, a sign that might reveal to me some secret of the hours he passed at the foot of his beloved mountain.

I thought of what must have been in his mind during the night before the battle, in that place so full of mysterious suggestions. A modern Œdipus, he stood before the sphinx of the Alps and the riddle it had challenged him to solve.

I was envious when I thought that he had not felt the peace of mind, the freedom from anxiety, that were ours that day. And yet the mountain had not changed since then; the same difficulties, the same perils awaited me on the same route. But the circumstances were altered for me; when the enigma is solved the sphinx dies. Let a man but know that one of his fellows has succeeded in performing any action, and that action appears less difficult. The real merit is his who first does the deed; but he himself, in doing it, makes it possible for others, and therefore less noble. The anxieties and the bold enterprise of the artist who creates are replaced by the mental calm and the slavish security of the imitator. And if it comes to pass that someone else repeats the deed, even though he bring it to greater perfection, he will not earn either the glory or the joy of the first. This is my small contribution to the much discussed Alpine theme as to the value of 'first ascents'.*

We were interested and on the *qui vive*, but nothing more. On that morning everything was at peace, both within us and without. We were in no hurry; no rival party obliged us to hasten in order to be the first on the top, no tiresome observer was watching through the telescope the time it took us to reach the summit. We were hidden from men's glances, we were free and alone; we had a whole day before us; a short day, if you will, for the middle of September was past, but the weather was fine, and I was determined this time to enjoy at my ease the ascent of the Matterhorn.

Round about us was a peaceful, impenetrable twilight; in front of us the snowy peaks had been bathed in a golden light, and then they had turned to silver by a thousand consecutive soft gradations. The waters were still in the grasp of the frost, and did not yet flow over the rocks. The top of the Dent d'Hérens was glowing, and the whole of its icy armour was sparkling in the sunlight, but the sun's

* [Rey always climbed behind a good guide. For a guideless party making its first ascent, or indeed subsequent ascents, of a great peak, I have found it makes little difference to the enjoyment whether anyone else has climbed the route before—R.L.G.I.].

rays had not started any avalanches; all that which was to fall from thence had come away in the summer, and the snows were beginning to consolidate once more in the cooler atmosphere and under the oblique rays of the autumn sun, and were preparing to return to their wintry state of immobility. There was not a breath of air; the sky was of deepest blue, perhaps too clear and too beautiful. When I consulted my guides as to whether there was likely to be a change, they invariably answered: 'Qui sait? On ne peut pas dire.' Guides never commit themselves.

It is said that climbers are sometimes childishly superstitious, and that they are inclined, before attacking a mountain, to toss coins in the air, just as once upon a time Roman generals consulted the flight of crows before a battle. I consulted the oracle by quartering a wretched, skinny fowl which mine host had put into the provision bag, and, judging by its flesh, it was to be expected that the day would be an extremely hard one.

And, indeed, hard and sharp were the rocks of the Z'Mutt buttress, which we started to climb immediately afterwards, and so was a certain chimney with ice-clad sides, devoid of holds, where we lost the first half-hour. Whilst we were busy inside it, the stones began to fall round about us, whistling as they came; down in the shadow where we were, everything was frozen stiff, but on the top of the ridge the sun's rays were already shining and loosening the pebbles — autumn leaves, as it were, falling from the Matterhorn tree! When we reached the backbone of the buttress, things began to go splendidly; the snow on the ridge was so good that it was not necessary to cut a single step. Seeing that the route was so easy and so good, we all rejoiced, and became more convinced than ever that we could ascend lazily, without haste.

The Staffel Alp stands at 7062 feet, the Matterhorn at 14,790; so there were little more than 7500 feet to ascend, of which we had already done one half. Perhaps this comfortable laziness was the remains of the fatigue we had undergone on the Weisshorn two days before; perhaps it was due to our preconceived idea that the Z'Mutt grat was not difficult. And Daniel, the only one among us who knew the climb, said that on the last part of the ascent, just below the final peak of the Matterhorn, there are certain slabs of rock, which are coated with ice that does not melt till late in the day, when the sun is on it. It was useless, he added, to be in any hurry to reach that point, and be obliged to wait there in positions less safe than our present one, and he promised to pay for a good bottle of wine if we did not reach the Jomein the same evening. Antoine and Ange, who were not quite so sanguine as he, took the bet, while I remained neutral. Daniel smiled in a mysterious manner.

Excellent pretexts were not lacking for stopping at every step. I kept looking down on to the Tiefenmatten glacier, whose white crevasses yawned far below in shadow, in everlasting tranquillity like that of a cemetery; or raising my eyes to the wall above, whose curving black lines gave it the appearance of the crater of an extinct volcano, I examined with curiosity its twisted strata. That which from afar had looked to me like the veins on a marble surface, waving in gentle folds like a wind-filled sail, now proved, as I scrutinized it close at hand, to be a mighty geological phenomenon; it appeared like the waves of a whirlpool that had suddenly stiffened into stone, but had preserved their crystalline transparency and the shape they had at the moment when they ceased to move.

In this place even the non-votary of science realizes the formation of the Matterhorn, which, strongly built though it be, consists of most delicate materials. My eyes kept turning somewhat anxiously towards the precipice that falls away from the summit to the Matterhorn glacier — a precipice that is in some places vertical, in others overhanging, and is one of the most wonderful in the Alps; the stones which fall down it drop over 2000 feet without striking the face.

We halted to take a photograph, and again to test an echo, known to Daniel, that was hidden away in this neighbourhood. My guides amused themselves like children by awakening with their loud cries the voice that dwells in the huge couloir, that was wont to reply only to the rumbling of thunder and the crash of the avalanche; but it awoke and answered us obligingly, as if it were pleased to hear unaccustomed voices, and it repeated them eight or ten times, stammering as if weakened by long silence. It seemed as if the spirit of the Matterhorn had recognized friends in us and was sending us greeting; its cries and ours were blended in the still air in a sound full of mysterious harmony. When we resumed our journey, the echo sank once more into silence, and who knows how long it will be before other human voices will awaken it again!

On the easy ridge a further temptation presents itself: a fine slab of rock, level and dry, protrudes from the snow; it seemed to have been made on purpose for us to rest upon. We stretched ourselves voluptuously out in the sunshine and went peacefully to sleep . . . I do not know how long I slept; I was waked by the guides shouting energetically with upturned faces, and seeming to converse with someone at a distance. There was a party on the top; every now and then we could hear the sharp sound of their axes striking against the rocks; at last a voice replied from on high, and my guides declared it to be a Valtournanche voice.

The thought that those others were already near the summit, while we were still so low down, stirred us up and made us start with renewed energy. It was eleven o'clock; we stepped once more into the shadow of the Matterhorn, and did not see the sun again till four hours later; the sun was just then hidden behind the peak, and its rays formed a luminous aureole about the dark summit of the Matterhorn. In half an hour we reached the end of the ridge, where it joins the actual peak; the easy snow came to an end and we reached the first of the mountain's formidable defences. These consisted of four pinnacles of rock, one after the other, which, as seen from below, appear a small matter, but when reached prove to be as high and smooth as towers. The difficulties begin with them, and the third and fourth are really serious. We climbed up and down, we sought to turn them on the left: there was a sheer precipice. We returned to the right: there the rocks were loose and came away at a touch. Our progress was infinitely slow; we took nearly two hours to negotiate the pillars and to reach the base of the wall.

I glanced round; we were but little higher than the Great Tower. On the left, towards Zermatt, was a deep and narrow couloir which flowed down the side of the mountain and fell away to the Matterhorn glacier; on its opposite side, quite close at hand, was the strange, overhanging wall which, seen in profile, resembles a huge, distorted, shattered nose. On the right we could see sideways the deep gap in the ridge between the Matterhorn and the Tête du Lion, a huge loophole left open in the wall that divides Switzerland from Italy; through this opening I perceived in the distance a small azure cone, that was Monte Viso. In front of me the wall rose steeply, and though it was quite close, I did not see how it was to be climbed.

Ange started first; Daniel wished him to be at the head of the party. 'Il est le plus jeune,' he said, 'faut bien qu'il apprenne à trouver son chemin'; and he was now watching him as he picked his way up the steep wall, testing with his hands the holds above his head, and drawing himself slowly upwards; he eagerly followed him with his eyes, like a master putting a beloved pupil through an examination, and I thought I read complete satisfaction in his eyes. We followed one by one, while the rope was slowly drawn in before us. It was strange but not excessively difficult climbing, though very steep, with hidden holes far apart from one another, which we could only reach with the tips of our fingers, stretching our arms to the utmost and extending our legs; but when once we had grasped them they held. I was reminded of the first part of the ascent of the Meije in Dauphiné, above the Duhamel stone man, but here the pitch was longer.

At first one climbs inside the dark couloir, and then, turning gradually to the right, one returns to the open face and to light and air, and one seems to climb more freely; also the rocks become more solid, and the strata better placed, and thus one reaches the ridge; but I think that if the rocks on this part were glazed, it would be impossible to ascend them. We had attained the lofty summit of the great couloir; just below we had traversed loose rocks that were most dangerous. During a halt Daniel told me of a Swiss guide who in that spot had been wounded in the head by a stone which the feet of one of the party had started; Daniel still remembered his painful impressions when he came past here a few days later, and saw the snow and the rocks all stained with the unfortunate man's blood.

We reached the Z'Mutt shoulder, the point where the ridge is joined on to the final peak. In the excitement of the climb we had failed to notice something which was going on, unknown to us, above our heads: certain fish-shaped clouds floating above us in the dark blue heights of the sky. Clouds of this shape are always of bad omen, but these were so high up that I did not think it possible that they could descend on to the summit; in my optimistic mood that day I thought that at the worst the morrow might not be so fine. Some of our morning's thoughtlessness was still about us; the guides were still joking about the good bottle for which Daniel would have to pay, but it seemed to me that Daniel was already less confident of winning his bet. Without looking at my watch I felt that it was growing late; the shadow of the Matterhorn marked the lapse of time for us.

No one who has not again and again explored the flanks of the Matterhorn at different hours of the day can imagine the solemnity of the shadow of its cone as it slowly and silently revolves on the vast field of snow; it lengthens and it shortens, fills a whole valley with darkness, or again it covers with a blue veil a vast glacier, and it stretches away to far distant peaks; at other times it casts itself in profile, like an apparition, over the mist of the dawn or the sunset, on the horizon. In the morning it is clearly outlined in the Tiefenmatten chasm, like the shadow of a Gothic cathedral whose long roof terminates in a sharp pinnacle; towards evening it lingers on the snows of the Theodul, sluggish and melancholy as the shadow of a huge cypress. The shepherds of the neighbouring valleys raise their eyes to this primitive sundial, and regulate their day's work by it; when it is touched by the sun's last rays, they bring their herds back to the stables; and the climber grows uneasy and hastens his steps.

Time was passing; it seemed as if the sun were hastening on his downward path; the fish-shaped clouds had increased in number and in length; as the weather changed so did our spirits. We no longer jested, we moved quickly along the base of the final peak, towards the Italian ridge and the Corridor that Carrel had followed on his first ascent. We did not, however, strike that famous place;[4] we returned towards the Z'Mutt ridge, traversing in a slightly upward direction. We then found the bad rock slabs of which Daniel had told us, and found them still glazed with a treacherous film of ice, the worst enemy of rock climbers; the sun had only just before come upon this place, and the thaw had scarcely begun. Icicles and stones were falling from above, and this was a thing Daniel had not told us. We would fain have run to get out of danger, but the difficulties of the way condemned us to a tedious slowness; we moved one at a time with the greatest care, and the man who was not moving always tried to put his head under cover, as best he could, right up against the wall.

Light puffs of mist came up at intervals. Our illusions about the length of an autumn day were being shattered. I was like one who has thoughtlessly reached the half-way point of his life, and become aware that life is not so simple a matter as he had thought in his over-confident youth, and that much remains for him to do before he can reach the goal that had previously seemed to him so near. I began to regret the time we had lost; Daniel must have been thinking privately that he would now have to pay for the bottle after all.

God so willed it that we won safely through on the Z'Mutt ridge. The last part was easy, and we made what haste we could; but the weather was rapidly growing worse. The huge, strange, fish-shaped clouds had disappeared from the sky, and a broad, grey veil, a lofty dome which covered half the horizon to the west, had taken their place; and from it small strips detached themselves from time to time and floated down suddenly till they rested on the highest peaks, and moved no more. The other half of the horizon was still clear, so that while the whole range of the Graian Alps and a part of the Pennine were enveloped in darkness, the mountains of the Valais and the Oberland and Monte Rosa were still resplendent with gorgeous light, that appeared brighter still by the contrast.

The final peak of the Matterhorn alternately donned and doffed a veil; its beauty and its mystery were enhanced thereby. Mists are to a mountain what a veil is to women: the colour of the rocks seems more rosy when a thin, white covering wraps them about; when the mountain's face appears for a second, it seems to smile more joyfully to us; when it is hidden, we are left with an infinite longing to see it again. But these were the last smiles; the sun sank out of sight; the dark curtain fell with incredible swiftness over the bright spectacle of Monte Rosa. The Matterhorn lost its colour, and became the livid Matterhorn that is seen in bad weather, full of shadows and sadness. Up from below over its lofty crags came waves of cloud, like a racing tide; they hurled themselves against the ridges, they broke, they returned in more serried masses, until they conquered and overwhelmed everything in their path. The highest rocks were swallowed up by them, and so were we, as we stood on the summit, which we had reached at last.

Few, perhaps none, can have had the experience of being on the top of the Matterhorn at about six in the evening of a day in late September, in bad weather. During the few brief moments I remained there, I reviewed the situation in my mind. It was serious; I rapidly thought of the experiences other parties had undergone when surprised by darkness and by storm up on the mountainside, and I did not disguise from myself how probable it was that we should have to spend a night up there under similar conditions. A slight shudder passed through my frame at the thought of the mystery of the descent; an undefined uneasiness like that of an animal that has a presentiment of danger; and at the same time there arose in me a great curiosity to see this peril, to learn what the terrible nights on the Matterhorn were like, how disasters came, what their setting was, what men's feelings were when they occurred, how I myself should behave in one. Perhaps I was never so near to learning these things. I understood then how certain accidents in the mountains originate and happen in the quietest and simplest manner, and how they certainly appear more tragical to those who hear them discussed than to those who are actors in them. Man's powers of resignation in the face of destiny's decrees must be unlimited.

Only an hour before I had been climbing upwards free from all anxiety, jesting with my guides, admiring, as I looked about me, the effects of light and shade, and the resplendent peaks; and now, amid the impenetrable darkness of the clouds, I was already debating in my own mind my chances of a safe return; a disaster appeared to me most probable; let the weather take a turn for the worse, the sleet change into drifting snow, and our fate was sealed. I should descend as far as I could, the cold would increase, till my hands were almost frozen and my body no longer under my control; I should then stop wherever I might be, in a place where I could not even sit down, and there await the sunrise with an infinite longing. Would the sun ever rise for me? And in what state would it find me? I thought of the labours and difficulties of the relief party that would be sent up to seek for me, and of the anxiety of those down below. Yet no! None knew that I was on the Matterhorn; I had told no one that I proposed to climb it, or whither I was going. I was alone, at an enormous distance from all human aid; my safety depended entirely upon myself and my guides. And it was the consciousness of this that gave me strength.

All these conflicting thoughts chased one another rapidly and almost unconsciously through my mind, in the mental duality that such circumstances produce; they contended with one another, and destroyed each other in turn, so that, when we resumed our journey, nothing remained of them in my mind except great anxiety to make a quick descent. We had briefly discussed the question whether to descend on the Swiss or the Italian side; the former was easier, on the latter the hut was nearer, and besides, we should be in our own country. We decided on Italy.

'*En route*', was the sharp command of Daniel, who had wrapped his head in a handkerchief and knotted it under his chin, thus making his face look like a woman's. He too was in a hurry now. We very soon reached the first ropes, and I was surprised to feel again my old instinctive reluctance to trust myself to them. I ought to have slid down the rope, holding on to it with both hands, whereas I grasped it with one hand only, and with the other I held firmly to the rock. One is advised to do so on ordinary occasions, but on that day the precaution was out of place. I thought the guides were grumbling; I heard one of them say behind me: 'Si on ne marche pas plus vite, nous dormons dehors.' The expression 'on ne marche pas' was meant for me; I quite understood that, and the thought of sleeping out, together with the wound to my vanity, immediately filled me with a feeling of surprising security; thenceforth I grasped the ropes with both hands, without hesitation, only desirous not to hear the same reproach again.

I have frequently observed that when the weather turns bad high up in the mountains, the guides become most ill-tempered. Those same guides who but a short time since were so obliging and so courteous, who were jesting with you, and treating you with so much deference, suddenly become rough and reserved, at times even almost brutal. This is their way of showing you that matters are growing serious; there is no longer any need for courtesy when men's lives are at stake. They know that the only hope of safety lies in rapidity of flight, and they have no patience with him who goes slowly, or with him who argues or complains. On these occasions you feel them pulling with greater force, almost with violence, on the rope that unites you to them; they seize you roughly by the arm or the leg, if in your haste you are about to make a false step; they do not hesitate to rebuke you if, through inattention on your part, your rope catches round a piece of rock, or to tell you plainly that you are 'going' badly. You may be sure that when the guides resort to these home truths, there is no time to be lost. The guides' rough and violent nature has resumed its sway, but, to be candid, the amateur is no whit behindhand in this respect; I remember on that day returning with extraordinary animosity my guides' tugs at the rope. Fortunately these ill-humours disappear directly we are safe, and they leave no trace of rancour; on the contrary, they are replaced by an affectionate feeling of greater intimacy than before. During that time of difficulty a feeling of complete equality has arisen, raising the guides to the rank of the amateur and making the amateur not inferior to his guides. And when the goal is reached, let one of them only tell you you have 'gone' well, and your anger is appeased, and the gloom of wounded *amour propre* disappears completely.

Our desperate descent was barely begun. I slid down, I crept along at one time on my back, at another with my face to the rocks; I hugged the mountain in the attempt to adapt my body to its shape; one moment I would go lightly in order not to put too much weight on a doubtful hold, the next I would let myself go with my whole weight, having seen out of the corner of my eye a place on which to put my feet. At times, at the bottom of a difficult bit, where the rope came to an end, my legs were too short to reach any hold, and kicked about in space and explored the rock; my bended knees did the work of my feet, my elbows were planted in the holds instead of my hands, until I found some Heaven-sent support, and then, arching my back, and supporting myself with the back of my neck, at last reached a place where I could stand in safety.

But where is the climber to whom the petty discomforts of such moments are unknown? The man below impatiently urges you to descend, while the one above protests that you are pulling him down; the rope of the party becomes entangled with the ropes that are fixed to the rocks, it becomes twisted by the damp and stiff with the frost; it hitches everywhere, winds round your legs, compresses your chest, rubs against your face. Everything gets in the way; your sack will not keep in its place, your camera catches at regular intervals, your coat impedes your movements; the very brim of your hat is troublesome. The axe is a real plague; you have tied it on to your arm with a piece of string in order to have your hands free, and it swings about on every side, turns upside down, smites your shins, squeezes your wrist or wounds your face; at times it hurts you so much that you cry out, and you are minded to abuse it as if it were a human being. It seems to be doing all this on purpose to aggravate the position of affairs just when they are at their worst; you could almost throw it away. With the axe it is as with certain friends: you wish to have them at your side in time of need; but when that is past, the first time they cause you any annoyance, you weary of them, and in your short-sighted human egoism you do not reflect that you may shortly need them again.

We were descending rapidly, but the terrible darkness fell upon us faster still; we had hoped for a short space of twilight, but owing to the thick clouds the night came two hours earlier. At the Col Félicité one single rift in the leaden clouds gave us a glimpse of the setting sun; it was a tiny shaft of orange yellow amid the gloom, like a tongue of fire in the smoke of a vast conflagration; then it too disappeared, dying sadly away like a last vain hope.

The darkness gradually increased, and the mountain's outlines became indistinct; at times a wreath of mist enveloped them as in a grey veil, but when clear they took on a darker hue. At the Enjambée the darkness was complete; of the wonderful precipice below I saw nothing at all. The Shoulder almost free from snow, dimly showed the lean structure of its crags; the rocks were somewhat iced, and prudence required that we should moderate our speed. Thanks to the violence of our exertions on the descent it seemed to me that the cold, which had been intense, was somewhat lessened; but my hands, which I had left ungloved the better to grasp the ropes, anxiously sought the warm depths of my pockets during those short moments when I was able to halt while the guide sought for the right way.

And so we descended, step by step, growing ever more doubtful of a happy issue, hastening where we could, spurred on by our anxiety. That headlong climb created a Matterhorn as yet unknown to me — a Matterhorn invisible, but tangible in its shape, in the smallest inequalities of its surface; and hands and feet groped for these and recognized them by sense of touch, and found the holds as if all my visual faculties were collected, by a phenomenal transfer of the senses, in my extremities.

We traversed the Crête du Coq, we passed close to the Cravate without seeing it. Each of us was thinking that if we could but reach the Grande Corde we were saved, but none had said so to the others; we were all silent now. Daniel led through the darkness with the wonderful precision of an old pilot, who knew well the perilous precipices of the Matterhorn.

Ah! the upper end of the Grande Corde at last! Down I slid along it — and there are about thirty-five yards of it — with boundless confidence; it was a regular leap down the precipice. A feeling of great strength and security had awoken in me; I hesitated no longer, I never made a false step; I was full of improvised stratagems, of incredible balancing feats, of leaps and halts of unheard of precision. I felt myself at that time the comrade of my guides, and not their 'Herr'. When man scents danger he becomes a man indeed, imbued with all the primitive excellence and valour of mankind;

brave as a small animal defending its life from a monster a hundred times bigger and stronger, impassive as the first man must have been, who won his livelihood among the obstacles of nature, as wild beasts do, who suffered and rejoiced, but perhaps did not as yet weep or laugh. In this hand-to-hand struggle with the mountain the sick man grows weak and apathetic; the strong man delights in the rough pleasures of the contest, and when he has succeeded in freeing himself from the monster's embraces he breathes as he has never breathed in his life before.

Little by little our eyes had grown accustomed to the darkness. After we had passed the Grande Corde there was some talk of lighting the lanterns, but I objected; I feared that their feeble glow would only make the darkness more profound, and that the lights and shadows dancing on the rocks would lead us astray. I did not even strike a match to see what time it was, yet I felt keenly enough the desire to do so; it was only when we were close to the Linceul that the reflected light from the snow allowed me to see the hands of my watch. We had taken little more than two hours from the summit to this point.

We entered the Vallon des Glaçons; this desolate couloir, which is dark even in the day time, was as black as a tomb. We groped our way across the *mauvais pas*, Heaven alone knows how; but as I brought my head against it with a fearful blow, we decided to light the lanterns, one at either end of the party. Time was required for this, because a breeze was blowing and the matches were damp, but at last the candle burnt with a tiny yellow flame. The scene changed; I once more saw by my side Daniel, whom I had not seen for more than an hour. Lighted up as he was from head to foot, his head wrapped in a handkerchief tied under his chin, he seemed to me a strange apparition, a man I did not know. Our range of vision was limited to a very few yards around us; I could see that only a few steps from me the rocks fell away into a dark abyss.

But my strange guide was already on the move, rapidly descending into the chasm with his lantern swinging to and fro as he held it in his hand; I followed close behind him, seeking the benefit of the light, like a moth round a lamp. From behind I felt a violent jerk at the rope and heard an oath; I turned round and out of the tail of my eye I saw the other lantern waving fantastically among the dark crags, together with other strange human forms. If the shepherds of Breuil had seen these tiny lights wandering along the arête, they would have thought them to be restless spirits in torment; but at that hour the shepherds were peacefully sleeping on their couches of hay.

A great confusion of ideas was beginning to form in my head; it was due to the mental distortion which comes to him who goes wearily by night. I saw holds where the rock was really smooth, and where there was a spot to place my foot I saw an empty space; sudden gleams of light dazzled my eyes; the rocks took on grotesque shapes of savage outline, like gaping jaws or fallen statues or open tombs, and among these ruins we hurried like men afraid; for an instant I thought I saw the roof of a distant house. . . .

'L'ancienne cabane' said a voice, and a few steps brought us up against an abandoned refuge. Two more ropes to descend before reaching our goal; down, down, without rest. In the shelter of the couloir we had not noticed the cold, but as soon as we had turned the rocks of the Tower and regained the arête, we were exposed to a violent west wind, and I suddenly felt chilled through and through; the very recesses of my pockets were frozen. But Daniel flees onward like a spectre, and I after him. I heard the sound of the lantern striking against his axe, or against the rocks; the lantern shot downwards, then rose again, spreading light and shade about it, and its leaps to and fro suggested to me what gymnastic feats Daniel was performing. The spectre and the light disappeared suddenly, to become visible again further on; the man's dark, lean profile stood out in an aureole of light. I felt the rope pulling me from below and I plunged downwards. It was a real race down the precipice. But the desperate descent was ended; the wandering light had stopped. I came up to it and my hand touched a dark wall; it was a wooden one. Oh! how pleasant was the touch of smooth wood after so much rough rock! A little door opened to our push; I found myself in the hut. We had descended the Matterhorn in less than three hours. Daniel had lost his bet; we were safe.

THE WEST FACE (*from the Air*)
showing the Tyndallgrat, Carrel's Gallery and (below on the left) the Z'Mutt Nose

1. Furggen Ridge
2. Hörnli Ridge
3. Swiss Summit
4. Italian Summit
5. Italian Ridge
6. Carrel's Gallery

7-13. Z'mutt Ridge

8. Z'mutt Nose
9. Head of Great Couloir
10. Gendarme
11. Almost level stretch
12. Three teeth
13. Snow Ridge

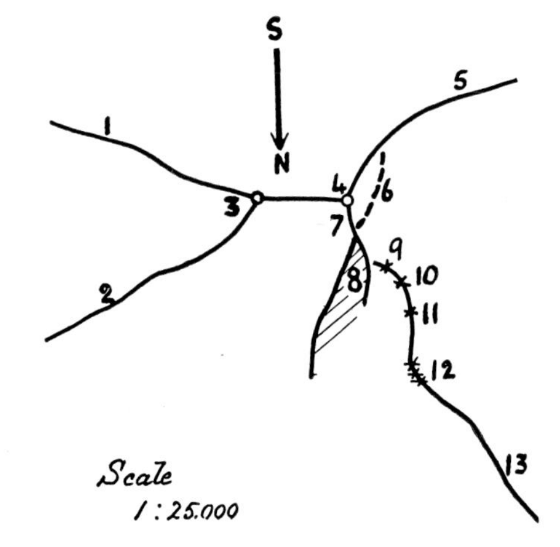

THE MATTERHORN (*from the Air*)
from the South-West

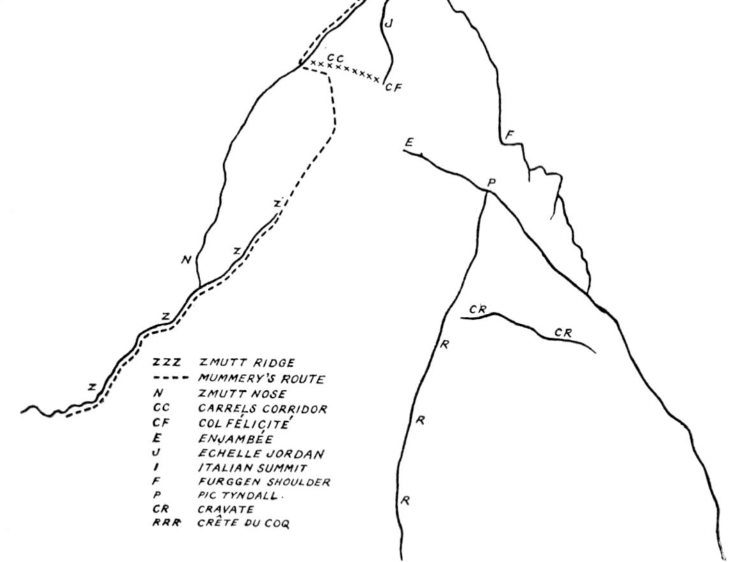

I cannot describe the feeling of relief, security, and peace which came over me as I entered. It was cold inside the hut; a thermometer would have indicated several degrees of frost, but to me the temperature seemed tepid compared with the cold outside. The two lanterns which in the open had given so poor a light, shone brilliantly inside between those narrow walls. Outside the wind rushed past in gusts with a roar like that of distant wagons being dragged over cobblestones; in the little hut complete quiet reigned. We were as if in our own home. Blessed hut! Blessed Alpine Club which built it!

Having crossed the threshold, untied the rope that had been on us for the last sixteen hours, and shaken from off our clothes and our boots the snow which had settled on them, we sat down and looked into one another's faces. Each of us was privately thinking of a good supper. Alas for our supper! Our sacks were empty, our bottles dry, firewood there was none. But by degrees we ordered our ideas. From the sack of one of the guides there issued a horrid piece of meat with more fat than lean, a few morsels of dry bread, and a squashed and shapeless slice of cheese. After searching in every corner of the hut, I found a paper packet containing — oh, blessed sight! — a small quantity of Neapolitan vermicelli. In the meantime Ange had recollected a secret hiding-place not far from the hut, unknown to all but himself, in which he had formerly concealed a little wood. We roped Ange, pushed him outside the door, and held him from inside the hut, paying out the rope gradually as he retired. Intense cold came in at the open door. In five minutes' time we received the order to pull on the rope, and at its extremity Ange reappeared, all numb with the cold, hugging in his arms a few precious pieces of wood. Very soon a fire was burning in the midst of smoke in the little stove, crackling cheerily and slowly melting the snow in the saucepan.

Round the fire we all four sat silently, in pleasant familiarity, and warmed our hands and feet. Not a word passed concerning our late adventures; we only watched with breathless interest the fat of our meat and the cheese melting in the boiling water, while a delicate odour of dishwater was wafted about the little hut. At length we were able to pour out the pale, thin broth, in which floated sparsely the vermicelli and a few streaks of cheese. The whole tasted of smoke; down in the valley we should have given the soup to a dog, but up there every one pronounced it a *chef-d'œuvre.* Two dried prunes, which I had in my pocket, completed the feast, and after this we went to bed.

As I wrapped my feet in one of the fur rugs that are in the hut, I noticed written on the back a few initials and the name of Jordan, a well-known one in the early pages of the history of the Matterhorn. He had presented that rug for the old refuge on the Cravate; from there it had been brought down to the hut at the Tower, and thence again down here. It had been for more than thirty years on the Matterhorn, and it seemed to me that it might, perhaps, have been wrapped round Giordano's feet during the five nights he spent on the mountain in the primitive refuge. Oh! progress enough had been made between that day and this, and this time I considered that progress, in the shape of our excellent hut, was not without its advantages.

Outside the wind howled at intervals through the clefts in the rocks; the Matterhorn slept a troubled sleep that night. I, my feet now warm, and wrapped in the historic rug, myself buried under the excellent coverings, was enjoying a sense of complete ease and comfort. I was not sleepy, but I was filled with desire to laugh at something — at anything, provided I might but laugh. I wished to chat with my guides, to tell them tales, but they were already sleeping soundly. Then I thought how delightful it was not to have to spend the night in the open, on the rocks of the Matterhorn, and during this my first hour's rest I reviewed the impressions received during the day — the impressions that were destined to remain indelibly stamped upon my memory.

Each one of our expeditions is fixed in our minds by some characteristic of its own; we may have forgotten all that occurred throughout the day, but some given episode, some spot, will ever recur to our memory, and always under the same aspect and with the same marvellous clearness. We remember one ascent by the cold we suffered in a bivouac, and by a splendid sunrise; another by a precipitous place where we watched for three hours a continuous rain of falling stones; another, again, by a cornice of snow which broke and fell away just as we were about to set foot upon it. Perhaps these were the moments in which the greatest number of emotions filled our minds, and so the name alone of the ascent reawakens in us in all its intensity the feeling we had then, and this even after many years. The sight of the cap we wore, the smell of the leather covering that protected our camera on that day, the taste of a prune, like those we turned about in our parched mouth during those hours of fasting, seem to take us back, as by magic, to those places, and to cause us to live again for an instant through those far-off times.

Perhaps I shall never forget the aesthetic emotions produced in me by the majestic circular chasm of Tiefenmatten and the fearful Z'Mutt face, nor the joy of the slow ascent, nor the curiosity I felt in ascending a Matterhorn that was free from huts and uncontaminated by ropes;[5] but the silent flight from the summit, the strange descent in clouds and darkness, our haste to reach our goal, my delight at touching the hut, will ever remain in the deepest recesses of my soul. It seems to me that it was only from that night onward that I really knew the Matterhorn. I had not seen the difficulties, I had touched them, and in the mental concentration produced by the darkness every rock had made itself felt by me.

That very evening I was reminded of this by my knees, which ached with the many blows they had received, and by my burning, skin-stripped hands. After a long rock climb the tips of the fingers, owing to the continual friction against the roughness of the rock, are reduced to a most delicate and sensitive condition, and are covered with little red spots like pin-pricks, so that touching the board of a table seems like stroking soap, and a glass feels like a piece of ice. For several days I carried these marks; my hands bore the peculiar, strong odour of the rocks; I took about with me in the pores of my skin, as in my soul, an infinitesimal part of the Matterhorn.

Our night in the hut was a cold one. We awoke before the dawn; I felt the frost in spite of the furs and rugs in which I was wrapped. The weather was very bad, the sky overcast; it was one of those days when the end of the world seems near, and when it appears as if the sun will never rise. A bitter wind was blowing, and sheets of drifting snow appeared from time to time; the hut and the rocks were covered with a coating of frozen snow that made them look like silver. We must needs wait till the cold had grown less before we could descend. The guides swallowed the warmed-up remains of our soup; I had not the courage to join them. Nine o'clock came; the wind had dropped, so we decided to start. I came out of the hut wrapped up as if I were starting for the North Pole; I had put on everything I had with me in my sack. The rocks and ropes were coated with ice, and therefore dangerous; we took more than an hour to reach the Col du Lion. The prospect was infinitely dreary: down in the valley all was dark; above our heads was one unbroken black pall; some opaque, whitish clouds, full of menace, floated about between us and the depths below, while a few hovered motionless above the hollow valleys.

On a morning drear as this, but far more terrible, Carrel the Bersagliere had left the hut at the Tower for his last descent, which came to an end not far below the Col, after a night and a day of fearful struggle, near a rock by which there now stands a cross. Ten years have passed since then. The pilgrims of the Matterhorn stop reverently before that rock. It was there that the old soldier, weary after his last desperate battle, his strength all gone, was laid by his comrades; it was there that he died.[6] Perhaps in the visions of his last moment he heard once more the trumpets sounding on the Colle di San Martino, and the shouts of victory on the conquered Matterhorn; these were the two glories of his life. Or perhaps his mind grew suddenly dark, and he was not even conscious of his own heroism which had saved his companions on that last descent. Such was the end of the long contest between the mountaineer and his mountain; a contest that lasted thirty years, full of ardent deeds of daring and of passive defence, of hard-won victories, and of defeats that were glorious as any victory. Carrel had ceased to conquer: his weapons were worn out with long use, blunt with age, and no longer served the valour and experience of the ancient warrior. The Matterhorn watched its opportunity and dealt him his death-blow. But popular rumour immediately lent a noble shape to the image of the first of the Matterhorn guides: 'Carrel did not fall; he died', they said in his native valley, and Carrel endured in legend invincible as he had lived.

No fairer death than this could have come to the conqueror of the Matterhorn. When I left that cross behind me, I think I looked upon my guides with a deeper feeling of affection and gratitude than before.

CHAPTER VI

THE FURGGEN RIDGE OF THE MATTERHORN

I REMEMBER as if it were a dream — a very vivid one, but still a dream — being in the courtyard of the Hôtel de Londres at Châtillon, when I saw, seated on a green bench, two men who were known to me. One of them was strongly built, stout, bronzed in face and rough in aspect, while the other was an aristocratic-looking man, with delicate features, a fine white skin, and a somewhat pallid countenance. They were smiling at me, and seemed as surprised to see me as I was to see them. They were Antonio Castagneri, the guide, and Count Humbert of Villanova, the climber, both of them my friends. We greeted one another with much cordiality, and they immediately told me that they were waiting for Jean Joseph Maquignaz from Valtournanche, and that they were all going up the Aosta Valley together to attempt a great ascent, which, however, they did not name.

Although Castagneri saw me armed with axe and rope, he did not inquire my destination; he simply told me that he knew it, and, drawing me aside, in a mysterious manner he traced with his finger a line that rose from my right shoulder to the top of my head, crossed it, and fell precipitously on to the other shoulder. He then stood and gazed fixedly at me, with smiling eyes full of kindliness and roguish fun, as if to ask me whether he had guessed aright. Indeed, he had guessed rightly! But how had he managed to find out? I had concealed my plan from everyone, for I realized how ambitious a one it was. How had he guessed it? Had he read an unwonted excitement in my eyes? Was it an unconscious suggestion from my mind to his? Meanwhile he repeatedly urged me to be careful, by means of certain dubious shakes of his head. I tried to baffle him as best I could, and I begged him to take good care of my friend and to lead him to a successful ascent.

Shortly after we said goodbye, for I was in a hurry to start. Before reaching Moulins, on the way to Valtournanche, I met Maquignaz coming down to meet the others, pipe in mouth, freshly shaven and cleanly clad. He looked as if he were going to a *fête*. He gave me a grave and courteous salute, we exchanged a few words, then shook hands, and he passed on. This was the last time he was to descend his native valley; I never saw either him or the other two again. A few days after I learnt that they had mysteriously disappeared on Mont Blanc.

I do not know why it is, but the figures of these men are as indelibly impressed on my mind as are the troubled figures we see in dreams, and every time I enter the courtyard of the Hôtel de Londres I seem to see those two brave men sitting on the bench and smiling at me, and to feel the pressure of Castagneri's powerful finger tracing the mysterious line upon my shoulder; and whenever I walk up to Valtournanche, in fancy I meet old Jean Joseph at the same spot with his pipe in his mouth, serenely descending his native valley for the last time, with all the vigour of a second youth. And now, when I compare the reality of what I saw with the imagined details of the subsequent tragedy, it feels to me as if the two I met were the ghosts of my friends, and as if the guide's smile contained at the time a touch of bitterness, whilst the pale, refined face of the climber expressed resignation to fate; as if old Maquignaz's grave salute were that of a wise man who knew that he was starting for a place whence there was no return. But more than ten years have passed since then, and it is so hard to distinguish between that which is real and that which is a dream in our lives, when grave and terrible events stir our emotions!

I went up the valley to attempt my secret climb, which was to be that ridge of the Matterhorn which rises from the Furggenjoch and faces south-east. It is the shortest and steepest[1] of the four arêtes of the pyramid, and it had remained unconquered; in fact, I think that after Mummery's attempt to scale it in 1880, it had not occurred to any climber or any guide to attempt it — to any guide, I say, except Daniel and Antoine Maquignaz, with whom I had agreed to try it.

I have described elsewhere[2] my adventures on that ridge, my three assaults delivered within a week, the nights spent on the Col and on the arête; my anxieties, my hopes, my bitter disappointment, and the terrible shower of stones which lasted three hours, catching us at a very great height, and finally obliging us to give up the attempt. Then I related my adventures but concealed my feelings, which I considered too intense to be mentioned. I had come down wounded and exhausted; at the time I thought my desire was quenched for ever, and I wrote to the *Rivista Mensile* a prudent declaration meant to convince myself and others of the folly of the attempt, and I said, using a phrase which I thought a happy one, that 'reason had at last overcome passion in me', and that 'neither I nor my guides would ever try again'. Possibly I was not believed at the time, though I spoke in good faith, and would have taken my oath on my assertion; but certain declarations should not be put down in black and white. And now, whenever I think of all my efforts and struggles to ascend the Matterhorn by that blessed arête, I cannot help fancying that the guide's finger, as it traced that mysterious line above my head, must have cast a spell upon me; and that the brave Castagneri wished before he died to commit me irrevocably to the Furggen ridge of the Matterhorn.

After my first attempts I tried to forget, but could not; the old longing would keep returning to me at intervals, when I least expected it, and with increasing importunity. How could I hope to forget, when that devil of a Matterhorn is so clearly visible from everywhere? If I went up to Superga, and put up my glass, I saw it through the lens, towering above the smaller hills that the distance had tinged dark blue; if I went into the mountains and dared show my head over the top of a pass, there it was again, beyond a line of valleys or behind a chain of peaks, its gigantic summit at one time white with snow, at another enveloped in a long headdress of wind-driven cloud.

It seemed to me to raise itself on tiptoe above the shoulders of the other giants, that it might look at me and mock me. But far or near it was always the same, straight and sharp and full of defiance, so different from all other mountains, so proud, so beautiful!

And that knife-edged eastern ridge, springing in three bounds to the summit, looked so short and easy, when seen from a distance.

Each time I looked upon it afresh two different kinds of feelings awoke imperatively in me; they were chagrin at my defeat and curiosity concerning the unknown. The question, What lay beyond the point I had reached? recurred persistently; it gave me no peace. How was the mountain fashioned beyond? One day – six years had passed since my first attempt – the question presented itself to me so clearly, demanding an answer so imperiously, that I hastened awestruck to my friend Vaccarone and made the great proposal to him. He saw that mine was a soul in torment, destined to wander up and down the Furggen ridge until such time as someone, ascending by that route, should have redeemed it from its sentence. And my good friend came with me. We thought we would try the descent instead of the ascent; we climbed to the summit by another route, as if to take the mountain by surprise; but on that day the weather was bad, and the abundance of snow made the rocks difficult. Our guides, whom we had not selected in the Aosta Valley, would not be persuaded. We returned without giving battle.

The disappointment produced by this pusillanimous attempt cured me of my desire for a time; my spirit seemed to be healed.

Ideas come slowly to maturity. If unhealthy they fall untimely from the parent bough; if healthy, they take on shape and colour, and one fine day we find, to our surprise and joy, that they are ripe.

But it is necessary that the idea should have hung long on its parent bough, and that it should be nourished with the best sap of our thoughts.

One morning in 1899 I awoke with the fixed idea in my mind that I was to make the ascent during that same year; this notion was inexorable – as a duty to be performed. At first I looked upon the matter with the calm eye of one who is familiar with the subject and without fear; I had six months before me. But as the time for putting the enterprise into execution gradually drew nigh, I was assailed by fresh doubts. That thought became my *bête noire*, which was always watching me at my work and speaking to me when I was thinking;

when I was in the company of my friends it sat importunate between me and them, and prevented my listening to their conversation. When I turned homewards, it was there awaiting me at my door, ready to spring upon me, for it knew that when alone I was weaker and less courageous. Often I found it comfortably seated at my desk reading a book. I knew that book, because I had so often read it myself: it was the story of the ascent of the Matterhorn, written by Whymper; and the *bête noire* with a fiendish smile would point to a chapter entitled 'The Seventh Attempt'.

'The brave Whymper made seven attempts to succeed, while you have only made three. For shame!' it would say to me.

Then it would open Mummery's book at the place where he describes his attack on the Furggen ridge: 'See how you may cover yourself with glory', it said, 'by conquering a ridge where another, and he one of the best, failed.'

There was no argument that the astute *bête* did not use to tempt me.

At night, when I was in bed, its presence was a torment to me; in my sleep I saw it more clearly than when I was awake, and it took on grotesque, ever-changing shapes, appearing at one time as a dark pyramid of enormous height, at another as an evil man who dragged me up a knife-edged ridge, up to a point where I seemed to have been already, long before; above it rose a dark, inaccessible wall of rock, whilst all around stones fell hissing through the air.

There my guide would stop and grin. He never led me any further, for dreams create nothing new.

Then I would fain have uttered, like Doctor Faust, the terrible exorcism of Incubus! Incubus!

I would seize the Gospel, the Gospel written by myself, in which appeared the wise words: 'Neither you nor your guides shall ever try again', and in which there was talk of the victory of wisdom over passion. . . .

It was all nonsense! Even I myself no longer believed in it. I decided to get rid of my terrible *bête noire* once for all; with resolute energy I took up my pen and wrote to my guides, to engage them definitely for the ascent in question.

While I wrote the *bête noire* assumed a benign aspect, it already looked upon me with respect, and directly I had dropped the letter in the post-box it disappeared.

It was only later that I became aware that whereas it had previously lived outside me, from that moment onward it had entered and freely taken up its abode in my brain.

In my letter to the guides I had made use of all the arts of suggestion which had served to convince myself. I had worked upon their feelings of patriotism, of local pride, and of personal *amour propre*.

I had pointed out that it was the duty of Italian guides — of Valtournanche guides, nay, of guides who bore the glorious name of Maquignaz — to make that ascent, the only one on the Matterhorn that was still virgin, that it would redound to their honour and profit. The guides to whom I had applied were the same pair who had accompanied me on my first attempts, and who had sworn with me never to try again. They agreed to come with me. It was settled that they should go up and examine at close quarters the unexplored part of the route, and report to me.

I bought 200 yards of rope, and sent it to Valtournanche. I hung a cross-bar to the ceiling of my little room, and exercised my arms at great length every day, for I knew that on the climb my arms would be much more in use than my legs; and I waited impatiently for news from my guides.

At last there came a letter from Antoine giving me, as his custom was, a short report, and ending with these words: 'Tenez vous prêt à partir, par télégramme.'

Ready to start! The idea! I had been ready for six months, and I had been yearning for this moment for the last ten years.

That letter threw me into a terrible state of excitement. I was anxious to start at once, to be up close to the difficulties, to see them and grapple with them. But now that which I had longed for was near at hand, I felt a sense of fear; yes, indeed, of fear. The project seemed to me a dangerous one, my strength inadequate.

I had never been assailed by such feelings before, and I caught myself endeavouring to cast them out of my mind by the help of other thoughts more terrible still of distant mountains enormous in height and perilous to the last degrees — Ushba, Kanchenjunga, and other monsters of their kind. I told myself that I was a fool to be thus agitated, but my heart beat more quickly for all that! No one in the world was acquainted with my secret, and this troubled me.

One evening I whispered it to a trusty friend, just as if I were confessing a crime I was about to commit. Would that I had not, for my friend shook his head and entreated me to be careful. This was not what I wanted. I was never before in such a haste for time to pass as during those days; I think that if the devil himself had come to ask for my soul in exchange for that ascent, I would have given it to him.

Such was my state of mind when the postman one day handed me a telegram.

I looked dubiously before opening it at the little square bit of paper with my name on it; I knew that it contained my sentence.

I plucked up courage and tore open the envelope; the telegram contained one word only: '*Venez*'.

A wave of joy impetuously flooded my heart.

Farewell to doubt, to hesitation, to fear!

All these vanished, and a sense of profound peace stole over me. I was like one who, having prayed long and fervently with bent head before the image of a saint, raises his eyes and thinks he sees the head of the stone image bending in sign of assent, and thenceforth feels certain that the boon he asks shall be granted to him.

I had waited so long! And the word was, 'Come'. It was the epilogue to my ardent, long-felt desire, to my rigorous preparation; it was the consequence of the decision taken months before, which had cost me such an effort of will. . . .

In the joy of that moment I rushed to the cross-bar hung up in my bedroom, and I climbed up its ropes to the ceiling four or five times with my arms alone. Yes; my muscles were in good training and worked well.

I was satisfied.

I picked up the yellow paper again and read a host of things into the letters of the one short word. I read that the guides had climbed to a great height, that they had discovered the secret of the route, and had seen close at hand the beyond which had caused me such anxious thought. It did not tell me as yet that the ascent was possible, but it did say that the attempt was possible.

I was tempted to tell all men, to cry aloud my hopes, to make my departure known. I kept the secret, and on the following day I dined at the Jomein.

The secret! It is easier to keep it in the city than in a little Alpine village. Even while I was driving up the valley it seemed to me that it was already divulged, and that men looked upon me with curiosity.

As I passed through the village I saw that every one knew; from behind a half-open door a great brown man was watching me, in whom I thought I recognized a guide who had contested the Pointe Blanche with me two years before. He was certainly not praying for my victory.

I saw another guide seated in the shade and smoking a pipe.

'You wish to climb that arête,' he said when he saw me, 'but you will not succeed.'

Immediately afterwards I met my own guides, Daniel, Antoine, and Aimé, who filled me with comfort. They gave me a full report of their reconnaissance, and said that they had hopes; the mountain was in good condition, but there was no time to be lost.

I looked searchingly in their faces, and they seemed to me to be easy in their minds.

But who can read the countenance of a mountaineer? I was calm, I even cried out upon myself for being so free from agitation on that day.

Perhaps my mind was by then sated with emotion, perhaps my brain was empty as a lodging that is free to receive a new tenant. My impatience had ceased; I could almost have wished for a day's rest in the excellent Jomein hotel, with the good company it contained.

There is nothing pleasanter than the day before a long-expected day.

But it was necessary to hasten our departure.

I ordered the provisions and arranged the plan of battle with the guides.

Daniel was to ascend to the summit by another route, with two men and much rope, so as to descend the Furggen ridge as far as possible, and throw down a long rope to us (Antoine, Aimé, and me), who were to come up the ridge; and the same night, while the whole hotel slept, I started.

'To-morrow evening at this hour?'

This is the only entry in my travelling note-book under that date.

'Io dico seguitando ch'assai prima Che noi fussimo al piè dell'alta torre Gli occhi nostri n'andar suso alla cima.' *Inferno*, VIII.	'I say continuing, that, long before we reached the foot of the high tower, our eyes went upwards to its summit.'

We three diminutive human beings, seated on the snow at the foot of the mighty Matterhorn, consumed our cold and frugal repast by the first uncertain light of the morning (at the base of the Furggen ridge, close to the Breuiljoch). I was resignedly and unwillingly satisfying a non-existent appetite after my five hours' night march.

In the mountains one must eat when one has time to do so; one never knows how things may turn out afterwards.

From that low level we could see nothing but the immense grooves of the wall in the shadow, and the last shining stars growing pale in the sky.

I gave way for an instant to the delights of sleep, that overmastering sleep which comes upon one at dawn after a sleepless night, unyielding and heavy as the rocks which lay about me.

But Antoine shook me. There was no time for sleep. 'We will sleep all right this evening,' he said.

'Where shall we sleep this evening?' I asked, yawning, and stiff from the morning chill. I had almost forgotten where I was and whither I was going.

Our side of the mountain was still dark as we climbed the first pitch, which is so difficult that it seems to have been put there where the ascent begins, as a warning to the imprudent and a barrier to the unskilled.

It is the gate of entrance to the Furggen ridge, and the dark words written on the gate of Avernus might be inscribed on the rock: 'Ogni viltà convien che qui sia morta.'

But when we reached the ridge, we looked beyond and saw the great east face all covered with the morning light and the peaks of the Oberland shining in the distance, and the bottoms of the valleys suffused with a rosy half-light that was a reflection of the first flush in the sky. And my glance swept eagerly up the face of the Matterhorn, whose summit was already aglow. The whole vast face of the mountain between the Furggen and the Hörnli ridges was exposed to our view. I could take in its whole expanse with one glance, and seen thus obliquely from below its height seemed to be diminished.

Hosts of memories that the years had lulled to sleep returned to me. I was no longer sleepy; the high mountain breeze played soothingly on my face, which felt cool and wholesome, as if I had dipped it into ice-cold water as soon as I had awaked.

There was a wondrous silence; our voices rang out strangely and crisply in that vast space. And as we gradually rose higher, the grand lines of the mountain's architecture were displayed to us in all their splendour as they sprang in their strength and daring up to the summit of the structure.

This eastern slope of the Matterhorn is built up of enormous, smooth, ruined steps, and appears, as seen from close at hand, like the dried-up bed of an immense waterfall that, springing from the summit of the mountain, and falling a thousand yards for a thousand years, has poured the weighty mass of its water on to these rocks, polishing them and wearing them away. But the cascade is not one of water, but of rocks, and the source of their supply is not exhausted. They start from above, from the top of the Matterhorn, as soon as the sunlight touches them, these unstable stones that are barely held in place by the frost of the night; and instantly the mighty dried-up bed becomes a practice ground on which the Matterhorn exercises its artillery, the finest artillery in the world.

And the ground is furrowed by the shells and the rock in places is shattered by the shock, and worn smooth by the continual passage of the missiles. The practice ground is almost perpendicular, and is

THREE OF REY'S COMPANIONS

1. Ange Maquignaz 2. Ugo de Amicis 3. Aimé Maquignaz

ALEXANDER BURGENER

he led Mummery up the Z'Mutt and Furggen Ridges

Looking up the Furggen Ridge
from near the Furgg-joch

4500 feet long. In 1890 I had witnessed one of these formidable practices, and I still remembered the awful grandeur of the spectacle.

I remembered the strange impression I had received from the smell of gunpowder which was prevalent that day, due to the shock of the falling stones as they were shattered against the solid rock, producing that odour of sulphur and saltpetre which the devil was said to leave behind him whenever he went by, in the days when people still believed in the devil.

But this morning the Matterhorn was quiet; the guides had known it would be so, otherwise they would not have come.

Up the ridge we went, keeping on its eastern side, climbing quickly, as one man.

It is a noble folly, this climbing to a height, a supreme delight, which would alone suffice to make life in the mountains fair and beautiful, were it not made so by a hundred other things. The day was coming on apace, it seemed to me that I was climbing up to the realms of light; and as I saw that the way was so free from falling stones, so unencumbered by ice or snow, and that the sky was so clear, hope entered my heart.

I was happy that the weather was perfect, that the Matterhorn was there in front of me, that I had it to myself, and that it gave no sign of life; happy that my legs were doing me good service, happy to feel so calm, to gaze freely round into space, to fill my lungs with the exhilarating air that purifies the blood and seems to lighten the weight of the body at every breath. Few words passed between us three, but those few were gay and light, the words of men who know no care.

Suddenly a whizzing sound disturbed the silence of the air; then a short, sharp crack like that of a whip struck our ears. We lifted our heads and looked inquiringly upwards. Another whiz, another sharp sound, which gave us the impression of something hard and dangerous passing close to us, invisible and swift.

I knew what it was: the little stones leaping from the summit at the first touch of the sun.

The ancient Matterhorn was jesting with us; we halted and looked anxiously around us. Nothing more came. It was a false alarm.

We resumed our ascent, which was exceedingly steep but not in the least difficult. This first part of the ridge, as far as the Shoulder, if in good condition, is no harder than the Hörnli ridge above the old hut, and is certainly easier than the Italian ridge above the Col du Lion.[3] We had reached without difficulty the first gendarme, which is about half-way up the ridge, and which is easily seen from Breuil, and is marked on its upper side by a small white snow patch.

I recognized this place as one where I had bivouacked nine years before, and I marvelled that three of us should have been able on that occasion to sleep in that narrow slit.

I remembered that Daniel's pipe had that night fallen to the bottom of the crack, and had remained there. I reckoned by my eye that we were on a level with the Little Matterhorn, which stood opposite to us, and that we were therefore at a height of 11,700 feet.

Antoine told me that a few days before, during his reconnaissance with Daniel, he had again slept in this place; and in fact there was still a little wood and a saucepan. We lit a fire and we rested while some wine was being warmed up, and talked of Daniel's pipe, which was at the bottom of the crack, irrecoverably lost.

In the meantime the sun rose, and with the sun there came a strong, cold wind from the north, so keen as to penetrate our clothes; it really seemed as if we had none on. Instantly, owing to the change from the rapidity with which we had hitherto moved, and our present immobility, I felt thoroughly chilled. For an instant I thought I should lose consciousness, and my life seemed hardly worth a penny's purchase. But when I had drunk a draught of hot wine I regained my strength, and even fancied that the short moment of physical and moral torpor had rested me.

Climbers are not wont to tell of their moments of weakness; not that they wish to conceal their frailty, but because in the final joy of victory their troubles and their exertions are forgotten.

And I too should have forgotten this little incident; I should have imagined that I had never been so strong and so gay as I was then, had I not later found these three entries in my note-book: 'Moment of weakness; hot wine; recovery.'

What is certain is that I took good care not to confess my condition to my guides, lest I should lessen the confidence which it was so important for them to feel in me that day; but I here honestly set down my slight lapse, as I desire to be candid.

The climber is not made of iron; a momentary physical weakness may assail any one, even a guide.

If the climber had not the frailty of a man, he could not realize the hardness of the mountain, he could not enjoy the sense of contrast which comes from his feeling the great disproportion between his own strength and the enormous strength of his adversary—a contrast which is perhaps, one of the deepest-seated causes of his passion.[4]

We started on again.

The warm sun was kissing the cold rock, and what little water there was burst its slender bonds of ice and melted with secret gurglings.

This was the mountain's first joyous cry as it awoke.

The completeness of my recovery made me throb with fresh vigour and with fresh impatience. I consulted the barometer every instant, as a man who is sick of a fever eagerly uses his thermometer. Rising rapidly from cliff to cliff, without encountering any great difficulty, we reached a second tower on the ridge; and the face had already narrowed like the bed of a river near its source, and had assumed the form of a hollow channel, the centre of whose curve enclosed snowy strips of extreme steepness.

On bad days this channel is swept by stones falling from the summit. I had once crossed it at the double under a hail of stones, and I now saw on the opposite side the rope which we had abandoned in our flight; it had been hanging from the rock since the day when our first attempt had failed, and the sight of it once more, slender as it was, and bleached by the sun of nine summers and the frost of as many winters, filled me with a feeling of profound discouragement. And yet that slender rope had saved us then in our hasty retreat before the threatening stones that whizzed through the air.

And it was with the most intense curiosity that I looked once more upon the rock in the centre of the channel, under which we had taken shelter, as in a safe casemate, for three long hours that day, while the Matterhorn bombarded us from above.

This year all was still; the rocks were free from snow, and on the top of the Matterhorn we saw no signs of those enormous icicles which then were hanging from its head, like a long white beard of ice. On this day the Matterhorn was brown.

We left the protecting rock on our right. The slope grew steeper; our hands now began to assist our legs; we climbed as it were a roof of slate, smooth and fearfully steep.

We reached the top of the third tower, the last on the ridge, and we named it the Furggen Shoulder.[6] At this point the huge buttress which rises from the Breuiljoch and supports the summit of the Matterhorn comes to an end against the final peak.

The architecture of the structure grew simpler; the ribs of the lateral grooves ran into the main wall and disappeared; only the final straight, smooth spire remained, rising majestically, in a last leap, to heaven; the daring, unparalleled creation of a superhuman architect. We were at about 14,000 feet above sea-level, and higher than the Pic Tyndall, which was visible from this point. So far all had gone well; the climb had been neither easy nor difficult; it was one of those on which an active climber can manage by himself, without looking for help to his guides or the rope. We had as a matter of fact reached this point from the Jomein in twelve hours.

Probably Mummery had come as far as this in his attempt in 1880; so far my guides had come in their recent reconnaissance. Beyond us was the unknown, the unexplored, dark, smooth, and perpendicular wall of the last cliff, which, as seen thus from below, seemed about to fall upon us. It was an old tower whose worn walls had been explored only by the lightning and touched only by the wings of eagles and crows.

Mummery considered it so formidable that he did not attempt to go any further, but preferred to make a dangerous traverse along the base of the peak, by which he reached the ordinary route on the Swiss ridge. It happened that he, like myself, made his attempt without proper preparation; this is not an ascent which can be carried out by ordinary methods.

As I scanned the wall I could not, near though I was, make out any practicable route up the smooth rocks; yet the guides were talking of a hidden chimney, by which the ascent was, they thought, possible, and they pointed out its base to me 120 or 130 feet above. By that time we supposed that Daniel's party must have reached the summit, and would shortly come over the top and down towards us, as far as a point high above our heads, whence they would let down the rope to us. We climbed up to a small platform about sixty feet above the Shoulder, and there I crouched with my back against the Matterhorn and my face turned to the mighty Furggen precipice. The guides left me there and climbed down to the Shoulder again, in order to see Daniel and his men, from that snowy buttress, as they reached the appointed place. From my lofty perch I could see Antoine and Aimé on the white terrace of the Shoulder, continually raising their heads aloft towards the spot whence help was to descend; though they were, perhaps, only about a hundred feet from me, they looked very tiny on that enormous pedestal. I photographed them and obtained a view like those one gets in a balloon ascent. And, indeed, I was as if hanging in a balloon car; I could see nothing but distant objects; the precipice fell away with marvellous steepness at my feet, and its base was hidden from me. Beyond the spur of the Shoulder was an immense void; the spur concealed the whole ridge up which we had come, and beyond it the chasm was so deep that my glance was able to travel unchecked along the utmost limits of the horizon from the Breithorn to the Mischabel. The huge glaciers of Monte Rosa, as seen from this lofty spot, assumed the appearance of a distant landscape in the moon, viewed through a telescope. The remoteness of those gigantic glaciers and the lack of objects of comparison near at hand gave me the impression of being at so great a height that I felt as if I were on a level with the sun. When I turned my head and looked upwards, I could see nothing but an endless stretch of vertical wall and the cloudless sky. One precipice fell away at my feet and another rose above me. I had now been so long without moving that I was cold, in spite of the sun's rays which were beating upon me. The guides, from their post, kept gazing upwards, and from time to time they shouted, like a sentry giving the alarm. But no sign came from above. In the mountains much patience is needed. When I consider that I was crouching in that sublime spot for nearly two hours, I fail to realize what my thoughts were and to analyse my state of mind during that time, which, moreover, seemed no more than an instant. I fancy that my boundless curiosity had been replaced by a kind of stupor that paralysed all my powers of thought. One alone of my senses had become exceedingly acute — my hearing; all my desires had become concentrated in my ear that awaited the signal.

After an hour and a half we heard a distant voice, which seemed to fall from heaven. We answered. Antoine and Aimé moved along the ridge, talking together with excited gestures; they had seen their companions from below, and long consultations now began between my pair and the mysterious men who were perched up aloft, vertically above me and invisible to me.

I did not doubt that the work of preparation was going on vigorously up there; that the rope which was to support us all throughout our whole ascent was being fixed firmly to the rock by means of an iron stanchion, and lowered in such a way as to hang down the chimney as desired. It is not easy to direct the movements of a rope a hundred yards long among the rough grooves of the mountain-side.

But I was not able to see these preparations.

At last the end of a rope appeared not far above my head; it was descending silently, as if it were a small snake crawling treacherously towards me with strange halts, leaps, and writhings.

It seemed to be alive; then it stopped a few yards from me. It was the thread that was to guide us out of the Minotaur's cave.

My guides had now left their post of observation, and were climbing up to rejoin me.

They spoke to me; 'Nous allons,' they said, and tied me very tightly to our own rope, leaving a great length between each of us. At last we were beginning the ascent, we were entering on the new part of the route, where no one had been before; our long-standing curiosity was about to be satisfied.

But I was free from emotion. I was in the grasp of a kind of calm fatalism. It was not courage, but an absolute inability to think of fear. In such moments as these I think one part of our minds, perhaps the wiser part, disappears, in order not to witness what the other is about to do. Antoine went first; he soon reached the end of the great rope, grasped it resolutely, and was not long in vanishing from our sight.

Then came Aimé's turn; I watched him climbing with hands and feet, and helping himself with the rope, but I could not understand how he managed to ascend.

I too approached the great rope, and heard the order to start. I hastily removed my gloves so that my hands might get a better grip; our own rope which bound me to Aimé became taut; my turn had come; I too began my attack. The first piece was a broken chimney with narrow sides, with rare holds of little value, since the strata of the rock trended downwards. I ascended, feeling with my feet for the knobs, one hand grasping the rock as best it could, and the other almost always clutching the great rope. The cross-bar exercises I had worked at before leaving home stood me in good stead at this juncture. But in my bedroom I had not had that little Furggen precipice at my feet. Such gymnastics were new to me, but I was doing my duty calmly and with the great strength that zeal imparts.

The sky was deep blue, the sun was shining, the new mode of climbing interested me. I whistled between my teeth a gay refrain which I had heard in town a few evenings before, and which had remained in my memory, I do not know why. But the narrow sides of the chimney were growing smoother, and at times, for lack of holds, I had to ascend by planting the soles of my boots against the rock and pulling myself up the rope by sheer strength of arm; on these occasions my body made a right angle with the wall, and swayed in rather an alarming manner. Being the last on the rope, I had no one to show me where to put my fingers or plant my feet. Antoine was leading and I never once saw him; of Aimé, who was next above me, all I saw most of the time was the nailed soles and heels of his boots scraping against the rock, and he was too busy to afford me any advice or assistance, except by holding the rope tight whenever I asked him to do so.

My axe, which was slung on to my arm, swung about confoundedly; the iron part pecked at my face, and the wooden became entangled with my legs. In some way or another I managed to ascend this piece and reached a spot where a few inches of protruding rock admitted of a short halt, during which I took breath with much satisfaction, but at each gasp the notes of the tune I had heard in town still issued from my chest against my will.

Everyone who is accustomed to long walks by himself is familiar with the strange persistence of some musical snatches that, after suddenly coming into the head somewhere on the way, cannot be suppressed. At first they seem a pleasant pastime, a relief from the silence of the walk, and you sing aloud, but by degrees they grow wearisome, you tire of them, you would be rid of them, but you are forced to repeat them softly. You close your mouth to prevent them from coming out, and they still sing inside you. You cannot free yourself, and the most beautiful musical airs thus become as odious as the sound of a barrel-organ in the courtyard of your house. The foolish refrain had that day already been with me on the lower part of the ascent, when I was still walking, and had forced me to sing it, my panting lungs beating time to it.

But up here, where all regularity had disappeared both from my gait and my breathing, it ran on disjointedly, without rhythm; and my muscular efforts, the jerks of the taut rope, and the shocks my body received as it came into contact with the rocks, imparted a mad emphasis to it; it was a debauched, savage kind of music, born of hell. Edgar Poe could perhaps describe the anguish of that struggle between a man hanging by a rope over a precipice and a musical *motif* relentlessly pursuing him.

And it was no place for singing.

Our route was growing more and more difficult. We had emerged from the chimney by which we had ascended the first 100 feet or so, and the slight assistance its sides had afforded us was now at an end. We were now on the rounded face of the cliff, and we were ascending the vertical route indicated to us by the great rope. I was suffering from a mad desire to call out to Antoine and ask him how things were going, but I dared not. And there, last on our rope, all alone (for so I seemed to be) I swung from side to side, as I ascended by means of struggles, contortions, and efforts of which I should have thought myself incapable. My hands tightly gripped the rope and struck violently against the rock, my feet kicked uncertainly in space, and from my lips there issued terrible curses at every blow I received. My hands were ungloved and numb with the cold, and I remember relinquishing the rope first with one and then with the other, in order to bring them to my mouth and warm them with my breath; then up again with both hands, and another step was won.

And I was under the illusion that I was acting on my own account, that I was overcoming the difficulties with my own energy alone, and I was proud of the thought. Men are wont in the difficult situations of their lives to think that they are acting on their own initiative, and conquering by their own unaided valour, whereas invisible threads are really supporting and moving them.

The wire-puller's box is hidden above. My wire-puller, the trusty Aimé, made me perform feats that day whose like was never attempted by the most disjointed harlequin on the little stage of the Lupi theatre. But the feeling of loneliness weighed upon me; at times I instinctively turned to look for some companion behind me, and I saw nothing but the sheer precipice, full of emptiness. I marvelled to find myself thus alone and in the rear; I thought it monstrous to advance thus at such a distance from one another; not to be able to exchange a word, not to see each other's faces, not to look into each other's eyes. I was aware of my companion's presence only by means of the vibrating rope, which squeezed my chest; but it was not the rope only which vibrated and united us — the hearts of our little party beat strongly and in unison with those of the invisible men who had been stationed up aloft for so many hours, at the mysterious head of the thread on which our lives depended.

Daniel told me some days afterwards that at that part of our climb a large stone had moved at his feet on the little platform where the rope was tied to an iron stanchion; the mass was about to fall, and would have come down sheer upon us, when Daniel, whose hands were guiding the rope, called out to his companions to hold him firm, seized the rope in his teeth, thus freeing his hands, threw himself on the unstable mass, and held it in place with his hands, and this piece of work cost him a tooth.

And when I think again of all we went through during those hours, of those men who worked with such steady courage for my victory, it seems to me that their self-sacrifice that day had something sublime in it; I feel that the confidence they had in me must have been unbounded for them to have ventured into such a place, that it must have been equal to the faith I had in them. And for this their faith in me I shall be for ever grateful. But up there I looked differently upon those two who climbed above me, who did not speak to me, and who went up impossible places. I thought then that they were two fiends who were inexorably dragging me bound to an unknown destiny.

Whither were those desperate men about to take me? My only comfort lay in the thought that down below, only a few miles away, Antoine had a dear young wife who had bidden him farewell but twenty-four hours before, and two fine children to whom I had given some sweets the previous day on my way through Crépin.

And for the youthful Aimé, too, I thought some maiden's heart was beating down in the valley with apprehension for his safety.

For ten to twenty minutes I rested, standing upright on a tiny platform, without relinquishing my grasp of the great rope, and then I heard a laconic 'Venez', and I started upwards once more, with my face turned towards the mountain. 'What in Heaven's name are you at up there?' I shouted. A small stone had been dislodged by the feet of one of my companions, and had hit me on the head.

I candidly confess that I had then to summon all my resolution in order not to relinquish my grip and let myself fall.

At that instant I was a double personality, consisting of myself and another man much greater and stronger than I, who spoke within me: 'Fool!' he cried, 'do you not see that if you let yourself go we shall all fall together?'

'Come, be brave! An effort, another, all right!' It was the imperious voice of animal instinct, a valuable friend that the comfort and security of our ordinary life has lulled to sleep in us, but that awakes in moments of need.

I had heard it before in other adventures in the mountains, but it had never spoken to me so loud and so clearly.

'Vous y etes, Monsieur?' shouted Aimé just then.

'Right,' I answered, though I was still shaken by my internal struggle.

'C'est bien; alors j'avance.'

As I climbed, each time I came into contact with the rock I received a wound, I felt a pain; the muscles of my arms were growing tired with the tension of continuous effort; I began to feel how heavy my body was. Something passed between me and the sun; it seemed the shadow of some body travelling rapidly through space. Another shadow passed, a swish of wings was heard; a black object glided past close at hand, falling from above and disappearing below like a falling stone. These were the crows of the Matterhorn, the lords of the place; there was a whole family of them, and one did not know whence they had issued. Up here, among the clefts of the rocks, they had hitherto been undisturbed by man, and when they saw the unaccustomed sight of visitors they flew restlessly to and fro, with ill-omened cawing, round about the intruders as they hung on the rope. They troubled me. One of them brushed my head with its wing; the horrible fancy flashed through my mind that they were like birds of prey hovering about a man on a gallows. . . .

I was evidently tired; it was fatigue that created that dark vision in my mind.

I have never understood as clearly as on that day how the excellence of a climber depends not only on his feet, his arms, or his lungs, but has a deeper seat in us — in our brains and our hearts.

But the long duration of our climb told me that we were at a great height, and that the end of our difficulties must be near.

And after a bit which seemed to me steeper and worse than all the others, I raised my head above the level of a ledge, and with a last effort I lifted my whole body on to it.

I had emerged on to a small and almost level platform, on which was still a little snow, the only snow I had met with on the cliff.

I saw my guides standing still at a short distance. Beyond them a staircase of rock, not quite so terribly steep, led up to the foot of a wall, which was, as far as I could judge, about fifty feet high, and on the upper edge of this wall I saw some heads appear and move about. They belonged to Daniel and his men. I remember these things with a marvellous clearness. We were about one hundred feet vertically distant from our comrades; we could recognize their figures; we could now easily talk to them and be understood, we were so near.

The great rope united us to them, the rope alone; we were separated by the low wall, whose upper edge overhung its base. I was with hesitation approaching the goal of my expedition, and I already ventured to believe I should succeed. I reckoned that from where we were to the summit it was not more than 110 yards.

Victory depended entirely on that last piece of smooth, slender rope that hung in space. Above that were our friends, and they would help us, and the Matterhorn would be mine!

Antoine had advanced without loss of time to the foot of the wall; there he stopped, and consulted with those above concerning the means of overcoming our last obstacle. I remained on the patch of snow, without sitting down. It was four o'clock; we had taken four hours to climb up here from the Shoulder, a height of about 300 feet. I do not know how long the consultation lasted. Meanwhile, with a view to lightening our load, Antoine had passed up to the others one of our sacks, which contained my Kodak.

I watched the sack as it ascended, tied to the rope, and swinging to and fro in the air, and I saw it received by Daniel.

Happy little Kodak! You had conquered the Furggen ridge of the Matterhorn.

I next saw Antoine advance a few steps, seize the rope which was hanging inside the curve of the cliff, climb three or four arms' length, raising himself by sheer pulling on the rope, and scraping the rock with his feet. He stopped with his boots planted against the wall; the rope was swinging uncertainly; he lost his footing, and came down again. I asked Daniel to throw him down a knotted rope, and forthwith the whole long rope was pulled up by Daniel, and in the upper laboratory he and his men employed themselves busily in tying two ropes together in such a way as to form a single knotted one. It kept us waiting a considerable time, but at length it descended.

Antoine fastened it below as best he could, in a fissure of the rock; then he began to climb vigorously up it. This was the attempt that was to decide our fate. Once more I saw him climb up a few yards, but the rope, though fixed at the bottom, was pulled out of its place by his weight, and began to swing to and fro in the air.

I saw Antoine's body, hanging by the arms, swung right and left. He was no longer ascending; his efforts were evidently paralysed by the uncertain oscillation of the rope. He held himself for a few instants more by one of the knots, tried to draw his body near to the rock, shouted a few words to those above . . . and then, what will you? Then he began to let himself down slowly, reaching the base of the wall, whence he had started, relinquished the rope, and came back towards us.

We were defeated.

Antoine, who had led us so bravely to this point, was unable to climb the last piece.

If he had failed, it was useless for us to try. I instantly and clearly realized this, and no one else can realize it unless he makes the attempt himself. It was utterly impossible to ascend by the strength of the arms alone, owing to the continual swing of the rope. The men above were in such a dangerous and circumscribed spot that they could not help us much; every movement of theirs would have sent down stones upon us.

The hour was growing late.

We had reached the point that we had feared to reach, namely, the point where difficulty became impossibility for us. We all kept silence, and a wave of sadness swept over me. I remembered that turning back meant a dangerous descent by the way we had come. I waited in the expectation that the guides would say something. Aimé was silent and depressed! Antoine shook his head, his face was stern and impassive. I asked if all hope were gone. He answered, as I expected, that there was nothing more to be done.

'Il faudrait une échelle,' he added.

But Daniel had none. I glanced round; there was Monte Rosa standing impassive in the distance; a few feet from us were the jaws of the precipice up which I had come and down which it behoved me to return. I turned my gaze away.

Ah! How nearly we had won our victory!

Perhaps less than ten yards had separated Antoine from those above at the moment when he was forced to retreat. We were exhausted; our muscles were trembling with fatigue.

Poor Icarus! who didst take the feathers of an eagle to fly towards the sun, and didst fix them on with wax. We exchanged a few words, and I gave the order to retreat. I looked at my watch; it was five o'clock.

The aneroid indicated 14,195 feet.

At about that time the following telegram was dispatched from Zermatt; I translate it from the German: 'A marvellous feat has been lately performed, namely, the ascent of the Matterhorn by the Furggen ridge. Several times during the past week men have been seen climbing daringly in that direction, and have reached a prodigious height.

'Finally, this morning, Thursday, three men well provided with rope were seen to gain the summit by the ordinary route, and to descend thence as far as they could on the Furggen ridge.

'From the point they reached they let a rope down the overhanging cliff to their comrades, who were enabled in this manner to make the ascent, hanging, as they did so, over the huge precipices that yawned at their feet. The whole thing was watched through the telescope from the Schwarzsee.

'Guides, both brave and experienced, shook their heads at such foolhardiness.

'The rash climbers are doubtless two Englishmen with many Italian guides.'

Now you know who the 'two Englishmen' were, and you know, too, of the defeat I had sustained instead of winning a victory, the news of which was telegraphed from Zermatt to the newspapers of Europe.[6]

'O virtù mia, perchè si ti dilegue?' *Purgatorio*, XVII	'O my virtue, wherefore dost thou pass away from me thus?'

That I should have any precise or clear idea as to how we managed the descent of the difficult bit is not to be expected. My mind was too much occupied with grievous thoughts; a feeling of great sadness weighed upon me, mingled with indifference, impotent rage, resignation, and revolt.

Yet the memory of certain moments remains impressed upon my mind as clearly and as deeply as the brand of a red-hot iron.

The knotted rope had been pulled up by those above, who had then hastily departed.

The day was nearing its close; the sun, the climbers' dearest friend, had long since left the ridge and hidden himself behind the mountain. I think the crows were no longer visible; perhaps they had already withdrawn to their nests.

Antoine fixed one of our ropes to a cleft in the rock on the edge of the ledge where I stood, and let it down the cliff.

I turned my back on the Matterhorn and went to the edge of the platform, to where the precipice fell sheer away, and as I looked down I seemed to be gazing into a bottomless well.

I can see myself again as I seized the rope and began to lead down in silence.

I remember that the guides fixed the ropes as we descended and that I told Antoine to cut off the lower end of the last at the bottom of the cliff with his knife. It was not unfair to prevent any others from trying to make use of it. But these ropes, fixed like this, did not serve us as well as the single great rope that had assisted us in the ascent, in those places where the rock was smoothest and most rounded they shifted their position and swung to and fro most abominably. Once, I remember, the oscillation was so violent that I was torn roughly out of the chimney on to the cliff, and I swung right and left in such a way that I was on the Swiss face one instant and on the Italian the next. I lost my balance; first my hands and then my forehead struck against the rock, while my feet vainly sought for a hold. I think I swore and shouted angrily to the guides. The only answer that came from above was a tug on the rope, which squeezed my chest so tightly as nearly to suffocate me. My hands were stiff and tired and of little use to me. Here again I was saved by an instinct: I seized the rope in my teeth and rested so. It was the affair of an instant, but the sense of security and comfort that this expedient afforded me is unimaginable.

Here was an extra organ, and a firm and unexhausted one, coming into play. I immediately regained my balance and was able to proceed. My men had not answered me, nor had they seen me; they were silently doing their difficult and serious duty, so full of boundless responsibility; and when, some time afterwards, I confessed my action to Antoine, as an offence I had committed, he laughed and in his turn admitted that he had been obliged to use his teeth two or three times as an aid to his hands, and he considered that no hand can be safer or stronger than the mouth.

The descent of those 250 feet or so appeared to all of us more difficult than the ascent of them, but urged on by the lateness of the hour we descended rapidly, and it cannot have been much after seven in the evening when the difficulties came to an end.

It was still daylight when we reached the snowy terrace of the Shoulder, and it was strange to us to be once more on an almost level spot after being so long on a vertical plane. Whilst we stood still on the Shoulder, we heard joyous cries coming to us from the Swiss ridge; they came from Daniel and his men, who had caught sight of us, and were expressing from afar their joy at seeing that we had passed the bad places.

I subsequently learnt that Daniel had been most anxious about us during the whole period of our descent to this point. We had still over 3,000 feet to descend before reaching the Breuiljoch, but it seemed to us now that we really had nothing more to do. For six hours we had been hanging at a height of between 14,000 and 14,300 feet, over one of the greatest precipices in the Alps; all the rest was child's play. Now the blind energy of our ascent and the desperate haste of our descent were followed by a dazed stupor and a strange indifference to everything. I did not talk to the guides of our past adventures, nor they to me; we refrained owing to a feeling of mutual consideration. I furtively looked round in order to see once

THE LAST STEP OF THE FURGGEN RIDGE

(Italian side)

THE SOLVAY HUT
and (above) the last step of the Furggen Ridge (Swiss side)

more from close quarters the dark wall, but I did it in such a way that my companions were not aware of what I did. The twilight lasted far into the clear summer's evening, the shadows deepened down in the valley, and ascended the mountain-sides by slow degrees; the sunset fires disappeared one by one from the beautiful snow peaks; a dark blue veil was drawn over the huge snow-fields that were so lately flushed with pink, and, as we descended, the darkness came on little by little.

We went in silence down the ridge for hours and hours, stopping now and then for a few moments to drink a draught of wine. We had now so much time to spare, and yet we were in haste to reach a safer and a warmer place.

When it became quite dark one of us suggested stopping and waiting for the moon to rise and light us on our way. We sat down where we were and ate some food, but without appetite; throughout the day we had felt neither hunger nor thirst; then, in our impatience, we rose again and started once more, without waiting for the moonlight.

We saw down in the Swiss valley a number of lights shining in long, regular rows; they were the lights of Zermatt, the Alpine capital, but so far off that they seemed like the reflections of the stars of heaven in a deep, dark lake. That glimpse of civilization and the haunts of men, seen from the desolate mountain-side after a whole day's isolation, first made me realize what an enormous distance had for so many hours separated me physically and mentally from mankind. Suddenly all the lights were extinguished, and only a few tiny twinkling points remained. It was the hour of curfew at Zermatt, and nothing remained to us but the stars of heaven. Henceforth we alone were awake in the whole vast region of the Matterhorn; travellers were asleep in their comfortable beds and crows in their lofty nests; we were walking on the back of the sleeping giant. But only our bodies were awake and moving by the force of inertia; the cold, light air of the heights kept them awake, while our minds were already asleep. Such exertions as ours had been can only be endured high up in the mountains.

At last the moon rose and clothed the night in white. It was almost full, and touched with light the neighbouring rocks and the distant snows; the huge streams of ice which are enclosed between the Theodul and the Weissthor shone cold and peaceful as they stretched down towards the shadows of the valley. In certain places on our route the rocks were covered with that thin coating of ice that is known as verglas. At night this appears to be the same colour as the rock it covers, and while descending one of the steep pitches of the cliff the first man on our rope put his hand on the glazed rock, slipped, and fell till the rope was taut. I had grasped the rope, and the shock came violently on my hand, but I held; we were fated not to come to any harm. Immediately afterwards I felt my cold hands grow warm, as if some tepid liquid were flowing over them and covering them. Later I perceived that it was blood. We halted once more, and I noticed that we were near the old bivouac. It was past midnight; there was a little wood left with the saucepan; we warmed some wine. A few minutes later three men were lying there huddled close together in a narrow cleft in the rock; their coat-collars were turned up and their hands were in their pockets. Their attitude was so strangely distorted, and they were so heaped up against each other, that they seemed like dead men. I fancy no other mortal men as weary as they lay sleeping in the moonlight at that hour. One thing only could wake them: the cold; and it came and waked them. They shook themselves, looked about them with dull eyes, striving to discover their whereabouts, and regained consciousness of life together with the sudden, acute, and painful remembrance of all that had happened on the preceding day. Then they started again in the moonlight.

Down below, on the Furggenjoch, and along the whole ridge that divided Italy from Switzerland, the usual battle was going on that night between the north wind and the south. The latter blew up white masses of dense cloud as far as the ridge; but there they stopped, unable to cross the frontier, for they met the north wind there, an invisible foe who defeated them; and the clouds retreated in disorder towards Italy, to reform under the shelter of the ridge, to return to the attack once more, and again to retreat. From above, by the light of the moon that was shed upon them, those rounded, distorted clouds resembled a dense smoke that had issued from the mouths of monstrous cannon. By now the shadows all round us had grown grey and transparent; the light was being slowly divided from the darkness, as in the Book of Genesis, and a little life was returning to us.

The dawn came on by imperceptible degrees, the cloudless dawn of an ideal day for an alpine climb, whilst we descended, saddened by our failure, by our defeat in a battle that we had fought with all our might, and such a one as we thought we should never fight again. The fine weather, which I had so ardently desired but thirty hours before, now seemed to me quite useless; I almost wished that a fearful storm might be let loose over the Matterhorn. But no, the Matterhorn was smiling calmly at the first flushes of the dawn — smiling, the same as yesterday, its impassive, everlasting smile. And from the same spot, for the second time, I saw the sun rise in his glory, and illuminate the invincible cliff with his rays. A few small stones fell from above; everything was as it had been, except my own heart. A day in my life had gone past. I felt a touch of bitterness, just as if some grave injustice had been done me. The guides and I had done all that was humanly possible, but the Matterhorn had been unjust to us this time, and as I gradually approached the haunts of men my defeat appeared more and more grievous and shameful. I unconsciously climbed down the difficult bit which forms the gate of entry to the ridge, and which now bore the dark words: 'All hope abandon', like the gates of Avernus. Then I hastened with long strides down the familiar paths leading from the pass down to the Jomein.

It was ten in the morning when I reached it, thirty-four hours after my departure.

As soon as I was seen from the hotel, a friend of mine, who was also a member of the Alpine Club, hastened courteously to meet me.

'Well?' he said.

His simple question affected me terribly; my throat contracted, a sob arose in it, and if I had answered I should have wept. But I did not weep, for human prejudices deny this noble expression of feeling to those who wish to appear strong. The climber wishes to be thought as hard as the mountain he climbs, and if I had wept I should have made others laugh. I entered the hotel and mingled with its denizens, wearing the mark of indifference. But my clothes, which hung in rags, like the sails of a ship that has made a long and stormy voyage, spoke for me.

I glanced at my burning hands: the skin had been torn off them and they were foul with blood, so that when a gentleman came civilly towards me with outstretched hands, I hid my own, like Lady Macbeth. Shaking hands would have been too painful!

'Dulcia nocturnae portans vestigia rixae
Quam de virgineis gesserat exuviis.'
CATULLUS, *La chioma di Berenice*

The instant a climber, on his return from a difficult expedition, sets his foot on the threshold of his hotel, he begins to be his guides' superior.

They leave him shortly before, discreetly disappearing without saying good-bye. They go modestly in by the servants' door and hide themselves in their underground room, while their Herr enters triumphantly by the front door, and is received with distinction by the landlord and his attentive waiters; and when he is nice and clean after his bath, he shows himself to the guests of the hotel, pretending he is not tired, and relates in his own way, and without inconvenient witnesses, the feats he has performed.

He estimates with calm superiority the difficulties he has met; he does not exaggerate them, but an occasional word he lets fall during his discourse sufficiently indicates that the situation must have been serious in places.

And he allows it to transpire that the guides were exhausted, that during the descent he held one of them who slipped — but he does not say how often he himself was held by the guide. At the *table-d'hôte*, near the end of a good dinner, the climber's neighbours, who mostly know nothing at all about Alpine expeditions, but who are nevertheless eager for sensation, are filled with wonder at the description he has given them; they unite in praising his courage, his coolness and his modesty, while no one thinks of the guides supping humbly by themselves in a dark room on the floor below. It is a severe lesson in modesty that the guides give us.

But these innocent triumphs on the small stage of the hotel are denied to a climber's vanity when he has failed.

The mountaineer who returns empty handed must digest his defeat by himself. He avoids talking about what has occurred, and tries to baffle the importunate curiosity of the friends who have been waiting for him, and who cannot bring themselves to believe that so great a climber can have spent two nights and a day on the mountain and then have nothing to tell.

These are unpleasant moments, and he is sick at heart; he feels so very small, and fancies himself unworthy to belong to an Alpine Club.

And yet he ought to bless these defeats: without them he would never have the opportunity of comparing the forces of the mountain with the undoubtedly superior ones of his own mind. If one is not beaten sometimes, one cannot appreciate the perfect delight of winning; and it is a noble, joyous, and most profitable thing to pass with steadfast faith through delusion after delusion until one reaches one's coveted goal.

But the climber who has failed does not reason thus. He hastens to hide his shame and his fatigue in bed until the luncheon hour; and lying on his soft couch, between the fragrant, newly-washed sheets, he stretches out his weary limbs that are all black and blue from the blows they have received, and as he luxuriously yawns before falling asleep, he reviews his position.

Here we have a man, he tells himself, a man who does not lack good sense, and is not without experience of life, making himself miserable about a matter of ten yards of rope that he was unable to climb.

If only this man were reasonable, he would say: what is past is past: let bygones be bygones, for you have done even more than could be expected of you. Let someone else go and try, and he will see, and yet . . . it would have been a grand thing to prevail, to be able to come down and tell one's friends that the Furggen ridge of the Matterhorn had at last been conquered by an Italian . . .!

And now, with this thought, other ideas form confusedly in the head of the weary climber, who falls asleep at last, and in his sleep again sees ropes swaying over tremendous precipices, black crows wheeling round his head, and dangerous slips by night.

An hour later the *table-d'hôte* bell awoke him. His limbs were aching, his muscles knotted with fatigue, his hands burning with their wounds, but his mind was calm and perfectly clear.

The sun's cheerful rays were shining in at the little window in the room and through the white curtains; the weather was fine; hope returned to him.

At the foot of the bed was seated the *b^te noire*, smiling and pleasantly whispering that now the difficult part was done, and that it behoved him to complete the work somehow and at any cost.

He understood.

He hastily dressed himself, and sent word to his guides that he wished to speak to them after luncheon.

Then he unconcernedly went in to *table-d'hote*, prepared to lie about his past, and to conceal his future, actions.

'Rem facias rem, si possis recte
Si non, quocumque modo rem.'
OVID

Two days later I once more entered the Jomein; this time I had negotiated all the last unexplored part of the ridge; the Furggen arête no longer had any secrets for me. And this is how it was done. I had not even dreamt of suggesting to my guides that we should follow our former route; I felt that they would have refused. That was one of the things that no man does more than once in his life. Moreover, it seemed to me that with regard to those few yards of cliff, it was all the same whether one climbed them up or down. Setting all pedantry aside, I reasoned like the fox with the grapes.

So we started off to ascend the Matterhorn by the ordinary Italian route, intending to descend the Furggen ridge as far as the point we had reached on the ascent, thus making our exploration complete.

We were provided with two long rope-ladders.

Early in the morning we started from the hut in two parties.

The morning was perfectly clear; not a cloud was visible anywhere on the vast horizon.

Our feet seemed to have wings; we passed the Grande Corde, the Crête du Coq, and the Shoulder without my perceiving them; my mind was so busy with what was to come that the ascent, fine though it was, made no impression upon me that day.

And this explains why it is possible to climb up and down the Matterhorn without seeing or perceiving any of its beauties, when the mind is either fearful or inattentive, too full of thought or too empty.

'Diable! Le Mont Blanc a mis son chapeau!' exclaimed one of us during a halt on the Shoulder for breakfast.

This was bad news, for it is well known how quickly a hat of cloud on the head of the monarch of the Alps widens its brim in such a way as soon to cover all the other mountains.

Our halt was a very short one, and we went on faster than before.

By seven we were on the Pic Tyndall, before nine we reached the summit. The wind had begun to blow from a bad quarter, and the clouds from Mont Blanc had reached our neighbour, the Dent d'Hérens.

On the top we found a single climber with his guide, and the former, hearing me address the latter in German, recognized me for an Italian.

He was an Italian too, and we shook hands with much pleasure; one meets so few Italians on the summit of the Matterhorn!

He was most cordial, and he offered me a cup of champagne.

When my party of porters appeared in a long line on the snow-ridge, he looked at them with curiosity and asked me who they were. I denied all knowledge of their identity.

Time pressed, and I cut the conversation short with another handshake and moved on.

I wonder what my compatriot's thoughts were as he saw us all starting down in a direction quite different from the one parties generally take.

I fancied I heard his guide shout out in German that that way would not 'go', but I did not turn round.

The first bit of the descent towards Furggen is broad and easy, but so broken that at every step one starts and sends down stones.

The storm was very near, and the tension of our minds was very great.

We descended about 160 feet, to where the slope begins to grow steeper as the head of the Matterhorn bends towards the precipice below.

At eleven we reached the exact spot where Daniel's party had taken up their stand on the day of the first attempt, and whence they had sent us down the rope. The iron spike which had helped in the work was still there, firmly fixed in the rock.

The porters had halted a few steps further back. I was left alone on the little platform whilst my guides went on to see whether it was possible to go down further in order to descend by ordinary means as much of the cliff as might be.

The first mists had meanwhile reached the Matterhorn.

They advanced capriciously, blown up by the gusts of wind, wrapped us suddenly about, and vanished again; it seemed as if the wind created them out of nothing and blew them back into nothingness once more. In the intervals when the mist encompassed us, the sun still shone warmly and pleasantly.

In the meanwhile my guides kept appearing and disappearing before my eyes; I could see them at a few yards from me, looking down on the Italian side for a way, and I could hear them talking together excitedly. But apparently there was no practicable route, or at least the mists prevented their finding it.

Down towards the Theodul everything was by now completely overclouded; the huge precipice dominating the Val Tournanche was wreathed in dense mist; there came thunderclap after thunderclap, each nearer than the last, and when the dark curtain was drawn by the wind round the Matterhorn I fancied I was enclosed in a very small space. Again the clouds were rent, and the sun shone through with a pallid light.

The rocks of the Matterhorn were still warm, but the cold breath of the storm had reached us. The Matterhorn was humming in the wind like a great organ pipe.

Twenty minutes had gone by when Aimé returned for the sack containing the ladders.

'Ça va?' I asked. 'Oui, ça va,' he replied; 'préparez-vous', and started down again with the sack. Then Antoine came to fetch me, and with him I went down the four or five yards that lay between me and the spot where they had fixed the rope.

This place, which I can see clearly in my mind's eye, was a narrow slab of rock, on which the guides crouched close together, not venturing to move, because the slightest movement would have been dangerous.

Their faces were very grave as they solemnly waited for the trial to begin.

We could see a few of the upper rungs of the rope ladder, which was fixed to the rock by iron spikes, but the rest was lost to view as it hung down the precipice.

Daniel told me to go down alone, but I insisted that Antoine should be the first to descend, as he deserved. While Antoine was tying himself on there came a rent in the clouds, which enabled us to see clearly enough.

Full of curiosity I peeped over the edge of the rock and, by the momentary gleam of light, I saw the whole piece down which we must go. It was overhanging. The ladder, which was about 16 yards long, hung down its whole length, and reached beyond the base of the pitch; its lower extremity lay unfastened on the rocky stair from which Antoine had tried to raise himself on our first attempt.

I recognized every detail; I saw a few yards off the spot where Antoine had swung to and fro, lower down the place where Aimé had waited, and lower still the patch of snow where I had stood.

I saw the scene again most clearly, just as I had seen it a few days before, but this time from above, not from below.

Meantime the ladder swayed gaily, as the wind tossed it to and fro like a light piece of ribbon. Then the clouds closed again.

Antoine descended the ladder, while we, his companions, held him by the rope. He was out of sight for four or five minutes, I suppose but I am not sure, for they seemed an eternity to me.

Then he shouted for us to pull on the rope, and a few minutes afterwards first his head and then his body reappeared over the edge of the cliff, like a diver returning to the surface. He was very much out of breath.

It was now my turn. I grasped the first rung and began to descend. I did not count the number of the rungs; there were certainly seven or eight of them; I felt the ladder stretching under my weight and swaying about.

The guides shouted to me to go slowly, and shortly afterwards that I had gone far enough. They meant that I had reached the point desired and that I might come back. However, I insisted on descending five or six more of the rungs, then I put my foot on a ledge of rock, but I did not let go the ladder with my hands. This was how I took possession. The guides up above were calling to me to make haste, so I climbed up the swaying rope and was soon by their side again. The ceremony was over.

And thus, in dismal mist, amidst the howling of the wind and the rumbling of thunder, the last great secret of the Matterhorn was revealed to man.

Now it behoved us to flee from the mountain's vengeance, so we packed up our baggage, but left our ladder hanging where it was as a witness to what we had done, and for the benefit of the Schwarzsee telescope.

The second ladder, which we had not used, we took to pieces, and carried off the rope with us, but threw the wood into the air, and saw it disappear into the unfathomed mist.

We hastened back to the summit, and it was high time, for the clouds were condensing and discharging an icy sleet, which the wind blew with violence into our faces. Nevertheless, on the top we consumed the last of our provisions, the clouds meanwhile wrapping us completely about: we could no longer see either precipices at our feet or horizon around us.

Of the sky we saw nothing, of the earth only the little snowy hump on which our feet rested.

We were utterly alone. The other party, which had left the summit more than four hours ago, was without doubt in safety by now, and, if they thought of us at all, must have thought it likely we had come to grief. It began to hail; we started off quickly down the Swiss side; it was a regular flight. However, below the top, we were sheltered from the wind; a storm of large and gently falling snowflakes replaced the driving sleet, and soon coated the whole Matterhorn with white.

The ropes and chains were iced and the rocks were slippery; our hands were numb and bruised, but now we neither felt fatigue nor perceived difficulties. One thought urged us onwards: that of reaching the Jomein the same evening.

Two hours after leaving the top we passed the old hut; at six we descended on to the Furggen glacier without going near the Hörnli hut, and we reached the Breuiljoch at seven. Thence we saw on the Italian side, amid that sea of stormy clouds, far away, in the direction of Aosta, the gleam of a gloomy sunset, which cast a strange, violet hue upon the mountains and the atmosphere; the Matterhorn, divided half-way up by a dark veil which added to its mystery, looked divinely tall and stern.

Far below the sound of a bell rang out, and the day drew to its close in an atmosphere of infinite sadness.

My heart was light and joyful; it seemed as if a heavy burden had been removed from me: my great curiosity was satisfied at last. And now, amid that majestic scene, a coarse vision presented itself to my mind: it was that of a clean white table in a warm, well-lighted room, with a steaming dish in front of me and a pleasant smell of cooking all round. And as I walked I thought of some particularly well-cooked toothsome dish that I should order on reaching the hotel.

A bright light appeared quite close to us out of the darkness of the night; we saw before us the door of the hotel, and dark shadows standing out against the light and seeming to await us. And as I passed among those shadows, I fancied I heard one of them express his joy at seeing us return alive, whilst another whispered a word of congratulation which went to my heart.

But I hardly answered the greetings and questions, for it seemed to me now that all I had done in those last few days had been nothing but madness.

The next day, when I reviewed the matter, calm in mind and rested in body, I had a clear comprehension of what had occurred.

I had been the first to climb, either up or down, the whole Furggen ridge, and I had so to speak, taken possession of it; yet I was not satisfied. I felt that I had taken the ancient Matterhorn by surprise, and that such warfare as this was not honourable; that a Cato amongst mountaineers would approve the cause of the vanquished, not that of the victor. All this was borne in upon me by the respect I have for my great adversary; I ought to have overcome him face to face, the first day.

No! the Matterhorn had once more defeated me, not I the Matterhorn.

But the most unexpected conclusion to my adventures was afforded me some time after by a Geneva newspaper, which dealt with a number of Alpine accidents that had occurred that summer (1899), and added: 'Le clubiste italien qui s'est fait hisser au Cervin par l'arête surplombante de Furggen mériterait une amende. C'est un fou dangereux.'[7]

On my word of honour I had never known it before; but then no man is a judge of himself.

'Ces airs dont la musique
a l'air d'être en patois.'
ROSTAND

That evening at dinner we were talking of guides and their songs, a pleasant subject and one that was full of local interest. One of the diners maintained that, after all, there is not much difference between the guides' singing and the coarse strains that one hears issuing from city drinking-shops on the evenings of fête days, and bewailed the fact that when the guides sing in chorus in their dining-room on the ground floor, they disturb the people who are reading in the salon; as if one came to the mountains to read!

The climber in his turn replied that he had heard the song of the guides in the open air, on high pastures, mingling with the sound of the cow-bells; that he had heard it amid the howling of the wind in lofty bivouacs, where it served to while away the long hours of the night and to induce forgetfulness of the cold, and that he had then found it full of poetry and vigour; but, he added, that one must have heard it in the heights and have sung it oneself in chorus with the guides, in order to feel the primitive spirit of the mountains vibrating in those songs, and to believe that those mountaineers had learnt them from the wind that whistles among the clefts in the rocks, and from the torrent that roars at the bottom of the valley.

These mountain songs are simple and slow: they consist of a few long-drawn-out notes, with sharp trills that are able to drown the roar of the waterfall, and to re-echo, like a distant call, from side to side of the valley. Theirs is not the sweet, almost voluptuous, cadence, in which the native of Capri lifts his voice to heaven on the shores of the deep blue sea, but a melody as grave and gloomy as the mountains themselves, a colourless cadence, which slowly ascends the lofty walls of the peaks, just as the smoke rises from a chalet in the peaceful valley at eventide. Where did they learn these songs, and who were their teachers?

Who were the humble Orpheans of the mountains? Some of these melodies undoubtedly come from afar, from the other side of the Alps, and they heard them when they went as children to tend sheep in the French Alps, whence they brought them to their native valley. One of the favourite songs of the Val Tournanche is about the Pyrenees; another, which is full of the sadness of the mountaineer when he is far from home, was composed by the great Chateaubriand from a musical *motif* that he had heard in the mountains of Auvergne — a *motif*, the poet says, remarkable for its sweetness and simplicity.[8] It is probably quite unchanged, as sung by our fellow-countrymen to-day. The one I love best of all, one in which I find the same sad expression of home-sickness, gives utterance to the complaint of a son of the East, who is languishing in a cold climate and follows in spirit the flight of the swallows towards the land of sunshine. How came this warm ray of southern poetry to find a home among the snows of the Alps?

Some of these songs are more than a century old, and have been handed down, they and their musical settings, from father to son, together with the tales and legends which form the modest poetic patrimony of these people. Others, again, are old songs in new settings; some are entirely new.

The songs of the city take many years to reach these remote spots, and when they do arrive — brought, perhaps, by some soldier in an Alpine regiment who has learnt them in winter quarters — their tunes, their rhythm, and sometimes even their words, change so completely that they become unrecognizable. Now and then the best singer in the village adapts an old tune to a few lines printed on a sheet of paper that he has bought at Aosta on a fair day; or he may compose a new song, which the others learn, and thus the village singer gradually acquires a reputation. Often enough the melody of these songs is beautiful even without words: the simple music is sufficient, for it is like the natural song of birds.

These men sing instinctively, like the birds, for song is the only means they have of worthily expressing sadness, joy, or love, giving utterance to the emotions that uncultured men can feel but cannot analyse. There is no other channel by which art can touch their laborious lives or shed its light upon their minds.

At this point two charming young ladies, who had attentively listened to what I was saying, begged me to get my guides to sing that evening.

I answered that guides suffered from an inborn reluctance to sing before gentlefolk, but, seeing that they were very much interested, I finally yielded to their gentle persistence.

Dinner was over, so we went down to the ground-floor, where the guides' quarters are; these consist of a dormitory and a refectory, like those of a convent. I opened a heavy black door, went in first, and ushered in my companions.

Ten or twelve strong, broad-shouldered men, with bronzed faces, were in the room, sitting all close together on wooden benches, with their elbows resting on a long, massive table.

They were all dressed alike in thick, well-worn clothes, of a colour between that of ashes and that of tobacco, the colour of rocks; some of them were in their shirt-sleeves, while their coats were thrown carelessly over their shoulders, and their flannel shirts, which were either red or of a large blue-and-white check pattern, alone broke the uniformity of colour with a warm note. Their hats were on their heads; they never take them off except in church, and when they do so you see on their thick, untidy hair a round mark, which makes you think of certain fifteenth-century heads as painted by Benozzo Gozzoli.

Under their crushed and shapeless hats we saw their rugged faces, on which it is difficult to discover the traces of any emotion, for they look as impassive as the face of a mountain.

All my men were there: Daniel, Antoine, Aimé, Joseph, Baptiste; also Perruquet, who had been my guide on the Pointe Blanche, besides other guides and porters, all Valtournanche men.

They had finished supper, and were spending the evening smoking and talking in their incomprehensible dialect. Their attitudes were those of tired men enjoying their rest and comfort; the joy of living brightened their dark faces, and their little cat's eyes sparkled with unwonted gaiety. These periods of pleasant rest after a toilsome ascent must be moments of rare delight in a guide's life.

The low room, with its vaulted ceiling, which had once been white, smelt like a damp cellar. They had drunk their basins full of hot broth mixed with wine, and the smell of this drink, of which the guides are very fond, mingled with the odours of the lamp, of wet clothes, and of bad tobacco.

A small lamp hung from the ceiling and shed a faint but picturesque light on the scene, in which the men's figures showed dimly through the dense tobacco smoke. Outside the night was dark but cloudless.

On our entrance the conversation ceased, and they all, with rustic courtesy, stood up and touched their hats.

The two girls, struck with shyness, sat down in a corner by themselves, away from the table, whilst I went towards the guides, who made room for me in their midst.

I called for some wine to wet my songsters' throats, and as soon as the glasses were filled Daniel lifted his towards me, and said: 'Monsieur, si vous êtes content, nous buvons ensemble à notre belle course.' I looked at him with astonishment; he had never made me such a long speech, for he was generally as unexpansive in temperment as he was lean in body. All present cordially clinked glasses and drank the toast. Then Perruquet insisted on paying for a bottle 'pour l'arête de Furggen', and lifting his glass, said simply, with an ultra-serious face, 'Je regrette que je n'étais pas avec vous.'

And now it was time for us to sing.

What a pity that Ansermin was not with us — Ansermin the graceful tenor, who could trill, and who knew all the songs of Savoy and the Valois.

But Perruquet, who was leader of the choir in the parish church, began to sing with his powerful voice:

> Montagnes de cette vallée,
> Vous êtes mes amours
> Cabanes fortunées
> Où j'ai reçu le jour. . . .

and the chorus swelled and rose to the low, vaulted ceiling and filled the narrow room with deafening waves of sound, interrupted by sudden pauses; the whole was a medley of strange discords, high trills, and deep bass notes which issued from the men's powerful chests like the music of a church organ.

They sang with the delighted fervour of great boys:

> Rien n'est si beau que ma patrie;
> Rien n'est si doux que mon amie.

Then the younger ones, who had at first shyly refused to sing, joined likewise in the joyful chorus, for they felt themselves carried away by the fascination of the music and warmed into enthusiasm by the wine they had drunk. That evening the duties of a guide seemed easy, gay, as if they consisted only of drinking and singing.

> Oh! montagnards, chantez en chœur,
> De mon pays la paix et le bonheur.

The whole repertoire was gone through, and in this manner the unassuming conquerors of the Matterhorn celebrated in their dark cellar-like room their own glory and that of the mountain.

And, between the songs, there was time for a sip of wine, an innocent jest, a hasty reference to the adventures of the past days.

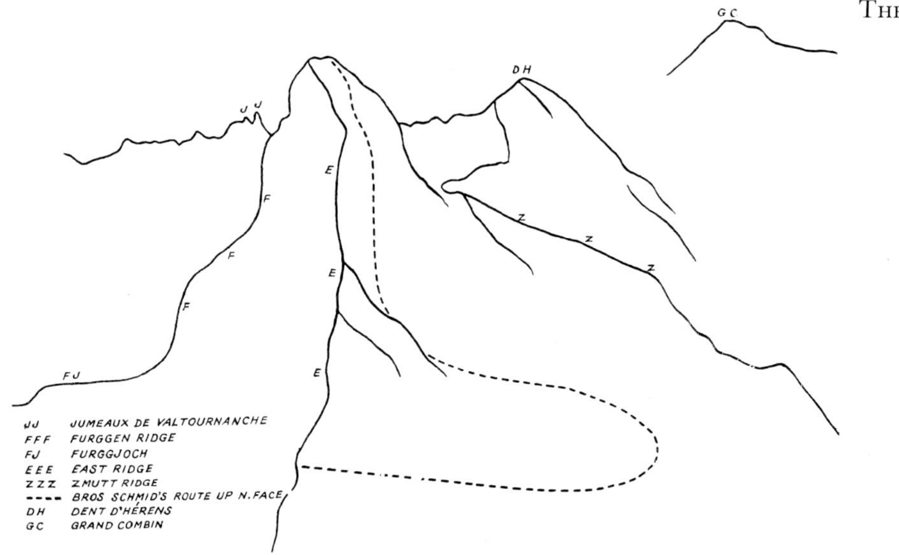

The North and East Faces
(from the Air)

LOOKING ACROSS THE NORTH FACE
from the North-East Ridge

One man jestingly asked me whether we had sung when we were up on the arête; another was slyly anxious to know whether I should be inclined to make the expedition again.

We laughed and jested because we felt safe, but the name of the Matterhorn kept returning to our thought and our lips, for outside the house, beyond the narrow walls of the room, amid the darkness of the night, towered the huge, dark pyramid. We could not see it, but we were all of us aware of its presence, because its influence pervaded our hearts, and we felt as if we were still ascending the sharp ridge . . . The Matterhorn was invisible, yet ever-present as God Himself.

The songs we were singing were in its honour; our voices vibrated with the memory of the things we had seen in the heights, and our chorus was instinct with the sympathy men feel for one another when they have struggled together against great difficulties.

There are some feelings that are not spoken of between traveller and guides, even when they are close friends, but during this pleasant, restful evening we made known to each other by means of the notes of our songs the feelings we had not ventured to express otherwise, and the emotions which our adventures had produced and which had been hitherto known to ourselves alone. It may be that some unwonted consciousness of the greatness of their calling had just then been vouchsafed to my guides, that a sense of the beauty of their lives, of the ennobling influence of danger, had pierced their rude exterior, that the low, dark room seemed to them to have become a vast hill, its walls to have disappeared, and the mountain songs to rise freely to the Matterhorn. I was so absorbed that I had almost forgotten the presence of the two girls, who were modestly sitting by themselves, intently studying that scene of primitive natural life, so free from sham and artifice; perhaps that humble music in those strange surroundings struck them also as something lofty and unusual.

I remember that one of the songs pleased us so much that we repeated it three or four times, and the last time, when we came to the final refrain, we heard two pure, silvery voices rising through the smoke and joining the deep tones of the guides. They belonged to the two girls, who, carried away by the mountain melody, had joined us in our song.

I glanced at the guides; they had not even turned their heads towards the quarter whence those sweet notes came, they continued singing the refrain to the end, but instinctively lowered their voices; but when the verse was ended they all rose to their feet and turning towards the girls, greeted our charming companions with a burst of rapturous applause which resounded through the room that their presence had brightened. They smiled a reply, thus amply rewarding our efforts on the mountain.

Music and the Matterhorn had filled our minds with peace.

From that moment the pleasures of the evening, which spring from the remembrance of past fatigue and from present content, were increased in number by that fresh, delightful incident.

We went out into the open air by the small door which leads on to the level space in front of the hotel.

In the perfect calm of that Alpine night the summit of the great mountain stood out in relief against the clear sky, and it seemed to me as if at that hour the light of the stars fell with a softer radiance upon the dark and rugged Matterhorn.

THE MATTERHORN IN THE TWENTIETH CENTURY

CHAPTER VII

BEFORE THE WAR OF 1914-18

THE story of the Matterhorn does not end with Rey's epic of the Furggen ridge. There is not a mountaineer worthy of the name who can look up at its towering form for the first time and not sense its challenge, whether he views it from Breuil or Zermatt or from the snowfields that surround it.

It is now more than a hundred years since men began to see beauty and a possibility of pleasure in such forms, and in the case of the Matterhorn it has proved a particularly provocative type of beauty. And it is with peaks as it is with women whose beauty is of this type, they generally have a history as long as the duration of their charms. Time and Nature deal very kindly with the charms of the Matterhorn, so, if man himself does not destroy them, its history may be long.

Moreover there is something in its challenge that is not found in the most forbidding-looking strongholds of the Dolomites. Dramatically defiant as these are, they barely raise their heads above the limit of perpetual snow. The Matterhorn rises more than four thousand feet above the glaciers at its base and climbing at fourteen thousand feet is different from climbing at heights below nine or ten thousand feet where snow rarely falls in summer. At the greater height storms are more formidable, ice adds perils to the rocks more often and more quickly, and he is, I think, an exceptional climber who does not find a difficult pitch takes longer to overcome and takes more out of him. Dr. Julius Kugy, the Grand Old Man of the Julian Alps, pays this tribute to the giants of the Western Alps: 'They demand a far greater development, a wider outlook from the climber; they give also a far richer reward.'

The two chapters that follow are an attempt to show how climbers after Rey have felt and taken up the challenge of the Matterhorn. They are little more than a bare record of the later struggles of men upon its grim walls and ridges; the glow of romance upon the scene of action must come from the outpourings of Rey's heart in the pages you have read.

In the first chapter, covering the early years of this century, I shall record adventures carried out in what might be called the classical tradition. Technique, equipment, and the standards of climbing, especially that of amateur climbers, had made their inevitable advance; the spirit in which those adventures were undertaken was essentially the same. The use of iron pitons to make an ascent possible and the deliberate acceptance of risks which no skill could avoid were still generally condemned. A new route was a sporting adventure; it was not undertaken as a 'death or glory' affair.

The second chapter, which covers the last two decades, will show how Nazi and Fascist ideology with its emphasis on racial predominance, its worship of force and its encouragement of contempt for danger as an asset in war, have influenced the history of the Matterhorn, so far as the making of new routes constitutes that history.

We parted from Rey in the hotel at Jomein, the bitterness of defeat forgotten in the warmth of friendship and in a recovered appreciation of what mountains meant to him. His final fantastic feat of exploration had assuaged the restlessness of a mind haunted by visions of those few feet of precipice that had eluded all his efforts to ascend.

It is difficult to imagine any English climber (whether north or south of the Border) going through this last performance of Rey's. Failure to climb an impossibly difficult rock pitch cannot be changed into success by being let down over it from above. As exploration in view of a future ascent the thing has been done on Welsh rocks and elsewhere, and as a rule, a discreet silence has been maintained about it till the ascent has followed. Rey never made another attempt. Perhaps he recognized that the place was not climbable by any methods he cared to employ. But the satisfaction he may have got from his descent over what he had failed to climb must not be judged by normal British standards. If we can divest ourselves of our rigid prejudice against the free expression of strong emotion—a prejudice that is said to have to have originated in imitation of the Duke of Wellington — and if we can understand Rey's passionate feeling for the mountain, the thrill that went through him as his fingers grasped its virgin rocks and halted for a moment on a ledge first trodden by Italian feet, we may be able to see the matter with his eyes. More than any other incident in his book it justifies what his great friend de Amicis wrote in the preface: 'In this feeling for the mountain Guido Rey lays his whole soul bare.' Moreover, it is an Italian not a British soul.

Yet in all Rey's writings there is not a word of resentment for the large British share of victories on the Matterhorn. Towards Whymper and Mummery his attitude is one of veneration, not of envy, though Mummery had seriously invalidated any future claims to conquest of the Furggen ridge by an ascent in 1880.

At that time no casuist thought of disputing a claim to the ascent of a great mountain by one of its main ridges because some apparently insurmountable step had been turned by a traverse on one side or the other. Such traverses might be extensive, as was the case in the ascent of the Dent Blanche by the south ridge. If a summit is approached by a main ridge from a gap at or near its foot, success may fairly be described as an ascent by that ridge, even if the party is forced off it for a considerable distance by a great obstacle at or near the finish.

On the other hand, in an ascent like that of Monte Viso from the east, the climb begins on the face and the main east ridge is only followed in the final stages. Ascent by the east face is the natural description of such a route.

Mummery, in attacking the Matterhorn from the south-east started from the Breuiljoch, and as far as possible followed the Furggen ridge rising from it up to the shoulder under the last vertical step. There is very good reason to regard this as the first ascent by the Furggen ridge and it is so described by Dr. Dubi in the *Guide des Alpes Valaisannes*, though Mummery's party passed the final obstacle by a long, difficult and dangerous traverse across the upper part of the east face to the Swiss Shoulder on the ordinary Zermatt route.

By the end of the nineteenth century first ascents by the main ridges of famous mountains were becoming very difficult to find and even more difficult to accomplish, while the number of climbers longing to add a few lines to Alpine history was larger than ever. Some of these longings were satisfied by promoting what had been nameless humps on ridges into peaks and the gaps between them into cols, and by finding routes up portions of ridges which had hitherto been regarded as obstacles to be turned.

Rey himself lays no claim to a genuine ascent of the upper portion of the Furggen ridge. His description of his exploit in being suspended over the front of the last terrific tower below the summit of the mountain drew more attention to the unsolved problem it presented, and stimulated the desire to gain the real victory, which he knew he could never claim.

A few years later a group of five redoubtable assailants were halted below the tower, two sitting astride of the snowy ridge of the small shoulder, three at the base of the rocks. They were Geoffrey Young, with Josef Knubel, V. J. E. Ryan with Josef and Gabriel Lochmatter.

Ryan had hoped for a traverse to the Italian ridge. The danger of trying to cross those precipitous unreliable rocks under constant stonefall was too obvious to justify such an attempt by men whose judgment imposed some restraint on reckless gambling with their own and other men's lives. Young says: 'That a later party should have actually started upon this route, after seeing what we saw, is even more surprising than their luck in escaping from it alive on to the summit. Down the only possible line of attack on the great nose which had defeated Rey a fusillade of stones hooted visibly.'

They agreed to attempt the traverse to the Swiss Shoulder. The cliffs of the Matterhorn's head gave some protection from stones at first, but the crossing had not become any easier since Alexander Burgener had led Mummery and Venetz over it, after making sure that the champagne was safely stowed inside them.

Young's description of their descent by the ordinary Swiss route,

'Our hurrying need not be excused to anyone who knows this ridge on a hot and populous day', may be compared with the remark of the famous Christian Almer to Whymper as they sat beneath the Matterhorn about forty years before. 'Why don't you try to go up a mountain which *can* be ascended?'

The problem of that last and steepest step of the Furggen ridge was still unsolved. Mario Piacenza had begun to look at it with longing eyes, and his longing grew with gazing till its conquest for himself and Italy became an obsession. Ange Maquignaz, one of Rey's guides in the ascent of his beloved Pointe Blanche in the south ridge of the Dent d'Hérens, gave him no encouragement: 'It's an idiotic route, you'll only break your neck!' Old Daniel Maquignaz, however, was not the man to admit impossibilities: 'Well, I've an idea a route can be found; it must go along those snow bands you see up there; where there is snow, there's always a way.'

There followed several years of exploration, carried out secretly, with all sorts of precautions to divert attention from the actual goal. The ostensible excuse for spending day after day at the Italian hut was love of fresh air, and photography of the Italian Ridge. Piacenza had found in Joseph Pelissier a guide as keen on the project as himself, and J. Carrel and J. Gaspard, both, like Pelissier, Valtournanche guides, shared in these explorations.

Long before other parties left the hut, these four would go up by the ordinary Italian route to the Col Félicité, where they traversed off to the right under the final precipices of the Matterhorn, looking for a practicable route near the vertical or overhanging edge in which the Furggen ridge drops from the summit. Ropes and pitons were fixed and left in position to help them across vertical gullies and facilitate retreat when the sun moved round and began to shine on the face and the deadly showers of stones began. On slopes as steep as those of the Matterhorn and topped by tiers of precipices the number and speed of these missiles is terrifying. Many of them hummed over the men's heads as they made their escape back to the usual route on or near the south-west ridge. There the camera would be taken out, sometimes even carried to the summit, to prove the *bona fides* of the photographers and obscure their true design.

The year 1909 was a particularly bad one for weather, the party on one occasion being imprisoned for six days in the Italian hut. It was Pelissier's last year upon the mountain, for in the following year he died in Piacenza's arms in the Caucasus after an ascent of Elbruz. He had been the keenest of all the guides to prove that 'although Italians had not been first on the summit, they were still capable of attaining the peak by the most difficult way'.

The first serious attempt was made from the Hörnli hut early on a Sunday morning, when few Swiss guides would be on the mountain. The ascent to the high Furggen shoulder from the Breuiljoch, nearly always dangerous in places from falling stones, was accomplished without mishap, but a tempest with hail and whirling snow precluded any thought of pushing the attack further. They returned to the Hörnli hut.

Next day they started while the other parties in the hut were asleep, and waited on the Breuiljoch for dawn. Climbing very quickly, unroped, they reached the foot of the first step in the ridge before the sun rose, but with the sun came the falling stones. Taking what shelter they could, they hurried up towards the second step. One chimney was passed 'at a run, amid the screech of missiles'. In climbing up to the second shoulder, where they were helped by a rope left by Rey, Gaspard dislodged a boulder which crushed one of his fingers. The finger was bound up and they went on, Gaspard still leading.

After two and a half hours of very quick going they reached the now famous shoulder where Mummery's and Young's parties found the traverse across the east face the only justifiable continuation of the climb. It was where Rey's guide had begun his attempt to scale the rope let down to him just on the Swiss side of the immense straight nose linking the shoulder with the summit.

Piacenza's men had many times surveyed the place and did not hesitate. They began their attack by a diagonal traverse of some twenty yards on steep loose rock, one of the bands on which Daniel Maquignaz had pointed out that snow could lie. Anyone who climbed in the Alps in 1911 will remember what a phenomenally fine season it was. The traverse brought them up against a rock wall devoid of hold of any sort. Gaspard mounted on Carrel's shoulders, Piacenza on Gaspard's; this human ladder brought a hold within reach and a belay for the rope. The two guides hauled themselves up over Piacenza's head and after a long struggle reached a stance from which he too could be pulled up. This passage was technically the most difficult of all.

Conditions were perfect, the weather calm and cloudless. Climbing nearly straight up they reached the snowbands that stretch across the south face immediately under the final precipices. But the last 400-500 feet of the ridge was still above them; there was ample evidence on the stone-strewn patches of snow on the cliffs that the climb ahead would be dangerous as well as difficult.

A rope was fixed and abandoned and an icy stone-swept gully was crossed. Cover was reached below a boss on the crest of the ridge. Piacenza wrote: 'From this spot we could see the Swiss parties on the Hörnli Ridge, who greeted us, without, I must confess, the cordiality of the Italian guides on the south-west ridge. The glory about to accrue to the men of Valtournanche is for ever lost to the men of Zermatt!'

Stones are easily dislodged by careless parties on the summit of the Matterhorn — do we not remember Whymper discharging some to convince the Italians of his victory in 1865? — so Piacenza and his guides remained under cover for an hour. They emerged to face fresh difficulties on the wall on the Italian side. A slab about a hundred feet from the crest was found unclimbable. Another smooth vertical rock was surmounted by means of the human ladder they had employed below. Another long, lonely wait followed for Piacenza before he could be drawn up to join the guides on a minute platform.

There seemed to be no way on. To add to the tension, a huge mass of rock close to them suddenly broke away and crashed down the gully they had crossed, leaving a cloud of dust. To climb up the bed of the gully with any prospect of avoiding death it would be necessary to wait till the night frost held back the loose stones. Was a traverse back to the ridge possible? It looked horribly risky, but they took the risk.

Doubtfully belayed by the rope Carrel crept across the crumbling face of rock up to a great boulder where he was safe. Another difficult slab was traversed and the ridge gained above the overhang. A proof that victory was won was the sight of the ladder used and abandoned by Rey in his last exploration.

At 1.30 'we attain the top — we are mad with joy; we embrace and wave a red flag to our friends at Jomein'. Needless to say, there was no political significance in the colour of the flag!

So the last great ridge of the Matterhorn had been climbed, as near the crest, perhaps, as it would ever be possible to climb it, short of constructing a piton staircase up the nose itself. Three years later came the war of 1914-18. Piacenza's ascent is the last noteworthy incident in the history of the mountain for more than a decade.

CHAPTER VIII

THE LAST TWO DECADES

THE Matterhorn is a pyramid with four faces. There are two reasons obvious to any mountaineer why it was climbed by its ridges. First, because the angle of ascent on the ridge is less steep and the line up the centre of the face steeper than on any other part of the faces forming the ridge. Second, because a ridge route, as long as the crest can be followed, is not exposed to stonefalls.

Even in face climbs, as for instance the great west face of the Weisshorn, the crest of a rib is preferred wherever possible as a protection against this danger, which technical skill can do little to avoid.

Now the faces of the Matterhorn are, for such extensive faces, exceptionally smooth; after a heavy snowfall they look like almost uniform sheets of snow, especially the two seen from Zermatt, the east and north faces. No prominent ribs show up on them as is the case with the fine rib that offers a direct route to the summit of Monte Rosa on the south face, or that which is followed by the Route Major on the Brenva face of Mont Blanc. Consequently, face climbs on the Matterhorn are particularly dangerous. Even at night I have seen a vast avalanche of rocks cover most of the east face in a moonlit cloud of dust. The precipitous steps in the lower parts of the Furggen ridge are passed by routes which parties who have climbed them have found anything but safe from missiles from above, apart from those that even a careful leader or his rope may dislodge, to the danger of those below.

Before the war of 1914-18 the faces had been generally left in their well-defended seclusion. Penhall's party, anticipated by a few hours by Mummery in the first ascent of the Zmutt ridge, chose a route lying almost entirely on the west face, approaching it by a couloir which forms a stone shoot for the discarded fragments of that face. What happened to Lammer and Lorria in their attempt to repeat Penhall's route showed what a trap it might be.

After the war of 1914-18, many young men, prepared for the adventure of war and having to live the most vigorous years of life in an atmosphere of disillusionment, found a need for excitement at any price satisfied by new and dangerous climbs. The unclimbed faces of the Matterhorn were made for such young men. The north face offered special attractions; it was in full view of Zermatt and it was plastered with difficulties from top to bottom.

In 1923 A. Horeschowsky and F. Piekielko made a serious attempt on it. They gained the ice slope at the foot of the face by following the ridge above the Hörnli hut for a short distance and then traversing glazed rocks. They crossed the ice slope diagonally upwards and then: 'A steep rib, consisting of loose frost-bound rock pillars, was very slowly ascended, the climbing being uncommonly dangerous. The only possible line of ascent which we could see was the narrow couloir which seams the flank to the right of the jutting-out Shoulder. Unfortunately we had to give up all hope, as the continuous stonefall made it impossible to gain a single inch of height in the couloir. So we sought to escape up vertical, at times overhanging, rocks below the Shoulder. We finally emerged at 5.30 p.m. at about 4000 m., a few steps from the Solvay hut. This section of 700 m. had cost us 12½ hours of hard, dangerous work.' We shall hear more of the narrow couloir, for it was followed for a great part of the first ascent of this face.

An attempt in 1929 enjoyed a shorter period of danger, but did not get off quite so easily. E. R. Blanchet with the guides Mooser and Lärjer found the rocks above the Matterhorn Glacier entirely ice-glazed. 'After 3½ hours slow progress the retreat was sounded. Mooser having been hit three times. The party was lucky to escape with their lives.'

In this same year an American tripper with a Zermatt guied made a 'record' ascent from the Belvédère inn on the Hörnli to the summit in 1 hour 50 min., and descended in 1 hour 5 min. The guide was ill for several days as a result. The comment of the editor of the *Alpine Journal* was severe: 'For such crimes the death penalty is inadequate.'

On July 28th, 1931, the brothers Franz and Toni Schmid pitched their tent on the pastures three thousand feet below the Hörnli hut, having bicycled most of the way from Munich. July 29th was spent in exploring the best way through the steep *séracs* of the Matterhorn Glacier on to its upper plateau under the north face. The next day was spent wisely, if unusually, in restful preparation for the great enterprise to follow.

They left their tent at midnight; on their backs they carried a good supply of rock and ice pitons, clasp-rings, two 130 ft. ropes, a rubber sleeping sack and a certain amount of food. At 2 a.m. they called in at the Hörnli hut to ask the guardian to warn any parties starting for the Matterhorn that there would be climbers on the north face. Stones dislodged by anyone above the Shoulder might mean death for the brothers Schmid.

Following the route already reconnoitred they reached the foot of the ice slope 1000 feet high which runs up towards the wall of vertical rocks below the upper north-east ridge. Before dawn they had climbed the slopes of avalanche snow at the foot of the precipitous north face and halted just below the *bergschrund*. Small fragments of snow and ice poured over the upper lip of the schrund as they tied themselves together with the two ropes and distributed the burdens.

The ice slope that rose straight above them is so steep that few climbers, even if comforted by the sharpest crampons, would hesitate to dispense with steps. However, this intrepid pair considered the saving of time more important than security, so Toni led off up the ice to the end of the rope's length and then drove in an ice piton to give security while Franz came up. In this way they climbed the great slope, presenting a good target to anything that fell from the rocks above.

The only feature of the middle stretch of the face that suggests a joint in the polished armour of the face is a long gully that starts near the top right-hand corner of the ice-slope and curves upwards till it is lost in steep rocks at about the height of the Swiss Shoulder.

Rocks began to appear, as they habitually do, through the ice as the top of the slope was reached. They were glazed and any holds on them had to be chipped out. A long traverse over these repellent rocks separated the leader from the entrance to the gully. For the last 200 feet Franz took over the lead and worked his way across to it.

In the hottest part of the day this gully streams with water, and is a favourite channel for falling stones; in the early hours of the day it is heavily glazed. A short way up it, the first stance reached since leaving the bergschrund permitted a short halt; Franz brought his brother up to it and a bar of chocolate was eaten. Hour after hour passed as they crawled up the gully, sometimes by the rotten rocks at the side, sometimes by the ice at the bottom of the channel. Attempts to break out of it only led to situations involving a hazardous return. They were lucky in finding themselves always where the stones did not fall.

The sun was dipping towards the horizon beyond the Col d'Hérens when Franz ran out a last rope's length that took them out of the gully by a difficult chimney and a short ice-wall on to the slabs above. They were now about level with the Solvay hut at over 13,000 feet. They looked round in vain for a possible spot in which to pass the approaching night. Toni relieved his brother and led up steep rocks and grooves of ice. They were tired and thirsty; their fingers had suffered badly from gripping the rocks and the close cutting in the ice, the rope was now frozen stiff, and it was getting dark. Franz took another spell at leading and at last at 8.30 a small projecting boss of rock was sighted. But before reaching it, they came within an ace of falling. Toni was belaying Franz, who was a few feet above him trying to move on to a better stance. Suddenly the rock on which he was standing broke clean off and crashed down the face. By desperately clawing on to a bulge of rock with his hands, he managed to hold on till Franz could pull him up on to a foothold.

The boss was reached, pitons were driven in and they tied themselves securely to the mountain with the rope. The aneroid gave the height as 13,600 feet. Axes and crampons were tied to another piton and they prepared for the night. Every movement needed care, for anything dropped was irretrievably lost. Food was extracted from the rucksacks and eaten and they crept into the rubber sack. All night long they lay crouched in it beside the boss, with ample time to contrast their position with those of the holiday makers down in Zermatt; the lights from its hotels may have reminded them occasionally how long must be the wait for dawn. It came at last and was greeted with shouts of joy, but it was another two hours before the sun rose above the clouds on the horizon and invited them to emerge from the sack and thaw the stiffness from their limbs.

At 7.0 Toni led off over the expanse of slabs and ice. Soon a promising rib took them up some distance and Franz relieved his brother in the lead. They thought the worst was behind them, but not for long. They came to smooth slabs where there was not a crack into which a piton could be driven. Franz had a very bad moment when he failed to find a hold after struggling up two or three feet and only just managed to get back on to his meagre footholds. It then appeared to him that a traverse to the left towards the Swiss Shoulder was their one chance of escape. Alexander Pollinger happened to come on to the Shoulder at that moment with a party. He shouted that the traverse was impossible, so Franz turned to attempt the traverse to the right which Toni had suggested, as arrival near the Shoulder would have meant failure to complete the climb up the face.

This traverse passed along a ledge of rotten snow, which behaved as such snow often does, looking as if it must collapse at any moment, yet not doing so. Beyond it came orange slabs on which the ice was sufficiently thick to let small steps be cut.

Meanwhile the weather had begun to threaten dire possibilities; clouds were forming about the summit and rumbles of thunder were heard. A bad storm on such a face could have only one ending for them. They reached a snow-filled crack which led straight up into the mist; there was only one thing to do, to follow it and keep on blindly upwards. Their crack was followed by others with short walls of rock interspersed. As the slope at last began to ease off, a storm of hail with thunder and lightning broke over them. But they knew they had won the battle with the face, and in a quarter of an hour they came out on the summit ridge close to the Italian end of it.

With lightning playing about them, they got rid of the axes and cowered under a rock. When a lull in the storm came, they hurried along the ridge over the Swiss summit and began to descend the fixed ropes. Here the storm returned worse than before; hail poured in avalanches over the Shoulder and the rope, thick and heavy with ice, became a menace. It was a hard struggle to make the Solvay hut. They entered it at 5.30 and got off their frozen clothes, which stood up of themselves like suits of armour. Then they wrapped every blanket they could find round them and lay down. They slept till noon next day. The snow lay thick round the hut and it continued to fall all that day. With some emergency rations kept in the hut for such occasions they made a scanty meal and went to bed again.

Next morning, August 3rd, the weather having cleared, they left the hut at 7.0. Deep snow covered the rocks and neither of them had been on this side of the Matterhorn before. They kept close to the ridge and found the going arduous. Soon after midday they were greeted by two of their friends who had come to meet them. The tracks and the company of these two friends made the rest of the descent a comparatively light affair.

At Zermatt a banquet was given in honour of the brothers Schmid. After a few days spent at the Hotel Mont Cervin as the guests of Dr. Seiler, they left on their bicycles for Chamonix, with intentions on the north face of the Grandes Jorasses. Perhaps it was well that they did not carry out those intentions. They must have arrived shortly before the bodies of two notoriously reckless climbers were found at the foot of the face, still roped together, with a piton hanging loose in the doubled rope. Toni Schmid was killed the following year, leading a very difficult ice climb on the Gross Wiessbachhorn.

It is worth recording two subsequent ascents of the north face, if only for the comparison in speed of working they afford between the good amateur and the good guide on a climb of this nature, where ice is a formidable obstacle to rapid progress.

The second ascent of the face was made on July 15th-19th, 1935, by two Munich climbers, J. Schmidbauer and T. Leiss. This party, hammering and nailing for three days, endured two miserable bivouacs before emerging on the summit. Only five days later the

Franz (left) and Toni Schmid

Matterhorn and Dent d'Hérens

(*from the Air*)

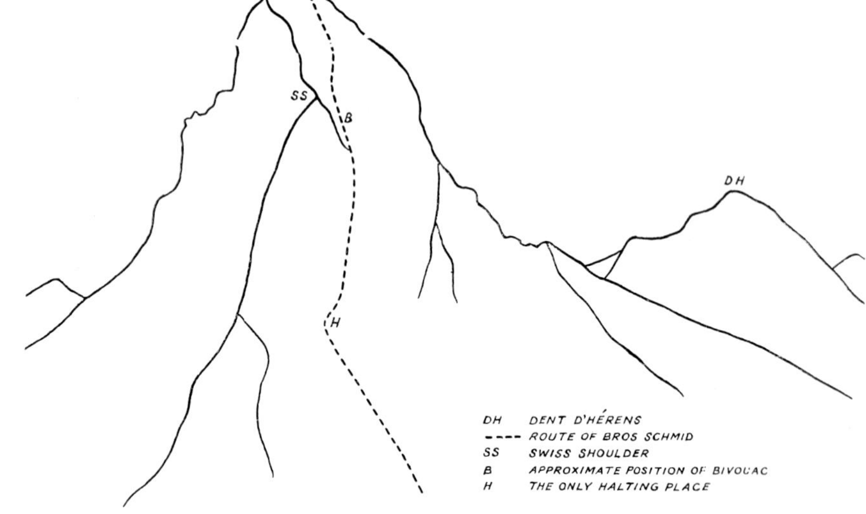

Grindelwald guide, Hermann Steuri, with Dr. Baur of Saxony, made the ascent and descended to the Belvédère inn on the Hörnli in a single day. These two left the Hörnli hut at 0.45, and reached the bergschrund below the face in an hour. A fall of stones occurred as they were cutting up the long curving gully, but they were not hit. By 10.0 the whole gully was behind them. After a short halt for food the difficult traverse to the right was begun; the only two pitons used on the climb were driven in here. At 11.30, the traverse passed, they were able to rest side by side for half an hour. From this point they found the going much less severe and at 13.45 they were on the Italian summit. Making a long halt there and at the Solvay hut they entered the Belvédère inn early in the evening.

Anyone familiar with the climbing literature produced under the Fascist régime in Italy will understand how keenly these victories on the north face stimulated Italian efforts to wrest the palm for reckless adventure from their Nazi rivals. Signor E. Benedetti began the task in 1930 by climbing the last step of the Furggen ridge by a route slightly nearer the crest than that taken by Piacenza in 1911. His guides were Louis Carrel and Maurice Bich.

The party left the Breuiljoch at 6.0 and climbed unroped up the dangerous stretch to the Furggen shoulder. One stone just missed Carrel's head; another, luckily from no great height, struck Benedetti on the forearm. The Furggen shoulder was reached at 10.30 and after half an hour's halt Carrel began the traverse on the Italian face. He ran out 150 feet of rope, but an overhanging nose of rock prevented the others from seeing what he was doing and also obstructed his own view of what lay ahead.

On this first exploration of the traverse he managed to change his scarpetti for boots, as the latter gave a better grip on the granite. He came back and was let down lower over the face, reappeared to take off his sack and then vanished once more under the projecting nose. A quarter of an hour passed, while the others waited in intense anxiety; then a voice came from above and a rope with knots in it began to swing to and fro across the nose. Bich caught it and swung like a pendulum over the abyss and then clambered up. Benedetti preferred to creep down a few yards till he could reach the rope hanging vertically. They all three came together again round a piton left by Piacenza's party.

Carrel then climbed up diagonally to the left, mostly on steep slabs, noticing rather below and further to the left a rope ring attached to a piton. The party then turned straight up, making a free use of pitons, the last man pulling them out after use. They were obliged to do this, as they only carried four pitons. Higher up they bore to the right up short chimneys and reached the crest of the ridge under the overhang, where they found Piacenza's card in a bottle.

Ten yards away to the left was a vertical crack 100 feet high; this was climbed and the crest regained above the overhang. The remains of Rey's ladder were still lying in a gully on the Swiss side of the crest. Keeping along the ridge from this point they arrived on the Swiss summit at 3.30. A long halt in the rays of the sinking September sun was made there before beginning the descent to the Italian hut. Back at Breuil next day, Benedetti soliloquized over the scars on his hands and his skinless knees, 'I must: however, regret that none of these wounds left any permanent signs to remind me that body as well as soul had made that ascent.'

The danger of stonefalls at so many stages of the ascent of the Furggen ridge will probably prevent it from ever becoming a popular climb. Piacenza's route was repeated by M. Auber's party in 1943. A fall of many hundreds of tons of rock occurred that year. It came from a point a little below the Furggen shoulder and the scar can be seen from the Riffel. Presumably it did not happen as M. Auber's party were on their way to the Shoulder. There have been at least three other ascents since.

While engaged on his partly new, piton-aided route on the Furggen ridge Benedetti had kept an eye on the Italian south face which had never yet been attempted. In 1906 Rey's friend Ugo de Amicis and Arrigo Trusta had made a new direct route to the point known as the Pic Tyndall on the south-west ridge. They followed a well-marked buttress, which is really the edge of the Matterhorn's south face. At times they had to leave the crest of the buttress and traverse on its south-west face. In certain conditions it forms a good alternative to the usual Italian route, but can hardly be considered an ascent of the south face.

The cliffs of the more westerly portion of the face under the Italian summit are sheer immense walls; it is the part under the upper Furggen ridge and the Swiss summit that offers some possibility of reaching the snowbands under the broad head of the peak.

In the fine October of 1931, ten weeks after the Schmids' ascent of the north face, Benedetti made his attempt. Louis Carrel, Maurice Bich and he left La Riende, the hut some 3000 feet above Breuil, at 5.0. After following the way to the Breuiljoch for some time they turned up the steep face, climbing first over 'a sort of pinnacle', then roughly parallel to the lower part of the Furggen ridge.

Benedetti's comments on the route are not reassuring as regards objective risks; he is moved to thank the previous bad weather for compelling them to wait for early autumn, 'thus making possible a climb which during the summer would have been dangerous if not impossible. With the rising sun stones began to fall methodically, and we had to put up with their unpleasant company for 10 hours. We were obliged to proceed by rushes, making for big boulders or anything that might afford shelter. But the stones were kind to us and fell only at regular intervals, thus permitting us to pass between successive showers'.

Have Fascists and Nazis some means of enforcing these methodical habits on stones? If not, Benedetti's apology suggests the tribute that hypocrisy often pays to virtue, or at any rate, used to pay while regard for the consequences of a man's actions, especially the consequences for others, was esteemed a virtue.

Coming to steep slabs and an ice cascade under the upper Furggen ridge, they went nearly straight up the face *in the main couloir* or some secondary small ones near it. When confronted by an impossible wall, they bore left over very steep rocks across a great rock rib that ran up towards the Swiss summit, then straight up again to the base of the last precipices under the Italian summit.

Benedetti thus describes the final climb up these cliffs. 'We stopped for a second time that day, then, after a most difficult traverse, reached the foot of the couloir leading up to the summit ridge near the Italian end. This couloir, about 250 feet high, was divided into three steps. It was very difficult, but perhaps we found it so through our being extremely tired at the end of the climb. Where the *passage d'Aymoned* cuts across our couloir there was a particularly difficult bit where we left a piton. Then we went straight up, still finding the climbing extremely hard. After 1¾ hours of strenuous gymnastics we arrived at a point a few yards below the summit ridge. There we put on a few extra clothes and emerged on the skyline at 6.0.'

I am inclined to agree with Benedetti's suggestion that fatigue may have made the last part of the climb seem so difficult, for I am pretty sure my party came down over it in 1906. We were then at our best at the end of a very good season, but we certainly cannot have been in the Carrel and Bich class. To avoid parties on the Swiss side, we had dined at the Schwarzsee and climbed through the night under an almost full moon, with a long halt at midnight on the roof of the old hut at about 12,000 ft. We reached the top soon after sunrise. A bit of rope hanging from the summit ridge near the Italian end of it led me to think it was the beginning of the usual descent on the south side. We found a succession of vertical chimneys with many loose stones; my head, as I led down, had a narrow escape from one of them. At one place, a small platform at the top of a steep drop, we found a sort of cat's cradle of thick string and boulders; it added more to our danger than our security. After a climb that to us was quite unexpectedly difficult, we reached the broad ledges, generally snow-covered, below the head of the Matterhorn. As we crossed these ledges towards the south-west ridge, we heard something whistle through the air and saw an ice-axe pitch and stick upright in the snow a few yards away. Looking up we saw the line of ropes on the Italian route and a party in the act of coming down the ladder. Later Mr. Walter Larden told me it was his party that had dropped the axe. Our route down the precipice must have been almost identical with that taken by Benedetti in his ascent.

I have mentioned the incident as showing how little actual difference there may be between making a new route and mistaking an old one! There is, I suppose, a morality of climbing and we know that, morally, it is the intention that counts. And there can be no question that in this case Benedetti made a new route, while I simply made a mistake.

One face of the Matterhorn was still unclimbed, the east face. It is the easiest and most stone-swept of all the four. In almost any part, it can be climbed and the obstacles turned without difficulty on one side or the other. In snowy years it hardly shows any bare rock and it may be less dangerous then than after fine weather. Late in the season it is often black, but for a few streaks of snow lying on ledges or in shallow gullies, and it is then in the most dangerous condition of all. Those who have climbed the mountain by the usual Zermatt route know that the occasional traverses on the east face offer little difficulty but need constant care to avoid dislodging stones.

Only men with a fanatical desire to place a new ascent to their own credit and that of their nation could be attracted to a route up this face. Benedetti had already shown himself to be of this mind. The ascent was made in the latter half of September. The party was larger than the trio who had climbed the south face the previous year. Besides these three it included G. Mazzotti, Lucien Carrel, and Antoine Gaspard.

The line chosen for the ascent was, as near as possible, straight up the middle of the face, a *dirittissimo* whose resemblance to a capital 'I' must have endeared it to Italians of that time. Attempts to avoid stonefalls by following such semblances of ribs as this side of the Matterhorn provides, were not wholly successful. Some of the party were damaged, though none was killed, before reaching the precipices that form the final defences of the peak at the top of the face.

Most of the day was spent in hammering a way up these last few hundred feet. Night fell before the leading guide had reached the rocks where the slope eases off near the summit. A wretched night was spent by the party in small groups separated from one another by stretches of precipice. Pitons were driven in, not securely enough to remove anxiety, to prevent their falling in the unlikely event of sleep coming to anyone. When morning came, the guides forced a way to the summit. More than 10 hours had been spent on this one difficult portion of the route, which has nothing at all to recommend it, unless danger alone be a recommendation. 'Death without glory' was a not inappropriate description of it by a distinguished mountaineer.'

All four faces as well as all four ridges of the Matterhorn have now been climbed. New routes can be little more than variations of those that have been made.

It was inevitable that a peak so dramatic in form and with a dramatic history should become a subject for the cinema. One of the earliest, as it was one of the few genuine films made upon it, was based on Charles Gos's novel *La Croix du Cervin.* Gos himself has described the making of this film of the ascent from the Col du Lion and the descent at night in a snowstorm, of the Zermatt side. Rarely can such a collection of guides of famous families have been engaged together; A Lochmatter, a Knubel, a Perren and a Pollinger; the worst of storms could hardly frighten one in company like that!

Later films have concentrated on the famous accident of 1865. One of the most popular — sad to relate — was *The Challenge*, which appeared in 1938. It purported to be the true story 'with certain episodes slightly altered'. A few comments from a critic who knows his Matterhorn and its history will show how true! 'All the climbing and the accident take place on the small rocky peak of the Riffelhorn near the two Riffel hotels. The only motion pictures taken on the Matterhorn are those of the party on the summit ridge. Hudson resembles the butler of low comedy and climbs correspondingly — a grotesque misrepresentation of the best amateur of his time. Croz is overwhelmed by Whymper and shows no sign of skill. Many details of the story are incorrect, some are frankly libellous. The actual order of roping is altered in order to make possible the suggestion that Whymper cut the rope. It is disconcerting to find Favre's inn (at Valtournanche) occupying the site of the present Riffelhaus and in full view of the Mischabel and Monte Rosa.'

If the film industry like to make a sensational climbing story, by all means let them do so, but it is not justified in representing as historical fact what is entirely untrue, and may be a gross libel on the character and conduct of persons whose near relatives may be living. Variations in the pace at which action takes place must occur in the showing of the most genuine films; there is harmless amusement in seeing clouds drift over the peaks as fast as a Mosquito plane and men marching up a glacier at 21,000 feet at 4 or 5 miles an hour, but the interpolation of scenes in which the conduct of — shall we say the Everest expedition — was grossly misrepresented, would be rightly resented.

Actual climbing of rocks or ice sufficiently difficult to be exciting is too slow to be a good subject for the cinema. And, perhaps mercifully, the staging of an accident that will give the impression of a real one to those who have witnessed such a thing must be almost impossible. The rôle high mountains play in popular film production is likely to be confined to snow scenes providing lovely backgrounds for the amorous adventures of the professional beauties.

Up to now none of the projects for hauling visitors to the summit of the Matterhorn by other means than the strong arms of guides have materialized, and its slopes are still considered unsuitable for ski-ing; though not by all. In 1940 a popular evening paper told us that 'a champion skier last spring enjoyed two days ski-ing on the slopes of the Matterhorn above Turin, going up in a funicular to a height of 14,000 feet'. This is a wider miss than usual!

There is, alas! no denying the fact that the Matterhorn is crowded in fine summer weather. It is, more than any other in these days, the mountain of which many tourists can say: 'In 19— I climbed the Matterhorn, since then I have climbed no other mountain.' In 1932 I remember meeting a party of two young Americans with two good guides coming down. It was the first mountain they had been on; both of them looked tired and scared; the leading guide told me they would have fallen fifty times if not held by the rope. From what they said, I think it will be their only high climb.

It is not so much the mere presence of a crowd that is disturbing; it is the danger of the loose stones they send down upon this Zermatt route that makes it the one climb in the Alps I should advise anyone to avoid in the height of the season.

And Breuil is not the simple place it was when Rey was climbing, or even when he built the Villa Rey to contemplate the Matterhorn in his old age. The commercial possibilities of the great snowfields south of the Breithorn as a ski-ing ground had not then been realized. Now the tourist can be pulled up there as he is to the Gornergrat.

And yet, the Matterhorn that Rey loved all his life is not really spoiled. It can give to the present and to future generations, if they approach it in the right way, the adventures and the memories it gave to the pioneers of the sixties, to Rey in the nineties and to myself and my young friends in the first decade of this century.

Thousands of tons may fall from its frost-assaulted rocks; the form it presents to countless future generations will be essentially the same as that which the pioneers of mountaineering saw as they came up the Val Tournanche with only the faintest hopes of ever climbing it. Its architecture is on the grand, simple scale that will always appeal to those whose souls are stirred by the appeal of height and beauty. Fashion and taste affect the esteem in which things are held, particularly those things that other men's hands have made. But what is simple and great invites the test of time. If its meaning has been temporarily lost by a too sophisticated, wrongly-educated generation, a generation that comes after rediscovers it and finds a new method of expressing it. When every rib of every facet of the Matterhorn has been climbed, it will still be climbed and still admired for what it is. And future climbers of it will not find their interest lessened because it has a history.

NOTES

CHAPTER I

[1] Josías Simler, in his work 'De Alpibus Commentarius', 1574, (p. 68), gives the following hypothesis on the etymology of the name of the Monte Silvio: 'Non nulli montes a ducibus et claris viris qui forte exercitum per haec loca duxerunt nomen acceperunt; . . . apud Vallesianos mons Sempronius qui et Scipionis dicitur (Simplon) et mons Silvius: a Romanis ducibus haec nomina accepisse videntur.' We do not exactly know at what period the new name of Mont Servin, or Cervin, replaced the old, from which it seems to be derived.

[2] On the Theodul Pass Roman coins have frequently been found, some lying alone as if lost by the way, others collected in a heap and stowed away in secret places. In 1895 a girl from the Theodul inn found fifty-four hidden under a stone; they were coins of the Imperial period, from 270 to 350 A.D., some of them with Christian symbols. In the collection of the Seiler family there appear many coins found on the pass belonging to various periods, from 200 B.C. to 900 A.D. (v. E. Whymper, 'Zermatt and the Matterhorn').

[3] The canonesses of the order of St. Augustine, called Dames de Sainte Catharine, established themselves at Aosta towards the end of the twelfth century. Their statutes show that they came from Loèche, a small town in the upper Valais, above Sion, where their original convent stood. They were forced to abandon it in times of civil war, perhaps during the troubles which laid waste the Valais in the reign of the Emperor Frederick II, when the barons of Raron, powerful local lords, attempted to oppress their native place, and to make themselves its masters. See De Tillier, 'Historique de la Vallée d'Aoste', edition 1888, p. 144. De Tillier writes: 'According to tradition they entered the country by the Mont Cervin, numbering only six or seven sisters, and took refuge first of all at Antey (Valtournanche).'

[4] Towards the middle of the fifteenth century, during the struggle between Catharine de Challand and the Duke of Savoy for the succession of Challand, Catharine had made a treaty with the Valaisans, to the effect that, at the first onslaught by the Savoyard troops, they (the Valaisans) were to come to her assistance and occupy the pass of the Mont Cervin, which was included in the territory of Challand, in the Challand valley, in the fifteenth century.

[5] The Wandering Jew the first time sees on the pass a great and thriving city, and prophesies that on his second passing by that spot woods and meadows will be growing on the site of the houses and streets; and that when his sad journeying shall bring him up thither for the third time, the woods and meadows shall be gone,

and all shall be covered with snow and ice (v. J. Grand Carteret, 'La Montagne à travers les âges').

[6] Vallis Tornina, or Torniaca, a name representing Valtournanche on the ancient maps, and derived from Tornionum, or Tornaeum, now Torgnon, one of the chief villages of the valley. Towards the middle of the fourteenth century there already appears the name of Vallis Tornenchia, which may be considered as deriving from Vallis Torniaca.

Praborno: Prato Borno, or Bornus, the old name of Zermatt; it appears in the ancient maps as early as the thirteenth century (v. W. A. B. Coolidge, 'Swiss Travels and Guide Books', p. 255). The Valdostans used this name till about 1860 in the form of Praborne, or Praborgne (Paraborgne in Grüner), probably derived from Pré borné, in allusion to the meadows shut in on all sides by the mountains. The German name of Matt is not found before about 1500. Simler ('Vallesiae Descriptio', lib. i.) latinises the name into Pagus Matta and Mattia vallis. Zurmatt and Zermatt (meaning near the meadows) are names of relatively recent date, De Saussure writes it Zer-Matt (v. also Coolidge, op. cit., p. 257).

[7] Aegidius Tschudi writes in his work, 'De Prisca ac vera Alpina Raethia': 'Sunt praeterea et aliae viae ultra Summas Alpes in Italiani nempe ex superiori Vallesia per montem Gletscher in vallem Ougstal (Aosta valley).' On his famous topographical map he marks the pass under the name of Der Gletscher. The date of Tschudi's ascent to the Col is not stated, but we may suppose it to have taken place about 1528. I am indebted for these and for the other notes on Tschudi which appear in the text, to the Rev. W. A. B. Coolidge. He also kindly showed me certain MSS. of the book on Josias Simler and the origin of mountaineering which Messrs. Falque and Perrin of Grenoble are publishing for him, from which I quote the following passage from Tschudi, translated from the German: 'Silvius Mons, appelé Der Gletscher par les Allemands, parceque sur son faîte s'étend sur une largeur de quatre mille italiens un champ de névé éternel, et de glace, qui ne fond et ne disparaît jamais; en été on peut toujours le traverser sans crainte soit à cheval soit à pied; le mont est très élevé et sépare les Sedunes (habitants du Haut Vallais) des Salasses (habitants du Val d'Aôste). Tout à fait sur le faîte de ce mont le chemin se bifurque pour descendre par le Val d'Aoste par deux vallées latérales, dont l'une appelée Aiaza (Val d'Ayas), est située à main gauche et mène à Eporedia ou Livery (Ivrée).' The latter is now known as the Col des Cimes Blanches (v. also Grand Carteret, 'Les Alpes dans l'Antiquité', p. 212). In Sebastien Münster's 'Cosmography', published in 1543, the name of Matter is given to the pass, and this is the origin of the present German name of the Cervin (Matterhorn). 'A Vespa (Visp) iter extenditur per montem Saser (Saas) et ab alio latere per montem Matter ad oppida quaedam Mediolanesis ditionis, item ad vallem Kremerthal (Val Tournanche) quae paret comiti a Zaland (Challand).' On Münster's topographical chart this group is marked under the names of Augstalberg (Aosta mountain) and Mons Silvius (v. Coolidge, op. cit., p. 256).

[8] As far back as 1760 Saussure had promised a reward to anyone who should find a way to ascend Mont Blanc.

[9] v. Saussure, 'Voyages dans les Alpes', vol. iv. pp. 389, 408, 438, 442, 443.

[10] 'Quelle force n'a-t-il pas fallu pour rompre et balayer tout ce qui manque à cette pyramide! Car on ne voit autour d'elle aucun entassement de fragments; on n'y voit que d'autres cimes qui sont elles mêmes adhérentes au sol, et dont les flancs, égalements déchirés, indiquent d'immenses débris dont on ne voit aucune trace dans le voisinage. Sans doute ce sont ces débris qui sous la forme de cailloux, de blocs et de sable remplissent nos vallées at nos bassins, où ils sont descendus, les uns par le Valais, les autres par la vallée d'Aoste du côté de la Lombardie' (Saussure, 'Voyages').

[11] 'Histoire naturelle des Glaciers de la Suisse.' Translated from the German and published in Paris in 1770.

[12] 'Nouvelle description des Glaciers, Vallées de glace et Glaciers qui forment la grande Chaîne des Alpes de Suisse, d'Italie et de Savoie' (M. T. Bourrit, 1795).

[13] ' . . . notre brave guide, chez qui nous avions logé aux chalets du Breuil, et que je recommande à ceux qui feront ce voyage' (Saussure, 'Voyages').

[14] Saussure found on the pass the remains, in excellent preservation, of a rude fort which was called the St. Theodul Fort, and which he believed to have been built by the Valdostans, centuries before, to prevent an invasion by the Valaisans. Describing the bivouac, he writes: 'La soirée fut très froide et nous eûmes beaucoup de peine à allumer le feu; nos guides n'avaient apporté ni amadou, ni allumettes. Je crois même qu'au Breuil ces inventions passent pour des objets de luxe. Cependant nous nous réchauffâmes sous nos pelisses, et nous passâmes une fort bonne nuit.'

[15] Mr. Cade, as Scheuchzer had already done in 1705, names the present Theodul Pass Monte Rosa. The word Rosa is a form of the ancient generic name given to the glaciers by the dwellers on the southern slopes of the Alps, which was pronounced roëse, roese, or rouïse; while the inhabitants on the north side called the glaciers Gletscher, and therefore the Theodul Gletscher mountain.

[16] *Alpine Journal*, vol. vii. p. 435.

[17] Professor Forbes relates that, during his first journeys among the Alps of Savoy, the simple fact of crossing the mountains in places where it was not customary to pass, was sufficient to make the traveller an object of suspicion to the vigilant police; when in addition he was addicted to sketching, or to the use of a hammer or a barometer, he ran the risk of rousing popular prejudice, of whose extent he would never have dreamt had not some of the extraordinary conjectures current about himself and his projects come by chance to his ears. (Travels through the Alps of Savoy).

Saussure, referring to his second visit to the St. Gotthard hospice in 1783, said of the monks there: 'Ils commencent à s'accoutumer à voir des étrangers qui étudient les montagnes. Dans mon premier voyage en 1775, ils crurent que c'était chez moi une espèce de folie. Ils dîrent à quelqu'un de ma connaissance qui passa chez eux peu de temps après moi, que je paroissais d'un bon caractère, mais qu'il était bien malheureux que j'eusse une manie aussi ridicule que celle de ramasser toutes les pierres que je rencontrais, d'en remplir mes poches et d'en charger des mulets.'

[18] The Commune of Châtillon used to pay 200 francs for the capture of a bear and 100 for that of a she-wolf.

[19] William Brockedon the painter, and author of an interesting volume — 'Illustrations of the Passes of the Alps' — came to Valtournanche for the first time in 1824, and again in the following year, crossing the Theodul Pass on the latter occasion.

[20] Brockedon relates that on his arrival, in 1824, at the village of Valtournanche where it was customary to engage guides for the crossing of the Theodul, they told him that the Col was impassable for miles on account of certain wide crevasses which had lately formed on the glacier; and that, in order to pass on foot, a great number of guides would be needed to ensure the traveller's safety, and they counselled him not to try. They said that a change in the glaciers was a rare occurrence, which had not taken place for twenty years; but that now the whole of the glacier on the Valais side was in motion. Attempts had been made to make another route, but the glacier's movement had destroyed it, and it was advisable to wait till the disturbance should cease. Brockedon renounced his project, and came back the following year ('Journal of Excursions', p. 48).

[21] For history of Zermatt and the Théodul Pass consult 'Swiss Travels and Guidebooks', by W. A. B. Coolidge.

[22] See *Alpine Journal*, vol. xvi. pp. 117 and 118.

[23] Dr. J. Forbes, 'A Physician's Holiday', 1847, p. 232.

[24] 'Excursions et séjours dans les glaciers', 1844.

[25] Christian Moritz Engelhardt, 'Naturschilderungen', 1840. 'Das Monte Rosa und Matterhorngebirg', 1852.

[26] In the course of his journey in 1842 Professor Forbes passed from Valtournanche to Gressoney, where he met M. F. Zumstein of Gressoney, the same who had ascended one of the peaks (the third in height) of Monte Rosa. Three weeks before Forbes's arrival, another peak (the fourth in height), had been conquered, also by an Italian, the Abbé Gnifetti, the parish priest of Alaqua.

[27] See 'Nouveaux Voyages en Zig-zag'.

[28] See W. G. Collingwood, 'The Life of John Ruskin', pp. 95, 96.

[29] 'The Stones of Venice', ed. 1898, vol. i. p. 59.

[30] The distance and the position of the places from which Ruskin studied the Cervin did not always allow of his conclusions being perfectly accurate, for which some climbers have reproached him, perhaps too severely (see Whymper, 'Scrambles', p. 155, and Hawkins, 'Vacation Tourists', p. 287). Ruskin was the first to daguerrotype the Cervin (see De La Sizeranne, 'Ruskin et la Religion de la beauté', and J. Bardoux, 'John Ruskin').

[31] Leslie Stephen, an English climber of the first rank, wrote on the occasion of John Ruskin's death: ' . . . Many people had tried their hands upon Alpine descriptions since De Saussure; but Ruskin's chapters seemed to have the freshness of a new revelation. . . .' (*National Review*, April, 1900). In his book, 'The Playground of Europe', he had written in 1871: 'Mr. Ruskin has covered the Matterhorn with a whole web of poetical associations, in language which, to a severe taste, is perhaps a trifle too fine, though he has done it with an eloquence which his bitterest antagonist must acknowledge' (p. 308). Ruskin was a member of the English Alpine Club from 1869 to 1882.

[32] John Ball made the first passage of the Schwarzthor from Zermatt to St. Jacques d'Ayas in 1845. He published the first series of that most remarkable Alpine work, 'Peaks, Passes, and Glaciers', in 1858, and in 1863 the first edition of his Alpine guide, which was at that time a true Alpine encyclopaedia, and earned him the name of the first of classical writers of the Alps.

[33] [Wills's most famous ascent was that of the Wetterhorn in 1854. His book 'Wanderings in the High Alps' was published in 1856. Blackwell published a new edition in 1937 — R.L.G.I.]

[34] Attempts: 1847, Ordinaire and Puiseux; 1848, Prof. Ulrich; 1851, A. and H. Schlagintweit; 1854, Bird, Smith, and Kennedy; First ascent, Smith and Hudson.

[35] Marshall Hall, referring to the year 1849, wrote: 'As for the giant Matterhorn, it has never entered the mind of man that its ascent was possible' (*Alpine Journal*, vol. ix. p. 174).

[36] 'Lettres sur les Vallées de Lanzo, 1823.' These letters were considered worthy of being republished, more than thirty years after, in the 'Alpine Journal' of J. T. Cimino (vol. iii, 1864), the first Alpine work published in Italy.

CHAPTER II

[1] Albrecht von Haller, A Swiss poet of the eighteenth century, who sang of the life of mountaineers in his poem, 'Die Alpen' (1732).

[2] 'Modern Painters', chap. xix. vol. iv. This chapter was first published in 1856.

[3] 'Le Ranz-des-Vaches était si chéri des Suisses qu'il fut défendu, sous peine de mort, de le jouer dans leurs troupes, parce qu'il faisait fondre en larmes, déserter, ou mourir ceux qui l'entendaient, tant il excitait en eux l'ardent désir de revoir leur pays' (J. J. Rousseau).

[4] With reference to the disafforesting which is, alas! going on in the Val Tournanche, as well as in the other Piedmontese valleys, I think it well to quote an emphatic warning uttered by the distinguished Genevese botanist, H. Correvon, a sincere friend of the Valtorneins: 'Un peuple qui déboise est un peuple en décadence: souvenez-vous en bien, messieurs de Valtournanche. C'est très

particulièrement dans le pays d'Aoste qu'on peut dire que l'avenir agricole dépend du degré de reboisement des pentes arides. Autrefois riche et prospère cette grande vallée, qu'arrosent les eaux provenant des plus hautes montagnes de l'Europe, est dans un état voisin de la pauvreté. La population s'en prend à tort au gouvernement et aux impôts. C'est le propre des faibles d'accuser les forts; il faut que chacun travaille et que tout individu collabore à la grande œuvre de réconstitution des forêts' (see *Bulletin de l'Association pour la protection des plantes*, Geneva, n. 14, 1896).

[5] This word in the Valdostan patois may be translated literally as 'cream-licker'; it means a child who is as yet helpless.

[6] See H. Correvon, 'Au pied du Cervin' (*Bull. Association pour la protection des plantes*, n. 14, p. 19). This legend seems to foreshadow the latest scientific theories of the formation of the pyramid of the Cervin.

[7] A place near St. Vincent in Val d'Aosta.

[8] I do not know whether the old painting still exists in the little church at Crépin. A fresco, touched up of late by a local artist, named Carrel, above the small door of the same church, represents the bishop in his robes, squeezing the juice of a bunch of grapes into a barrel with his hand; by his side is a monster bearing a bell.

[9] The name of Mont Cervin, as also that of Matter or Matternbeg, was given to the Theodul Pass and in general to the whole group before it was restricted exclusively to the principal peak of the group. The name of St. Theodul, first bishop of Sion, and patron of the Valais, was probably given to the Col by the Valdostans, who wished by this means to indicate the pass which led to the land of those who were under the protection of the holy bishop. In the same way on the Valais side it was called the Augstlerberg Pass (pass of the Augusta mountain), as being that which gave access to the valley of Aosta (see Coolidge, 'Swiss Travels', p. 179).

[10] Grüner, in his 'Description des Glaciers de la Suisse' (1760), wrote: 'Le Mont Cervin (der hohe Mattenberg), s'entrouvrit en 1595, et forma une crevasse de six pieds de largeur, qui rendit impraticable le passage qui conduisait en Italie.' And a tradition has survived that formerly the pass between Zermatt and Valtournanche was nearer the base of the Cervin, where the pass called the Furggen now is, which was well known to the smugglers, or that of Breuil, and that in fact it became impracticable through the cataclysm. [The Breuiljoch is the pass ordinarily used by parties who traverse the Matterhorn and wish to return to the side from which they started the same day. I remember that in 1906 a bergschrund on the Swiss side was rather formidable, a sufficient obstacle to stop any party before the era of ice-axes. — R.L.G.I.]

[11] See Hinchliff, 'Summer Months Among the Alps', and Longman, 'Journal of Six Weeks' Adventures'. In Mr. Coolidge's 'Swiss Travels', the death of six men which occurred on the Theodul glacier in 1669 is recorded, and that of others again in 1795, in 1816, and in 1848. The Italian *Alpine Club Review* relates the

discovery, made by a Pession of Valtournanche in 1885 on the Italian side of the glacier, of some beams and a shoe; digging down into the earth, Pession found two corpses, eight shod horses' or mules' hoofs, and a little silver cross like a reliquary, a few medals and other articles, one of which was marked with the date 1582. See also in the *Alpine Journal*, vol. vi. p. 99, the curious discovery made by Mr. Gardiner on the Verra glacier.

[12] I suppose him to have been that Joseph Brantschen of Zermatt, of whom Engelhardt and Desor speak, and who replied as follows to the latter, when he proposed to him (in 1839) to cross the Weissthor: 'It is impossible, sir, it is only crossed by those who go on pilgrimage to Macugnaga, and you, sir, are not a pilgrim.' And he refused, saying with the deepest conviction that he would never attempt the passage except with that holy object.

[13] It was an ancient privilege of the Duchy of Aosta that the French language should be used in its official documents. De Tiller ('Historique de la Vallée d'Aoste', p. 352), writes in 1738: 'Les édits doivent être conçus et publiés en langue française, et non italienne, pour qu'ils puissent être entendus par chacun, ainsi qu'a été disposé par les articles 6 et 7 de la patente accordée au pays par S.A.S. le Duc Emanuel Philibert sous la date du 24 Juillet, 1578, confirmée par la réponse at 9me article du mémorial du 4 Octobre, 1650.' The said petition, presented by the General Council of Aosta to Charles Emanuel II, besought the sovereign to direct that edicts published in any other language but the French should be considered void, and that the inhabitants of the Duchy should not be obliged to observe them. The feeling of the Valdostans about their right to use the French language in their churches, their tribunals, their schools, and their public offices, has remained strong to the present day, notwithstanding the changed conditions of the valley. [Under the Fascist régime great efforts were made to abolish the use of French. Names were Italianized, Villeneuve into Villanova, and so on. In the post office at Cogne in 1931, the officials had to pretend not to know French. Many of the inhabitants seemed to resent it. — R.L.G.I.]

[14] Wills writes: 'We saw him only out of the window, working away, like a common labourer, at some repairs which were being done to the church.'

[15] 'Italian Valleys', p. 202, published in 1858.

[16] 'Summer Months', p. 153.

[17] 'Journal of Six Weeks' Adventures', p. 97.

[18] The Mont Cervin Hotel was founded in 1852. But many years before that, Herr Lauber, a sort of local doctor, had opened a small and picturesque wooden chalet of his for travellers. Desor mentions his hospitality as early as 1839. On to this chalet, which was sold in 1864 to Mr. Seiler, was grafted the Monte Rosa Hotel (see Coolidge, 'Swiss Travels').

[19] R. Browning, 'The Inn Album'.

[20] I have an old advertisement of the Zermatt Monte Rosa Hotel, belonging to the Seiler brothers, copies of which were still being distributed among travellers in

1862, although it had probably been printed some years before. Among the beauties to be admired in Zermatt and its environs, which are accurately set forth in the advertisement, there is no mention of the Mont Cervin. The great Matterhorn speculation had not yet begun.

[21] [This is the first prominent point north of the Dent d'Hérens on the ridge connecting that peak with the Matterhorn. After failing to reach it from below, Rey reached the sharp snow crest and its most northerly highest point from the Col des Grandes Murailles and a ridge descending from the Dent d'Hérens. — R.L.G.I.]

[22] Murray's 'Guide-Book' mentions the new chalet as early as 1853. See 1854 edition, p. 259, where the following appears: 'The quarters at Valtournanche are execrable. The new chalet built at Breuil is, perhaps, better, cannot be worse.'

[23] The hotel was opened in 1856 (see 'Guide to the Aosta Valley', by A. Gorret and E. Bich).

[24] 'A Lady's Tour', p. 579.

[25] The historians Rivaz and Boccard relate that the Valdostans took to barricading themselves on the Theodul Pass as soon as the inhabitants of the Valais began to make frequent raids over on to the Italian side (see *Journal of the I.A.C.*, vol. iv. p. 257). In the valley there is still a tradition of long struggles between the Valaisans and the Dukes of Savoy, and both Saussure and Durandi mention it. The following tale, which was still current not many years ago among the mountaineers of the Visp Valley, testifies to the animosity that existed between Piedmontese and Valaisans; I quote it from Alfred Ceresole's work, 'Zermatt und Umgebung': 'Once upon a time all the men of Zermatt who were able to bear arms had gone down to make war on the banks of the Rhone, from castle to castle. No one was left at Zermatt but children, women, and the infirm. One day a report was spread that a handful of Piedmontese was about to cross the St. Theodul Pass and to come down and sack Zermatt. A terrible panic seized the defenceless population, but a youth named Charles kept his head. He caused the women to assemble, ordered them to dress up in their husbands' clothes, to arm themselves as best they could, and to follow him to the pass. When they reached it, they built a stone wall and awaited the enemy, who soon appeared, but, seeing the wall crowded with defenders, understood that victory could not be easy; they thought the whole army of the Valais was opposed to them, and sent a spy to learn what was the strength of the garrison. The spy, who had never before seen warriors with swelling bosoms, asked Karl whence his troops came and why they looked like that. 'My soldiers', proudly answered the young captain, "have these swelling bosoms because stout, brave hearts beat in them." The spy was satisfied and returned to Italy, and neither he nor his comrades were seen again.'

[26] In F. A. Arnod's narrative it is written that the glacier was very difficult to pass, 'à cause des crevasses fréquentes qui obligent les passants à porter des ais pour les traverser'.

[27] At the sight of the ruins Saussure uttered the following exclamation: 'Ce sont vraisemblablement les fortifications les plus élevées de notre planète. Mais pourquoi faut il que les hommes n'aient érigé dans ces hautes régions un ouvrage aussi durable, que pour y laisser un monument de leur haine et de leurs passions destructives?'

[28] 'I was surprised at the vigour and originality of his thoughts, and the force and elegance of his phraseology, both of which would have done credit to an educated man' (Wills, 'Wanderings', p. 212).

[29] Hinchliff, who came past in 1855, describes Meynet as follows ('Summer Months among the Alps', p. 152): 'We found the hut in the possession of a very fine old man, who must be either the ghost or merely the successor of him who Mr. Wills has reason to think perished by some unfair means. Our friend was very busy about his house; and its situation, at more than eleven thousand feet high, did not seem at all to cool his satisfaction about it. He said he intended to have another room ready for the next season, and he promised to make the roof waterproof at the same time.'

Mr. King, too, was glad to describe Meynet, who struck him as 'a most singular character', and he adds that the custom of the few travellers who came that way during the short season could not repay the host for his trouble and for the labour of bringing everything up to such a height, if he had not other resources; 'but,' continues Mr. King, suggestively, 'the custom of the few travellers who pass in a season, if even all stayed, could not pay him for his trouble, and the labour of transporting every article to such a vast height, if he relied on nothing else; but that matter we left to his own conscience and the vigilance of the *préposés*' ('Italian Valleys', pp. 208-213).

[30] In the visitors' book at the Theodul, which was begun in 1857, there is an emphatic inscription written as an epigraph by a certain Signor Bich, who was the postmaster at Châtillon, and seems to have been a fervent admirer of Meynet. The inscription begins as follows: 'Riches et savants voyageurs qui passez par ces déserts glacés, vous tous dont le cœur tendre et généreux aime éprouver la douce satisfaction de faire du bien, dites à vos riches cœurs que le bon Jean Augustin Meynet est digne d'un rayon de votre science, de vos richesses at de votre pouvoir, . . .' and actually ends with the words quoted below: 'Oui! Dans un pays où les ressources sont très limitées, il a fallu tout le dévouement du brave Meynet, digne successeur et neveu du courageux et habile feu Pierre Meynet, qui fonda l'asile du Col St. Théodule sur un des murs de l'ancienne tente que fit construire l'immortel De Saussure, pour braver tous les dangers et soumettre à son action philanthropique la rigueur du climat. Enfin puisque des milliers de familles, d'amis, et les Gymnases, les Académies, en un mot les sciences, et l'Europe entière ont les yeux et les cœurs tournés vers le brave Meynet pour lui recommander un fils, une épouse, un père, une fille et un savant; que des cœurs donc, désireux du retour de leur objet aimé, daignent aussi se souvenir du Guide qui les a conduits, de ses soins empressés,

et de son modeste confortable dans son habitation la plus élevée de l'Europe, à 3351 mètres au dessus du niveau de la mer.' Other exhortations follow, written by the same Signor Bich in Italian, German, and Latin. The Latin one is even more curious than the French: 'Ego autem sum ille qui nihil est et nihil habet, praeter desiderium magnum, id est fiat salus hominum, sit gloria montis Cervini, et fiat fortuna Johannis Agostini Meynet.' The signature follows ! !

[31] It is worthy of mention that the brothers Schlagintweit stayed on the Theodul Pass for three days in 1851, and that Dollfus-Ausset was there in the same year, and afterwards founded a meteorological station, maintaining there for more than a year (1864-1865), at his own expense, three keepers, one of whom was the Abbé Gorret's father.

At that time there were two huts on the pass, one of wood and the other of stone; the wooden one was named Noah's Ark by Dollfus-Ausset.

[32] To this expedition belongs an anecdote, which Sella loved to relate: His companion in the ascent was Count Paar, Austrian Chargé d'Affaires at the Court of Sardinia. The strained relations that existed at that time from the end of one war to the beginning of the other between Austrians and Piedmontese are well known; but Sella and Paar had in common their geological studies and their love of mountains. Well, during their march over the glacier, Paar and the guide fell into a deep crevasse. Sella quickly dug the point of his alpenstock into the snow, and was able to withstand the pull and hold his companions by means of the rope. Sella's position was critical because, if the alpenstock had given way, a disaster would have been almost inevitable. After many efforts he succeeded in pulling them out of the chasm. It is said that when Count Paar thanked him for having saved his life, he replied, with a sly smile, that he would keep and value the alpenstock which had supported them; 'if it had not been for this stick,' he added, 'perhaps the German nation would have cursed Latin perfidy' (see Guiccioli, 'Quintino Sella', vol. i. p. 33).

[33] Murray's 'Handbook' was careful to warn its readers that 'The Châtillon guides are not trustworthy'. 1854 edition.

[34] Whymper, the first time he came to Valtournanche, gave utterance to the following unflattering and perhaps unfounded verdict on the Valtournanche guides: 'Up to this time my experience with guides had not been fortunate, and I was inclined, improperly, to rate them at a low value. They represented to me pointers out of paths, and large consumers of meat and drink, but little more.' Those who offered themselves to him at Châtillon seemed to him 'a series of men . . . whose faces expressed malice, pride, envy, hatred, etc.' Whymper had to change his opinion when he came to know Carrel.

CHAPTER III

[1] Amé Gorret writes: 'M. le chanoine Carrel, vrai valtornein, sortit la première idée: si l'on pouvait gravir le mont Cervin, ce serait de l'argent au pays. Nous, ses parents, nous avons recueilli sa parole, et avons voulu voir si ce n'était qu'une simple utopie, ou bien s'il y avait peut-être du bon et du practicable le long de la Becca.'

[2] He personally knew John Ball, Adams Reilly, W. Mathews, Nicolls, Tyndall, Tuckett, and Whymper. See the description of him given by Tuckett, who visited him in 1859 ('Peaks, Passes, and Glaciers', vol. ii. p. 261).

[3] Amé Gorret writes in 1865: 'Le goût pour les courses et les ascensions ne date pas de bien longtemps chez nous; aussi entourés de montagnes magnifiques, nous les ignorions; les chasseurs seuls connaissaient les cols, et les touristes étaient régardés à leur passage comme des merveilles. Le mont Cervin, cette montagne si fière et si belle, que nous pouvions voir tous les jours, le mont Cervin devant lequel les étrangers s'arrêtaient frappés d'admiration, le mont Cervin ne nous frappait pas' (*Feuille d'Aoste*, 1865).

[4] 'A. Gorret, J. Antoine et J. Jacques Carrel ont gravi la Tête du Lion, mais leur course ne fut qu'une velléité' (Chan. G. Carrel, 'La Vallée de Valtornenche en 1867').

[5] I obtained this information from the late lamented G. B. Rimini, who was a friend of the Chanoine Carrel. Even in the last years of his life the chanoine was wont to say: 'Je finirai par faire mon panorama du haut du Mont Cervin.'

But his wish was never granted. He died in 1870.

[6] See 'The Italian Valleys of the Alps'.

[7] Very little is known about the later attempts made by the men of Valtournanche.

It is certain that in the same year, 1857, Gabriel Maquignaz and Victor Carrel le peintre, also started to try and find a route. They took the shortest way, up the east face of the Tête du Lion, but were prevented from going on by the falling stones in the couloirs.

The Abbé Gorret says of this attempt in a letter: 'Au fond du névé glacier de la Tête du Lion se trouve un étroit couloir, une cheminée, et une espèce de barme, où l'on a porté des ollines, et où l'on a dormi quelques fois depuis.

'Je pense que c'est jusque là que sont allés Gabriel et le pentre Carrel, et non plus loin.'

The chimney reached by them has nothing to do with the chimney to which Whymper afterwards came. There is no doubt that Jean Antoine Carrel tried again several times by himself and with Jean Jacques. Old guides relate that after his first attempt he made himself a sort of axe with which to cut steps in the ice on his expeditions.

In one of his letters Whymper writes that the Valtournanche guides in 1860 were excellent rock-climbers, being accustomed to hunting, but that on ice or steep snow-slopes they were very poor, as they had no experience whatever of the same. They had no ice axes. Possibly there was not a single one in the whole valley at that time.

He states that J. A. Carrel had no axe for several years after he began to accompany him, and he had a photograph, taken about 1863, in which Carrel appears with an ordinary stick in his hands.

Whymper puts the early attempts made by the Valtournanche men into one group, dated 1857-1859; it seems that Jean A., Jean J., and Victor Carrel, Gabriel Maquignaz, and the Abbé Gorret took part in them. He mentions as the furthest point reached the chimney at 3450 metres (11,385 feet), probably confusing it with the other chimney, which was much lower down. He mentions, however, that several attempts were made before this height was reached, but that those who had taken part in them did not remember how many times they had tried (E. Whymper, 'The Ascent of the Matterhorn', 1880, Appendix E).

[8] H. Warwick Cole, 'A Lady's Tour round Monte Rosa', p. 379.

[9] 'Vacation Tourists', pp. 283-289.

[10] Hawkins, however, admits that J. J. Carrel did his duty with much goodwill and courage, and seemed ready to follow him as far as he pleased.

[11] The point they reached was probably that where the hut at the Great Tower stands.

Whymper estimates its height at about 3900 metres (12,870 feet), and states that this party went about 100 metres (300 feet) further than the farthest point attained by the early explorers.

This information confirms Carrel's having made attempts later than 1857.

According to the statements of some old guides, J. A. Carrel had attained the spot where the Luigi Amedeo di Savoia hut now stands before Tyndall did so, and had made this place his usual bivouac.

[12] See 'Mountaineering in 1861', pp. 86, 87. Tyndall says, 'Bennen was evidently dead against any attempt upon the mountain'. It is curious that Tyndall and Bennen, observing the mountain from Breuil, mistook the extremity of the Shoulder (afterwards named the Pic Tyndall) for one of the two summits of the Matterhorn (Whymper, 'Scrambles', p. 97).

[13] Peter Taugwalder asked for 200 francs, whether the summit were attained or not.

[14] Whymper wrote concerning J. A. Carrel: 'Jean Antoine was . . . the finest rock-climber I have ever seen. He was the only man who persistently refused to accept defeat, and who continued to believe, in spite of all discouragements, that the great mountain was not inaccessible, and that it could be ascended from the side of his native valley' ('Scrambles', p. 89).

[15] As the exploration of the mountain gradually proceeded, the most striking

The South Face
(after snow)

South Face and Furggen Ridge

places received names. Of these names some were suggested by Whymper, but the great number were due to J. A. Carrel's imagination, see 'The Ascent of the Matterhorn', E. Whymper, p. 305).

Here are the names in order of ascent:

Col du Lion, 3577 metres, or 11,804 feet.

La Cheminée (Lo Ciarfiou in the dialect), to the east of the Col du Lion.

La Tente (about 3800 metres, or 12,540 feet), where Whymper pitched his second tent, and where the Luigi di Savoia hut now stands.

Degrés de la tour (Whymper's Great Staircase), the part between the Tente and the Grande Tour.

La Grande Tour, the conspicuous gendarme on the south-west buttress; at the base of this Whymper pitched his third tent. Here the second Alpine Club Hut was built (3890 metres, or 12,837 feet).

Le Vallon des Glaçons, to the east of the Grande Tour.

Le Gîte Giordano, a little platform on the ridge of the buttress, where Ingegnere Giordano passed the night in 1866.

Le Mauvais Pas, a narrow ledge of rock at the top of the Vallon des Glaçons, which is negotiated with the aid of a fixed horizontal rope.

Le Linceul, a very steep slope of névé, which is either climbed or skirted on the ascent.

Corde Tyndall, or *Grande Corde* (4080 metres, or 13,464 feet), a stretch of almost vertical cliff about 30 metres (100 feet) high, at the upper end of the Linceul. Tyndall was the first to place a rope there.

La Crête du Coq, the stretch of jagged ridge on the south-west buttress, which goes from the Grande Tour to the base of the Shoulder.

La Cravate (formerly called Le Collier de la Vierge by the natives of the valley), a ledge of rock which was always covered with snow, and which runs from east to west under the extremity of the Shoulder, and is slightly inclined. The first Italian hut was built there (4122 metres, or 13,602 feet).

L'Epaule, or *The Shoulder*, and the Pic Tyndall (4245 metres, or 14,008 feet).

L'Enjambée, the cleft which separates the north-east extremity of the Shoulder from the final peak.

Le Col Félicité, a little gap in the ridge, half-way up the final peak, and so called after Félicité Carrel, who ascended as far as this point in 1867.

L'Echelle Jordan, the rope ladder below the summit, called after the English climber, Leighton Jordan, who had it put up at his own expense by the Valtournanche guides.

Le Gîte Wentworth, a small level space near the summit, where Lord Wentworth spent the night in 1871.

Le Pas Thioly, the last corner on the ridge to the south-east before the summit is reached, at about 20 metres (66 feet) from the latter; so called after M. Thioly, who passed it in 1868.

[16] This inscription is still visible on the cliff at the foot of the Crête du Coq, after the Mauvais Pas is passed. On the same rock, beside the initials of J. Antoine, E. Whymper and Luc Meynet carved their own in the following year, 1862.

[17] The Abbé Gorret writes in 1865: 'En 1862 MM. Tyndall et Whymper donnèrent plus que jamais vie au problème de l'ascension, et légitimèrent les tentatives aux yeux du peuple, puisqu'il y avait gain et journée.'

In the winter of the same year Kennedy made his attempt on the Zermatt side; he reached a height of 3300 metres (10,890 feet) (see *Alpine Journal*, vol. i).

[18] Corona, 'Aria di Monti'.

Luc Meynet was wont to relate the following anecdote about his adventures with Whymper:

On their return from one of their many adventurous attempts, in the course of which the whole party had all but been swept away by an avalanche of stones, Whymper, Croz, the Chamonix guide, and Meynet were resting on the Furggenjoch. Whymper was making barometrical observations, Croz was smoking his pipe; Luc waited patiently till Croz had finished, and then, taking off his hat, most respectfully, asked him to lend him his pipe because he had left his own at home.

'You might as well have left your head there too, *drôle de bossu*,' was Croz's reply. 'Do you imagine I am going to lend my pipe to a half-man like you?'

The poor man did not answer a word, but Whymper, who had overheard the dialogue, came up to him with two cigars. 'Here,' he said, 'you smoke too.'

And Luc proudly lit a cigar, straightened himself to the best of his ability, and strutted about in front of Croz, puffing clouds of smoke into his face.

They started for Breuil, and on the way down the Furggen glacier Croz walked quickly, hoping to make Luc, who was laden with the tent, slip, but Luc managed the rope in such a way that he saved himself from being pulled down by the insidious jerks.

It happened that Croz fell into a crevasse and was held up by the strength and foresight of Luc.

The moral of the story was then pointed by Whymper, who turned to Croz and said: 'Sachez, Croz, qu'on a souvent besoin d'un plus petit que soi.'

This tale shows the keen antagonism which existed at that time between Valtournanche guides and those from other places.

[19] The account of the attempt should be read in Tyndall's work, 'Hours of Exercise in the Alps'.

The old Bich said that when he ascended the peak with Carrel and Gorret in 1865, he found at the base of the part called the '*grande corde*', a few pieces of the ladder which Tyndall had used to climb this place.

As regards the Enjambée, we must correct Whymper's error in ascribing this name, or, as he wrote it, 'l'Ange Anbé', to a pinnacle of rock which rises between the gap at the end of the Shoulder and the final peak (see 'The Ascent of the Matterhorn', Whymper, p. 90).

[20] Tyndall did not fail to recognize the excellent qualities of Carrel as a most useful companion and a first class cragsman. In Carrel's book he wrote the following statement:

'Jean Antoine Carrel accompanied me up the Matterhorn on the 27th-28th of July, 1862. He proved himself an extremely good man on this occasion. He is a very superior climber, and, I believe, an excellent guide. Many times during the ascent I had occasion to observe his skill and activity. He has served in two campaigns, has been at Novara and Solferino, and the discipline of a soldier's life renders him acquainted with many things which are useful to a mountaineer. I can express without reserve my entire satisfaction as regards Carrel's conduct through a very difficult day. — Breuil, 29th of July, 1862.'

[21] On the occasion of this attempt, Whymper wrote the following testimonial in Carrel's book:

'. . . He is a first-rate walker, very good indeed on rocks, and very good at anything. He is a most desirable man for any one who wants to make new excursions. — Valtournanche, August 11, 1863.'

[22] Giordano afterwards declared in a letter to Bartolomeo Gastaldi, that the attempt on the Matterhorn in 1865 was chiefly made with the object of making its ascent feasible for Quintino Sella, who wished to make some important observations on it.

[23] See *Alpine Journal*, vol. v. p. 329. The editor of the *Alpine Journal* concluded the controversy between Tyndall and Whymper by pointing out that it was only natural for Carrel to look with a somewhat jealous eye on any one who came to snatch from him the honour he had so ardently desired all his life, and that he must not be judged too hardly if he did not show much anxiety to assist a foreign guide to ascend the mountain.

[24] I owe these valuable letters to the courtesy of the Sella family.

[25] Giordano's other guides were Caesar Carrel, son to Jean Jacques, Charles Gorret, brother to the Abbé Gorret, and Jean Joseph Maquignaz. The latter was only in his first mountaineering season, and was enrolled in order that he might make himself useful in his quality of miner and stonemason by fixing the steel spikes in the rock.

[26] It is well known how the minister Sella was beset at that time by innumerable difficulties of the gravest description, in the matters of the application of serious financial measures which he himself had proposed in March, and of the transfer of the capital to Florence (see Guiccioli, 'Quintino Sella', vol. i. p. 107).

[27] The messenger was the Abbé Gorret.

[28] Whymper relates that Croz, catching sight of the Italians from the summit, exclaimed: 'Ah! les coquins, ils sont loin en bas.'

[29] See Gorret, 'Ascension du M. Cervin', and *Alpine Journal*, vol. ii. p. 239. I have followed the Abbé Gorret's account; he wrote: 'Ils n'étaient encore que sur l'Epaule à quelque distance au deça du Signal Tyndall quand Whymper et sa

bande les avaient appelés par leur cris du sommet de la pyramide.' From this it is evident that, when Carrel and his companions saw Whymper on the summit, they were still ascending. Others, Whymper among them, gave a different account; Whymper says, after hearing Carrel's story, that the party had reached the extremity of the Shoulder, at the base of the final peak, that there opinions became divided; J. A. Carrel and J. J. Maquignaz wished to proceed, whilst the others were unwilling, and the result of the dispute was that they all retreated, and it was only when they were on the rocks near the Cravate, on their descent, that they heard Whymper's shouts. The cause of their retreat was, then, the dispute between the guides, and not the sight of the Englishman's victory (E. Whymper, 'The Ascent of the Matterhorn', p. 304 D). The first version seems, however, to be the true one, and it was verbally confirmed to me by the Abbé Gorret himself. Another complete confirmation of it appears in Felice Giordano's diary, in which, dated July 14th, is the following note: '. . . At 2 p.m. they saw Whymper and six others on the top; this froze them, as it were, and they all turned and descended. . . . ' Carrel's conduct on that day, July 14th, was commented on and discussed in Italy and abroad.

[30] Gorret was suggesting the route afterwards discovered by J. J. Maquignaz.

[31] On the descent Carrel and Bich, having rejoined their companions, who were awaiting them, followed as far as the Shoulder a route that was somewhat different from the one they had used on the ascent, and rather easier: that is to say, they traversed the whole length of the ledge of rock on the north-west face of the mountain, which ledge they had named the Corridor, and thus reached the point where the arête of the Shoulder comes to an end against the final peak. This variant was afterwards used by Mr. Craufurd Grove, both on the ascent and the descent. [There is an interesting article with diagrams of Carrel's and other routes on this Z'Mutt Face in vol. xxxvii of the *Alpine Journal*. — R.L.G.I.]

[32] Sella did not ascend the Matterhorn till twelve years later, at the age of fifty, and then he took his sons with him. 'What a beautiful mountain!' he wrote after his ascent, to a friend of his; 'you understand beauty . . . but you can form no idea of beauty such as that of the Matterhorn.

'I thought that by now I had a fairly good knowledge of mountains, of their attractions and their poetry; but when I ascended the Matterhorn I was forced to confess to myself that I knew nothing, so great is the difference between this unique mass and other mountains. Therefore you may all scold me as much as you will, but if the opportunity presents itself I shall climb the Matterhorn again. A little risk does not matter. At any rate up there a man does not merely hurt or cripple himself: if his foot slips he takes a leap of perhaps half a mile. You will agree with me that that would at least be a decent death.

'I regretted somewhat having taken my sons with me, for, as regards myself, I have passed half a century, and there would not be much harm in ridding Italy of my person; but it would be a pity to lose vigorous youths. But they, too, were so happy, so enthusiastic over the stupendous spectacle! If you only saw their faces when they speak of it.' (This letter is quoted by Guiccioli.)

The ascent was accompanied by an incident which might have resulted in a terrible disaster. J. A. Carrel, when he reached the rope which is before the part called the Echelle, suspected that the rope was not firmly fastened, and climbed up the rock in order to make sure. His foot slipped, however, and he was obliged to have recourse to the rope to support himself, when the rope became suddenly detached, with the result that the guide fell 12 or 15 feet, over Sella's head. Fortunately Carrel was able to clutch the rocks firmly and to bring himself to a standstill on a small level space, whilst Sella had been prepared to withstand the jerk on the rope which bound them together. Antonio Castagneri, who was in the party, used to tell how the guide Imseng then tried in vain to climb that piece, which was now without a rope, and how they had to wait till Carrel had recovered from the shock and was able to take his post as leader again, and overcome the difficult bit. Stains of his blood were seen on the rocks by those who followed.

[33] I quote from the letter written at that time by Whymper to the *Times*.

'As far as I know, at the moment of the accident no one was actually moving. I cannot speak with certainty, neither can the Taugwalders, because the two leading men were partially hidden from our sight by an intervening mass of rock. Poor Croz had laid aside his axe, and, in order to give Mr. Hadow greater security, was absolutely taking hold of his legs and putting his feet, one by one, into their proper positions. From the movements of their shoulders it is my belief that Croz, having done as I have said, was in the act of turning round to go down a step or two himself; at this moment Mr. Hadow slipped, fell on him, and knocked him over. I heard one startled exclamation from Croz, then saw him and Mr. Hadow flying downwards; in another moment Hudson was dragged from his steps and Lord F. Douglas immediately after him. All this was the work of a moment; but immediately we heard Croz's exclamation, Taugwalder and myself planted ourselves as firmly as the rocks would permit; the rope was tight between us, and the shock came on us as on one man. We held; but the rope broke midway between Taugwalder and Lord F. Douglas. For two or three seconds we saw our unfortunate companions sliding downwards on their backs, and spreading out their hands endeavouring to save themselves; they then disappeared one by one and fell from precipice to precipice on to the Matterhorn glacier below, a distance of nearly 4000 feet in height. From the moment the rope broke it was impossible to help them.'

Whymper wrote also at the time to Signor Rimini, the Secretary of the I.A.C. His letter ends thus:

'A single slip, or a single false step, has been the sole cause of this frightful calamity . . . But, at the same time, it is my belief no accident would have happened had the rope between those who fell been as tight, or nearly as tight, as it was between Taugwalder and myself.'

Their rope was a weak one; it does not appear to have been cut by the rocks, but to have been broken by the shock and the weight it was called upon to sustain. It is said Croz held Hadow for an instant, and still tried to check the fall even after Hudson and Douglas had been pulled out of their steps, but in vain; his last word was 'Impossible!' so the Taugwalders said (see G. Studer, 'Ueber Eis und Schnee').

[34] Byron, 'Manfred', Act i.

[35] Mr. Hadow was nineteen years old, and this was his first season in the Alps.

[36] Craufurd Grove writes that in 1867 it was the guides' opinion that the north side was better for the ascent and the south side for the descent, and that at any rate the southern slope was the more difficult.

The *Alpine Journal* made the following observation: 'However much the guides may have improved the southern arête, it is not probable that this route will be often followed, as the southern side of the mountain is raked night and day by incessant falls of stones, while on the northern side no risk is run from this source' (vol. ii. p. 154).

F. Giordano, after his traverse of the Matterhorn (in 1868), rightly considered the Swiss side to be easier but more dangerous than the more laborious Italian side.

[37] The modest refuge on the Cravate was erected in 1867, and sufficed for many years; in fact, until the hut at the Grande Tour was built. The proposal for the construction of the latter came from the Aosta section of the I.A.C. in 1878, and was warmly supported by Sella, Budden, and Corona, and the hut was completed in 1885. In 1893 the present hut, which is called after Prince Louis Amadeus of Savoy, was built by the Turin section in a more suitable spot, about 330 feet (100 metres) lower down. The first refuge on the Swiss side (Alte Hütte) was constructed in 1868.

[38] 'It is hardly necessary to say that the difficulties to be encountered in ascending this mountain are of the worst kind. I cannot speak too highly of the admirable skill with which they were overcome by Carrel and of the care with which, during the expedition, he provided against every chance of accident.—Zermatt, August 16, 1867.'

[39] A proof of the enterprising spirit of the Valtorneins was given by the discovery of a new passage in July, 1887, by the guide J. B. Aymonod. In the preceding year a fall of stones had swept away the rope-ladder at the Passage Jordan; the ascent of the Matterhorn on the Italian side was hindered by this, and the local guides suffered. Aymonod, accompanied by J. R. Perruquet and J. B. Maquignaz, climbed to a point about sixty metres (200 feet) below the Passage, and, turning off to the right, reached the base of the chimney which comes down between the Italian summit and the Swiss. He went up this chimney by very difficult rocks to the summit.

This new route was followed in August of the same year by Signor J. Pigozzi, of the Bologna section of the I.A.C., and shortly afterwards by Signor P. Morani, of the Milan section, both of them accompanied by Aymonod.

Dr. Güssfeldt used it to descend in the same year.

The rope-ladder was subsequently replaced on the old route, and Aymonod's variant was no longer followed.

[40] Vittorio Sella, leaving the Jomein at 11 p.m. on March 16th, reached the summit at 2 p.m. on the 17th, and the Swiss hut at 7.30 p.m. The *Alpine Journal* declared that this expedition was undoubtedly the most remarkable one that had ever been made in the winter season (vol. x. p. 494).

[41] See Emile Javelle's fine work, 'Souvenirs d'un Alpiniste'.

[42] In 1890 the Federal Government was asked simultaneously by the same contractor for a concession for the Zermatt-Görnergrat railway, and for a Zermatt-Matterhorn one. The Görnergrat railway was constructed, and has been working since 1899, but fortunately there has been no more talk of the other. An account of Ingénieur Xaver Imfelds' bold project was published in Th. Wundt's valuable work, 'Das Matterhorn'. It essentially consists of a line which goes up to the Hörnli, and continues thence in a rectilinear tunnel about two kilometres (one and a quarter miles approximately) long, built under the ridge, and issuing near the summit on the Zmutt side.

CHAPTER IV

[1] 'Lofty Alps, like lofty characters, require for their due appreciation some elevation in the spectator' (Leslie Stephen).

[2] This range, which comprises peaks of exceeding difficulty, had been partly explored about that time by G. Corona.

Subsequently it was examined by Italians and others, and now the names it has received make it appear like a page out of the almanack de Gotha of Italian mountaineering: there is a Punta Margherita; there are the Punte Budden, Giordano, Sella, Lioy, Carrel, and Maquignaz.

[3] The first man to accomplish the difficult and dangerous passage of the Col du Lion, from Zermatt to Breuil, was A. F. Mummery, with A. Burgener as guide, on July 6th, 1880.

[4] Whymper, having revisited the scene of his battle, wrote as follows in Notes to the Preface of the fifth edition of 'Scrambles Among the Alps', which was published in 1900:

'In August, 1895 (?), I ascended the S.W. ridge as far as the base of the Great Tower . . . More than thirty years had passed since my last visit, and I found that great changes had taken place in the interval.

'The summit of the Col du Lion was lower than it was formerly, from diminution of the snow; and the passage across it was shorter than it used to be. For the next 150 feet or so of ascent there was little alteration, but thence upwards the ridge had tumbled to pieces, and many familiar places were unrecognizable.

'No spot on this ridge is more firmly fixed in my recollection than the Chimney.

'Only a remnant of it was left — more than half of the Chimney had disappeared; and from that point upwards everything was altered. Difficult places had become easy, and easy places had become difficult.

'The angle in which a thick, knotted rope is now dangling, which is now one of the steepest bits of the ascent, did not exist in 1864.'

(Whymper here means the pitch above Seiler's Slab, the little platform on which the Swiss climber's fatal slip occurred.)

About a fortnight after this visit of Whymper's, on September 9th, a terrible fall of rock took place on a part of the ridge below the Great Tower, wreaking havoc on the ridge underneath, destroying and carrying away the fixed ropes, and quite altering the appearance of this part of the mountain.

Traces of this fall are still visible.

A great English climber, Mr. W. E. Davidson, who has climbed the Matterhorn six times and traversed it five, relates that he was that evening in the Refuge at the Great Tower, and found himself unable to proceed any further on the descent, owing to the dangerous condition of the mountain between the hut and the Col du Lion, the whole distance being continuously swept by falling stones.

He says that the sight was a most extraordinary one. He descended the next morning before the sun touched the rocks and started the stones falling again. Under normal conditions this stretch, like the whole of the Matterhorn on the Italian side, is free from this danger.

[5] The ropes on the Italian side of the Matterhorn are provided by the Italian Alpine Club, and are fixed by the Valtournanche guides every time it becomes necessary to renew them.

On an average, and barring exceptional cases, they last eight years.

[6] Emile Javelle wrote: 'Du côté de Zermatt, le Cervin n'est qu'une immense pyramide unie et régulière. Plusieurs touristes qui n'ont pas compris le caractère grandiose de cette simplicité, en ont déclaré l'ascension tout à fait monotone; autant vaut dire que Dante n'est pas amusant, ou que la mer est uniforme.'

[7] Not all these ropes are indispensable; as far as the Italian side is concerned it seems to me that only four should be retained, namely: the one in the new chimney below the Luigi Amedeo di Savoia hut, the grande corde below the Shoulder, the rope before the ladder, and the ladder itself; the suppression of the others would make the ascent harder, but not more dangerous.

CHAPTER V

[1] The history of the development of Zermatt is exhaustively dealt with in the Rev. W. Coolidge's work, 'Swiss Travels and Guide Books'.

Mr. Alexander Seiler, starting from quite small beginnings, succeeded in

South Face
The last thousand feet

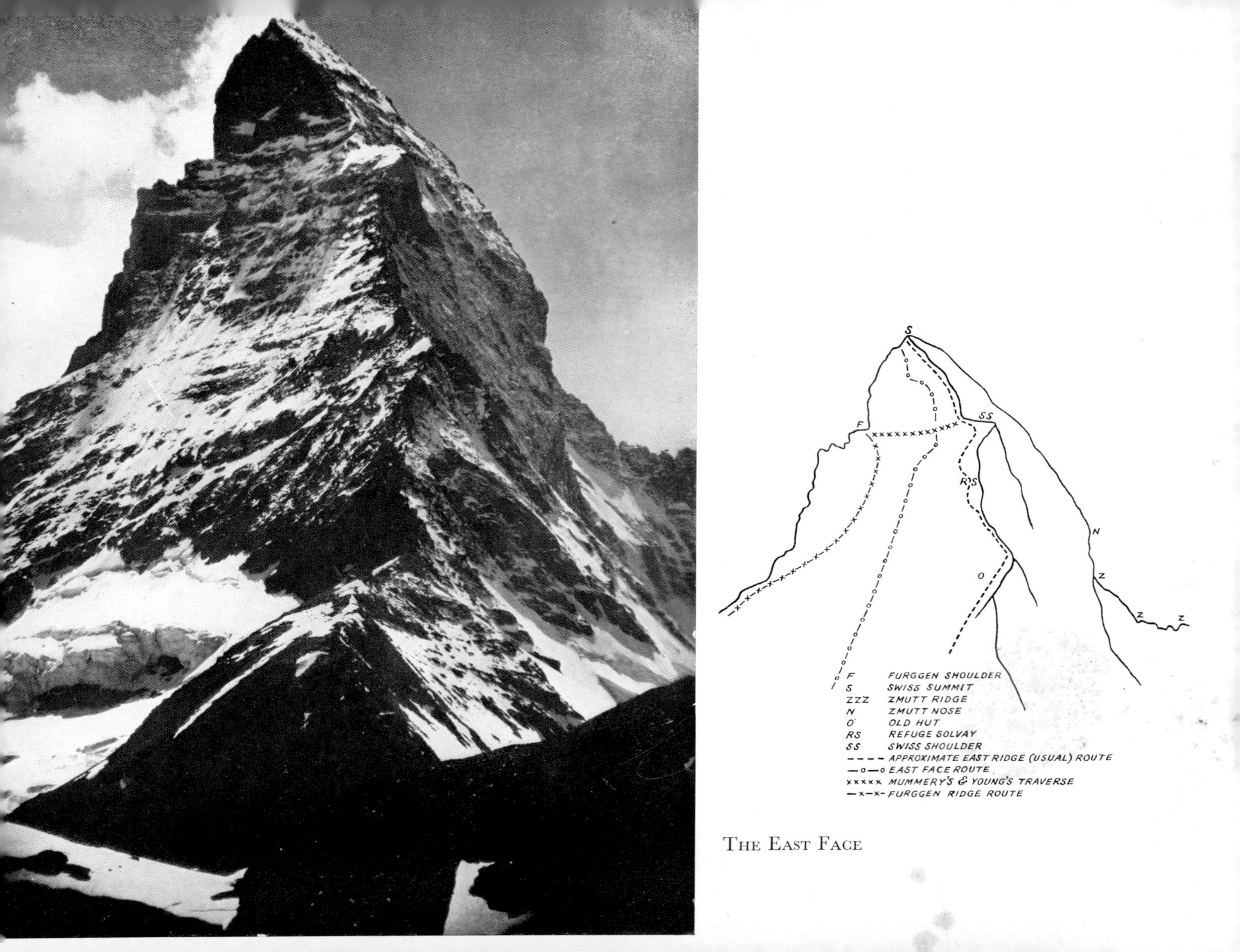
S
F
SS
RS
O
N
Z
Z
Z
F FURGGEN SHOULDER
S SWISS SUMMIT
ZZZ ZMUTT RIDGE
N ZMUTT NOSE
O OLD HUT
RS REFUGE SOLVAY
SS SWISS SHOULDER
- - - - APPROXIMATE EAST RIDGE (USUAL) ROUTE
—o—o EAST FACE ROUTE
xxxxx MUMMERY'S & YOUNG'S TRAVERSE
—x—x- FURGGEN RIDGE ROUTE

THE EAST FACE

building up a most important industry in his Alpine hotels, of which he founded several, among them the Riffel and the Riffelalp.

In his later years he frequently had to provide for two thousand guests daily.

Honest and cordial, he was much beloved by travellers. It was said that, just as one could not imagine Zermatt without the Matterhorn, so it could not be imagined without Seiler.

He died in 1891 (see *Alpine Journal*, vol. xv. pp. 491-493).

The Monte Rosa Hotel was called by Matthews 'the mountaineer's true home'.

[2] See Penhall's and Mummery's accounts, *Alpine Journal*, vol. ix. pp. 449 and 458.

[Mummery's party chose the route described by Rey and almost always taken by the numerous parties which have made the ascent since Rey wrote. Penhall's route up the west face is unquestionably a worse route as regards avoidance of danger and difficulty.

On September 1st, his party had climbed up by the route followed some hours later by Mummery, as far as the third of the great teeth above the ice ridge. They descended below the ice ridge to bivouac. In the morning the weather looked bad and they went back to Zermatt, meeting Mummery's party coming up. The weather cleared, so Penhall and his guides started up again from Zermatt after dinner. It was not because they knew Mummery was ahead of them that they chose a different route. Penhall himself wrote: 'When we got nearly opposite the Stockje we waited and consulted; I wanted to go much further up the glacier and try the middle of the face. Imseng's only objection to this was that if we went that way we should find no suitable place to pass the night, while on the arête we should. This seemed reasonable, so I gave in.'

In descending from their bivouac they left the crest of the ridge high up and went down the rocks nearer the great couloir (Penhall's couloir) which forms the angle between the west face of the Matterhorn and the great projection of the lower Z'mutt Ridge. They did this 'so as to get a better view of the face'. Next day they climbed the rocks near the couloir, crossed it about half-way up and ascended the west face.— R.L.G.I.]

The aspect of the wall Penhall climbed is anything but encouraging, and Messrs. G. Lammer's and A. Lorria's experience of it on August 3rd, 1887, confirms the report of its difficulty, and also shows up its danger.

Dr. Guido Lammer described the events of that terrible day in the *Oesterreichische Alpen Zeitung*, vol. ix. no. 188, p. 205.

The two skilled mountaineers, without guides, were ascending the Tiefenmatten face by Penhall's route.

At 1 p.m. they were on a level with the teeth on the Z'mutt spur. The face was glazed with black ice, and in a most dangerous condition.

They decided to turn back.

About five o'clock they were crossing the Penhall couloir when a small snow avalanche fell towards them from above. It did not strike them, but flowing down at their feet, it made them lose their balance and carried them down in a leap of 150 to 200 metres (500 to 600 feet).

Dr. Lammer related that during those very short moments a crowd of the most varied thoughts flashed through his mind with extraordinary clearness; and, while the consequences of such a fall were thoroughly evident to him, he had time to think of his home, of a certain Alpine and literary controversy, of india-rubber balls rebounding with prodigious elasticity, etc. etc., all which led him to the conclusion that death by falling must be quite painless.

When at last they stopped Lammer felt an intense pain in his foot, which had been dislocated.

His friend was lying motionless a short distance away. He had a terrible wound on his forehead and a broken leg; the rope, which had become much entangled during the fall, was compressing his neck; he was unconscious, and when he recovered consciousness he was seized with delirium, unbroken by any lucid interval. Dr. Lammer attempted to drag him down-hill over the snow, but his companion howled with pain, cursed imaginary assassins, clutched himself with his hands, and rolled about on the avalanche snow. Lammer was prevented by his own condition and the difficulty of the place they were in, from making any other efforts to convey his friend downwards; he laid him on a mound of snow, threw his own jacket over his shoulders, and put his hands into a pair of stockings. He wished to tie him to a rock with the rope, but it seemed to him cruel to make it impossible for his friend to move if he should recover consciousness.

He shouted loudly and frequently for help, but no voice was heard in reply. He then descended alone, without an axe, without his coat, and without a hat; he dragged himself across the glacier to the Stockje hut on the opposite side. Finding no one there he resumed his journey, and limped and crawled, as best he could, down the long Z'Mutt glacier, till at nightfall he was knocking, quite exhausted, at the door of the Staffel Alp.

The relief party which he sent off reached the spot where Lorria was lying at eight in the morning, and found him still unconscious. In his delirium he had torn off his clothes.

Lorria suffered long from the effects of his fall.

This event was followed by a violent controversy. Some firmly maintained that the accident was due to the absence of guides, while others were convinced that it would have occurred just the same if a guide had been with the climbers. [Dr. Guido Lammer's writings show him to have had a morbid attraction for dangerous situations; hence, perhaps, the choice of Penhall's route. — R.L.G.I.]

[3] H.R.H. the Duke of the Abruzzi made the ascent with Mr. A. F. Mummery and Dr. Norman Collie with young Joseph Pollinger on August 28th, 1895.

According to Mummery the weather was threatening, and, the Prince climbing very well, they went exceedingly fast, so that their time was probably the quickest possible. They left the bivouac at the foot of the snow ridge at 3.40 a.m., and reached the summit at 9.50.

[They took to the upper Z'Mutt ridge below Carrel's ledge—R.L.G.I.].

A few days afterwards the first descent of the ridge was accomplished by Miss Bristow, with the guide Matias Zurbriggen, of Macagnaga.

[4] Mummery, on his first ascent, went nearer than we did to Carrel's route, and found on the rocks a piece of rusted iron, which had belonged to the 1865 party, or to Craufurd Grove's in 1867.

[The upper parts of the routes on the Z'Mutt Face are well shown in the *Alpine Journal*, vol. xxxvii. pp. 221-232. — R.L.G.I.]

[5] All things considered, the ascent of the Z'Mutt ridge is not excessively difficult; it is certain that no part of it presents the difficulties which would be encountered on certain passages on the Italian ridge if they were not roped.

There is some danger of falling stones on the first part of the ascent, before the snow ridge is attained, and in the last bit when the slabs under the summit are being crossed, there being no shelter there.

Although at certain points the rock is rotten and unstable, the structure of this side affords good holds; the position is, however, most unfavourable. On cold and windy days the climber suffers more in the shade than on the other sides, where the sun strikes early; and it is quite likely that the rocks in the middle and upper part will be found so glazed with ice as to make it impossible to continue the ascent.

This is, perhaps, the reason why the guides do not recommend this route to the travellers who come to Zermatt; the travellers themselves do not think of it, and so this 'northern widowed side' of the Matterhorn is still reserved for the few real adorers of the mountain. 'Tourists, like trade,' observed Whymper in this connection, 'drift into the easiest channels' ('Guide to Zermatt and the Matterhorn', p. 182). It is said that immediately after the first ascents of the Z'Mutt ridge a proposal was made to construct a hut on that ridge to facilitate the ascent of it. Mr. Baumann thought that that route would become the favourite one of those who intended to traverse the Matterhorn.

[6] Leone Sinigaglia was with Carrel and concluded his account of this terrible descent with these words:

'Carrel died, like a good and brave man, on his own mountain, after having summoned up all the energy he possessed in order to save his employer. He died after bringing him out of danger to a place of safety, exhausted by the supreme effort of sixteen hours of assiduous work, amid continuous struggles and difficulties, in a snowstorm which several times appeared irresistible.

'I shall never think of him without infinite emotion and gratitude.'

[Readers may read his description in vol. xv of the *Alpine Journal* or in *The Mountain Way* (an anthology by R. L. G. Irving).]

CHAPTER VI

[1] Dr. Paul Güssefeldt gives the following comparison of the inclinations of the different ridges of the Matterhorn:

S.W. ridge (Col du Lion)	length	Kilometres	1.5	inclination	36.°
S.E. ridge (Furggen)	,,	,,	1.7	,,	43.5°
N.E. ridge (Hörnli)	,,	,,	2	,,	39°
N.W. ridge (Z'Mutt)	,,	,,	3.01	,,	37°

[2] See in 'Alpinismo a quattro mani' (Climbing with Hands and Feet), by G. Saragat and G. Rey, 'An Attempt on the Matterhorn'.

[3] The general inclination of the Furggen face, which appeared to be almost vertical as seen from the Theodul, and at an angle of 70° from the Riffel, is not really greater than 40°.

'Forty degrees', says Whymper, 'may not seen a formidable inclination to the reader, nor is it for only a small cliff. But it is very unusual to find so steep a gradient maintained continuously as the general angle of a great mountain slope, and very few instances can be quoted from the High Alps of such an angle being preserved over a rise of 3000 feet' ('Scrambles').

[4] De la disproportion même entre l'infini qui nous tue et ce rien que nous sommes, naît le sentiment d'une certaine grandeur en nous. Nous aimons mieux être fracassés par une montagne que par un caillou . . . L'intelligence, en nous montrant, pour ainsi dire, l'immensité de notre impuissance, nous ôte le regret de notre défaite' (Guyau).

[5] Times of our ascent:

Left Breuiljoch at	4.45 a.m.
,, first tower (old bivouac) at	6.15 a.m.
,, second tower at	8.30 a.m.
Reached third tower (Furggen Shoulder) at ..	10.0 a.m.

[6] Our descent was not visible with the Schwarzsee telescope because that side of the mountain was then in shadow.

It was also alluded to in the *Monthly Review* of the I.A.C., vol. x. p. 210; in Whymper's 'Guide to Zermatt', 1900 edition, p. 182; and in the preface to the 1900 edition, p. vii, of Whymper's work, 'Scrambles Amongst the Alps'.

Monsieur M. Paillon mentions it also in his translation of Mummery's work, 'Mes Escalades', p. 31.

[7] *Journal de Genève*, September 15th, 1899.

[8] We find this song on the lips of Lantrei in 'Les Aventures du dernier Abencérage'.